To CARMACK W,

Enjoy the issue!

July 2007

COME HAVE FUN

with

FRANK RUSH

at

Craterville Park

and

Sandy Lake Amusement Park

By Frank Rush III

Come Have Fun
with Frank Rush
at Craterville Park
and Sandy Lake Amusement Park

ISBN-10: 1-58752-282-9
ISBN-13: 978-1-58752-282-6

Printed in the United States of America
1 3 5 7 9 10 8 6 4 2

Printing coodination by
Personalized Priniting
Carrollton, Texas

Front cover: In this photo the train at Sandy Lake Park is driven by Ramon Mireles. Dad was responsible for helping Ramon and his family to become naturalized citizens, and Ramon drove the train for over 20 years. He is one of our closest family friends.

To order a copy of

Come Have Fun

or contact
Frank Rush III
Phone 214-725-6727
or e-mail
frankrush@aol.com

Contents

Hey, Cowboy! Let's Talk! ix
Introduction xiii
    The Rush Family Tree xv
    Where Did this Train Come From? xviii
    Where's this Train Going? xxi

Track Section #1
(1971-2005)

1. All Aboard for Sandy Lake Amusement Park 3
2. Pulling Out of the Station in 1971 12
3. The Rush Family Takes a Ride on the Sandy Lake Park Express . . 14
    Whistle Stop for Traditional Amusement Parks 32
4. Laying Track with Special Events 35
5. Football Camp 41
6. More Special Events 48
    Whistle Stop for Uncle Fred 53
7. FunFest 64
    Whistle Stop for Dr. Dri and the Other Bandmasters 69
8. Fun Facts 76
9. High Diving Mules, Security Lions, and Trained Buffalo 78
10. The Family Circus 84
    Whistle Stop for Sandy 85
11. The Show Goes On 92
12. Company Picnics 95
13. They've Been Working on the Railroad 100
14. Steep Grades and Rough Track Along the Line 110
15. The Rail Yard Keeps Getting Smaller 115
16. Side-Tracked on the Interstate 119
17. Nearly Derailed by the Bush Tollway 121
18. Trees Along the Track 127

Contents

19. Birds on the Track 131
20. Famous Passengers on this Train 133
21. Frank Rush Productions 141
    Whistle Stop for Mr. Binion 149
22. Hunting with Dad and His South Dakota Connection 155
23. Unwinding with Dad and Santa Claus 165
24. Sandy Lake Park Christmas 169
25. The Reason We Own the Train 171

Track Section #II
(The Late 1800s-1957)

26. Turning Back the Clock. 177
27. Remembering Old Craterville Park. 198
    Whistle Stop for Jimbo 203
28. Indian Stories. 207
29. More About Old Craterville Park 214
    Whistle Stop for Papa Jack 229
30. Let's Rodeo 231
    Whistle Stop for Ridin' and Shootin' with Mom 236
31. The Rodeo Showdown with the Turtles 240
32. Around the World in 80 Days and National Geographic 243
33. The First Rocking R Ranch. 249
34. The Land Grab. 258

Track Section #III
(1958-1971)

35. Moving on Down the Track to New Craterville and Beyond 265
36. Cowboys and Indians at Cache 274
37. Rocking R Ranch Rodeos 275
    Whistle Stop for Wild Willy 290
38. The Rocking R Ranch at Meers 293
39. Hollywood Visits the Rocking R Ranch 296
40. Home on the Range. 301
    Whistle Stop for Merle. 315
41. Horsing Around. 317

Whistle Stop for Big George, Pete, Punk, and Bill Hill 319

42. Meers Store 323

Whistle Stop for E. Paul Waggoner 326

43. Meanwhile, Back at the Ranch 332

44. What Would Mr. Bicket Do? 334

Whistle Stop for Herschel Boydstun 338

45. Making the Grades 341

46. Take Us to Texas 343

Whistle Stop for Mr. Hunt 357

47. Going Once, Going Twice, Sold! 360

48. The Wrong Track 365

Track Section #IV
(2004-2005)

49. A Round-Trip Ticket 369

50. Nearing the End of the Line 370

Whistle Stop for Vista Ridge 375

51. The Last Stop 376

The Last Whistle Stop for Beans and Badges 380

Acknowledgements 381

Hey, Cowboy! Let's Talk!

Driving a miniature train around an amusement park would top the list of exciting jobs for any child or adult. Announcing, "Allllll aboard," pushing the throttle forward and hearing the engine roar, ringing the bell and blowing the whistle would thrill anyone with a sense of adventure and fun.

Just as an engineer directs the operation of a train to its next station, Frank Rush enjoyed directing the annual preparation and opening of his amusement parks for sixty-eight years. Even after months of work, the day before the Park opens for the season is always hectic and filled with last minute chores. In 2003, opening day was set for March 20. Little did we know, March 19 was the eve of Dad's final opening day.

The winter's leaves had been raked and removed. The Park lawns were cut smooth, and the picnic tables were painted and lined up under the pavilions. Each ride had been put back in operation, painted, lubricated, and inspected for safety. The refreshment stands were stocked. Wieners, ice, and ice cream were stored in the freezers. Cheese and chips for nachos, Sno-Cone juice, cotton candy sugar, and soft drinks were ready for hungry kids and adults. The ovens at the smoke house were already slowly cooking the brisket and ham for catered meals. Arcade machines were tested, and the miniature golf course had new carpet on the greens and fairways. Under the big white tent in the center of the Park, the FunFest performance stage was decorated, and sound equipment, lights, judge's platform, folding chairs, and music stands stood ready for use. The schedule for the next day's band competition and group picnics was posted, and employees were issued new uniforms for the season. New American and Texas flags fluttered in the breeze on the flagpole near the front of the Park. A thousand other jobs had been completed. It was a perfect day, and a perfect Park, waiting for excited students and families to pour into the gates, looking for a day of fun and fellowship.

Late in the day, as I drove my golf cart past the pool entrance, Dad hollered, "Hey, Cowboy! Come sit down here. Let's talk." Dad sat there in his favorite chair, a vantage point from which he could keep track of the activities. As usual, he wore his dark, wrap-around glasses, a hunting coat, and ball cap. His Wrangler jeans were tucked down in the top of his brown Justin ropers, cowboy style. I pulled over and asked him what was going on. He said, "Well, the Park is ready to open. It never looked any better. We'll have a good day tomorrow and a big season."

I asked, "Dad, have you heard the weather? They're predicting a one hundred percent chance of heavy rain tonight, and we'll be in a tornado watch before midnight. We've got thirty bands coming tomorrow. A picnic committee for a group of eight hundred people will be here at noon to taste our food and tour the Park. A news reporter will be here to do a story on the FunFest, and things don't look too good because the Park will be soaked."

With the same unflappable optimism that had guided Dad though life, he said, "Go home, eat dinner, and don't worry."

"Don't worry? How can you not worry?" I asked.

"I'll bet you a gallon of ice cream everything will be okay," was his response.

During the night, before Dad's last opening day at the Park, it thundered, the wind picked up, and the city's storm sirens sounded. By dawn the next day, less than one tenth of an inch of rain had fallen, and only a few green leaves, blown down by the wind, littered the ground. As the sun rose over the Park, the lawns had just enough left over raindrops to sparkle like fields of diamonds. The sky was Texas blue as buses began to arrive and unload. The smell of fresh popcorn and pizza wafted out of the refreshment stands. All of the band groups performed on time. The company picnic committee loved the barbeque and was so impressed, they asked to have a contract prepared. The news reporter had an emergency story to cover and called with a promise to come the following day. The lines at the rides and refreshment stands were steady until late afternoon, and we had plenty of seasoned help to serve our customers. Dad drove around on his golf cart and made sure things were operating up to his expectations. After the customers left, the boys gathered the trash and washed down the picnic tables while other employees got their areas ready for the next day.

Late in the day, I still had a few chores to finish when I heard Dad holler at me, "Hey, Cowboy, come sit down here. We've got a problem."

I walked over and took a seat. I was wondering what he was concerned about. Could it be the bank calling for a much-needed deposit? Was there a problem with the help or a ride? He seemed in a somber mood and deep thought, and I figured he was reluctant to give me the bad news. The clock ticked off thirty seconds, then forty-five, as Dad studied on what he was about to say.

"What's the problem, Dad?" I finally asked.

He looked glum for a few more seconds, then he asked with a wry grin, "Where's my ice cream?"

Frank and Genelle Rush

Introduction

There are special characters or acquaintances you remember all of your life. It may be a close friend, a co-worker, a teacher, a preacher, or just someone who crossed your path. My father, E. Frank Rush, is one of those people everyone seems to remember or to know. He may have been responsible for some pleasant experience with your family at a picnic in one of his amusement parks, a rodeo, a parade, or a Wild West Show. You may have heard someone relate a Frank Rush story, or you may have your own story to tell. Whether you did or didn't know him personally, you will enjoy this journey through his life and his business dealings, and meeting people he touched in one way or another.

Many people recall Dad's energy and enthusiasm for work. Some think about Dad in relation to the amusement parks, his promotions, and the special events he was involved with during his life. Many remember Dad as a talker. He loved, more than anything, to visit about almost any subject. A tough trader, an easy friend, a gift giver, and a mentor with the ability to be at ease with anyone great or small. That was Dad.

This collection of stories and family history includes old Craterville Park and new Craterville Park in Oklahoma, and Sandy Lake Amusement Park in Texas, along with remembrances of some of Dad's dealings. Since Dad always had more than one iron in the fire, there are whistle stops along the way, where we can stop, stretch our legs, and learn more about Dad's friends.

One thing about Dad that impressed people was the huge number of notable people he had been acquainted with during his long life. He crossed paths with cowboys and Indians, movie and TV stars, wealthy people, politicians, and noted business people as well as people of little notoriety. They all drew his attention for some special reason. Dad considered each friendship a treasure.

Introduction

A close friend, former Carrollton Mayor Milburn Gravley, recently related this Frank Rush story: Mayor Gravley said, "When I first met Frank, I thought he was telling tall tales about who he knew. There were too many stories about his friends, things he had done, and places he had been to be believable. Over the years, I discovered he wasn't making anything up."

Dad's personal appearance was not remarkable. At five feet, ten inches tall and of average build, he was not imposing, but he had an outstanding feature: his voice. It was so recognizable that he seldom introduced himself on the telephone. Most people could identify him by his voice, and if not, they were left scrambling to recognize him by the subject of the conversation. He had another unique habit. He rarely said "goodbye" at the end of a conversation. Generally he would end a visit and simply hang up, a custom that his friends became familiar with. If he was talking to you in person he would invite you to "come back soon" or some other pleasantry, but he seldom said goodbye. Once, I asked him why and he said that he didn't like the word. He said, "Goodbye is too final, and besides I'm not finished talking to people."

By the end of Dad's life, there were countless stories and tales buzzing around in his head. His life was full. His experiences were varied. He overcame problems and basked in the glory of success. Some of his stories may sound improbable, but Dad was an improbable person. Dad lived thirty-two thousand, two hundred and seventy days, and his life spanned the most remarkable age in world history. Some would consider Dad old fashioned, and others would say he was a man ahead of his time. I choose to think of him as a man who took the time he had and used it in his own unique style. One can identify an individual cowboy by the unique crease in his hat, and there are lyrics to a country song that say, "I wear my own kind of hat." Dad wore his own style of hat, and he can sure be identified by his own style of life.

Dad often quoted *his* father, "Always tell the truth, and you will never forget what you said." Then Dad would add, "That's what I'm a'fixin to do."

The Rush Family Tree

Perhaps the most noted Rush of all, Doctor Benjamin Rush (1745-1813), was known as "The Father of Psychiatry." He was a member of the Continental Congress in 1776 and signed the Declaration of Independence. Our family genealogy goes back directly to Doctor Rush.

Franklin S. Rush (Granddad Rush) was listed in "Who's Who of America" Vol. 15 1928-1929. He married Effie May Seymore (Mamo) on December 24, 1895. Granddad Rush's history notes include the titles of cowboy, ranch foreman, farmer, stock raiser, forest guard, forest supervisor (Wichita National Forest and Game Preserve) and owner/operator of Craterville Park. Granddad Rush was the origina-

The Sandy Lake Park family left to right back row:
Frank Cuccurullo holding Taylor, Jodi Cuccurullo, Frank Rush III,
Vickie Rush, Annesa Self, Tom F Self, (Big) Tom Self, Suzy Self,
David Rush, Tori Rush. Front row: Whitney Rush,
Genelle Rush (Grammy), Frank Rush (Grampy), T. J. Self.

tor of the five-year farm plan for the 4-H Club. He was a member of the Cherokee Strip Cow Punchers' Association and was a Republican, Baptist, Mason, Odd Fellow, Modern Woodman, and naturalist. Granddad Rush would, no doubt, list his only child, E. Frank Rush as his crowning achievement.

A brief history of the family members in this book will serve to explain the often puzzling order of names:

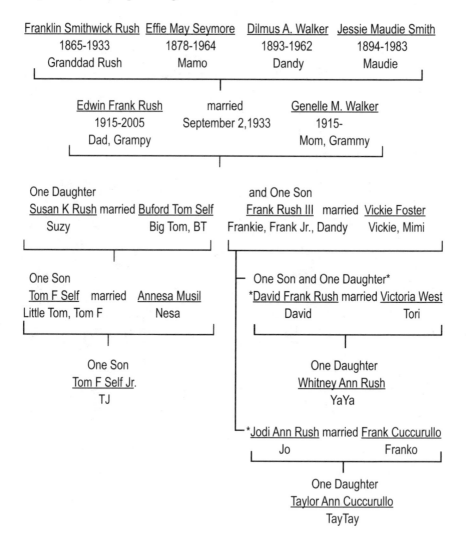

Franklin Smithwick Rush   Effie May Seymore   Dilmus A. Walker   Jessie Maudie Smith
1865-1933   1878-1964   1893-1962   1894-1983
Granddad Rush   Mamo   Dandy   Maudie

Edwin Frank Rush   married   Genelle M. Walker
1915-2005   September 2, 1933   1915-
Dad, Grampy   Mom, Grammy

One Daughter   and One Son
Susan K Rush married Buford Tom Self   Frank Rush III   married   Vickie Foster
Suzy   Big Tom, BT   Frankie, Frank Jr., Dandy   Vickie, Mimi

One Son   One Son and One Daughter*
Tom F Self   married   Annesa Musil   *David Frank Rush married Victoria West
Little Tom, Tom F   Nesa   David   Tori

One Son   One Daughter
Tom F Self Jr.   Whitney Ann Rush
TJ   YaYa

*Jodi Ann Rush married Frank Cuccurullo
Jo   Franko

One Daughter
Taylor Ann Cuccurullo
TayTay

Our names have always been confusing. Why I was named Frank Rush III when the exact name of my father, or his father before him, is different, has never been fully resolved. Granddad Rush, Dad, David, son-in-law Frank Cuccurullo and I have the same name, Frank, in common. Big Tom, Little Tom and Tom F Jr. have the name, Tom, in common as well. Adding to the confusion, we have lived at Sandy Lake Park since 1971, so we have the same address, business phone number, insurance companies, doctors, etc. Vickie's and my son, David, married a girl named Victoria, who now has our last name, Rush. Luckily she goes by Tori rather than Vickie like my wife. Our daughter married a man named Frank. Dad gave him the nickname of Franko to help keep us straight. A few of our older friends in Oklahoma still remember my grandfather as the original Frank Rush. Some "Okies" still refer to Dad as Frankie, although I am called Frankie by friends and family. When we moved to Texas, Dad started using Frank Rush Sr. on his business cards, so I started going by Frank Rush Jr., even though his signature is E. Frank Rush, and my signature is Frank Rush III. In this book, I will refer to my family by the names our family uses on a daily basis. In most cases, I will refer to the subject as Dad.

Where Did this Train Come From?

Frank and Genelle Rush, C. 1944

Granddad Rush and my grandmother, Mamo, were living at the headquarters of the Wichita National Forest and Game Preserve in Southwest Oklahoma when Dad was born in 1915. Granddad was appointed United States Department of Agriculture Supervisor on August 8, 1907, by President Theodore Roosevelt. His assignment was to develop the fifty-nine thousand acre wilderness area for public use and to reintroduce native buffalo to the refuge. Granddad and his work had a historical impact on that area. Some details about Granddad will be addressed in this book; however, there are a number of good books about his life as well.

It was in late spring, 1915, when the doctor surprised my grandmother with the news she was pregnant. Apparently, Mamo was not aware she was going to have her first, and only, child until she went to the doctor for an examination. Granddad was fifty years old and Mamo was thirty-seven years old when Dad was born August 31, 1915.

As a forest supervisor, Granddad laid out roads, picked locations for lake dams and began construction of the tall game fence around the perimeter of the refuge land. He went to work immediately preparing for the arrival of the buffalo. Once the refuge was ready, he established the buffalo (American Bison), Texas Longhorn, and elk herds that are still there today. During his tenure at the refuge, he accomplished all this and a great deal more.

Upon his retirement on June 30, 1923, Granddad and Mamo moved to a site just outside the south gate of the refuge, and began to establish and develop Craterville Park and Dude Ranch.

There were two parks owned by the family in Oklahoma, both named Craterville. The original park, old Craterville (1923-1957), was located fifteen miles west and north of Lawton. It was a beautiful park surrounded by granite mountains. Old Craterville would eventually embody many attractions plus a working cattle and horse ranch of several hundred acres. Tourists and campers began to frequent the Park in larger numbers as attractions were added. Dad and Mom met at old Craterville, and they were engaged in 1933 when Granddad passed away unexpectedly. His death left Dad, Mom, and Mamo to continue Granddad's dream of building and operating the Park. Two days after Dad's eighteenth birthday, on September 2, 1933, Mom and Dad were married. Suzy and I were born at old Craterville.

In 1957, old Craterville was condemned by the Army Corps of Engineers in Federal Court and taken into the Ft. Sill military base. The Park moved, and new Craterville (1957-1966) was established at a location about twenty miles north of Altus, near the entrance to Quartz Mountain State Park. At the same time, the Indian Curio Store, Trading Post, and rodeo grounds were moved three miles to the south of old Craterville in Cache, Oklahoma. Our home and the cow and horse operation was moved fifteen miles north to the three thousand, six hundred acre Rocking R Ranch near the community of Meers, Oklahoma.

New Craterville was never as successful as its predecessor, and Dad and Mom found themselves strapped for time trying to manage all three operations. The economy in Southwest Oklahoma began to sag in the mid 60's, and the cow and horse market went into a major slump. When the Government condemned old Craterville, the courts appraised the property at a value far less than the cost of moving and establishing the various branches of Dad's operations and our home. Between the cost of defense lawyers, stressful condemnation hearings and some double-dealing politicians, Dad never completely recovered from the economic inequity of the land grab and eventually went broke. In late 1966, he had to liquidate his assets to pay his creditors, and he was looking for a way out.

A friend asked Dad to come to Texas and meet with Angus Wynne, the founder of Six Flags Over Texas, about producing a Wild West Show. Things worked out, and we moved to Texas in April of 1967. After two seasons, and more than eight hundred performances at Six Flags, Mister Wynne sold Six Flags to the Pennsylvania Railroad Corporation. Dad did not want to continue to work at Six Flags without Mister Wynne, though we continued to live in Arlington. Dad, Mom, Suzy, and Tom moved to a small acreage on Baird's Farm Road a couple of miles north of Six Flags where there was room for our horses and equipment.

In 1969, Dad, Big Tom, and I went to work for the G.C. Walters Real Estate Auction Company in Dallas. We obtained our real estate licenses and sold farms, ranches and unusual commercial properties in Texas and Colorado. While working for Mister Walters, we also found Sandy Lake Park. We parted company with Mister Walters; and Dad, Mom, Big Tom, Suzy, Vickie, and I began the operation and ownership of Sandy Lake Park as six equal partners in January of 1971.

Where's This Train Going?

The first section of this book will include Sandy Lake Park history and our family involvement since 1971. We will then journey back in time to some stories that have captured my fascination for the earlier events and history of Dad's life. Specific years which events occurred may be jumbled; however, the background and juxtaposition of the stories seems to me to be more important than chronological order.

Most people love a miniature train ride. Over time, Dad owned several miniature trains, so I have chosen a train trip metaphor to reflect some of the many interesting events in his life. Perhaps your train trip will be made more enjoyable as you look out across the countryside, whistle stops, towns, events, and people along the way. As our train driver, Bob Bryce, says in his welcome to riders on the Sandy Lake Park miniature train, "A good way to start this train ride is to give the one next to you A GREAT BIG TEXAS HUG, then sit back, relax, and enjoy your trip around the Park!"

Track Section #I
(1971-2005)

1. All Aboard for Sandy Lake Amusement Park

The property that is now Sandy Lake Amusement Park never had a grand opening until we arrived in 1971, but people camped here as early as 1930. At one time, it was a dairy farm and has had various other uses over the years.

The building and alignment of the Bush Tollway began to get public attention in 1998. At best, the tollway would take ten less-critical acres of our property. At worst, the alignment would cut through the heart of the Park, meaning we would be out of business. News about the possibility of the Park closing spread quickly.

During the process, a car pulled up at the main gate early one morning. The driver honked the car horn until I asked our gate man, Jeff Harlan, to go out, open the gate, and see what they wanted. Jeff opened the gate, and the car drove in and pulled up to the office. An elderly woman got out of a big green Buick and wanted to see the owner. I introduced myself to the lady (Mrs. Roxie Record), at which point she poked me in the chest and said, "Don't you let Mayor Gravley close this place up!"

I said, "Well, Ma'am, it's not Mayor Gravley. It's the North Texas Tollway Authority."

She said she had known the mayor and his family since she was a child. Her grandmother had lived in Lewisville, Texas, and in 1932, the two of them walked the old railroad track from Lewisville and camped "right over there under the big pecan trees by the lake." There were other campers from a 4-H club and a group of Boy Scouts. "There were grapevines loaded with purple grapes. Granny and I ate them and carried two peck sacks home to make jelly," she recalled.

I told her the grapevines were still there and she could pick some if she wanted. She said, "Sonny, I'm too busy to pick grapes, but this place is too important for families like mine to let Mayor Gravley shut it down." (Poke, poke.)

I was cut short when I again tried to explain, "Ma'am, it's not Mayor Gra...."

She got back in her car, slammed the door, rolled down the window and told me not to worry, she would write Mayor Gravley a letter. Then she roared off in her big Buick.

True to her word, I received a letter for Mayor Gravley from Mrs. Record, hand-written on the back of her church bulletin. It stated in part, "M. Gravley, know this. I would like to put this in the paper and go to the City Council and tell them this. There has been a rec. park on this land, long years ago in 1932 and longer. This was a place the Boy Scouts set up a camp and 4-H club camped out. This is the only thing in the travel magazine in Carrollton. Don't close it up. Roxie Record." It was clear. Unless "M. Gravley" wanted a poke in his chest from Mrs. Record, he best listen up!

We have learned from conversations that there was, indeed, a camping area and a dairy farm on the property. Prior to that, they had built the old highway from Dallas north toward Oklahoma. The construction contractors needed a gravel and sand source every few miles and tried to use local supplies along the way. The state made deals with nearby landowners to mine the necessary materials.

Over thousands of years, river channels change and leave rich deposits of sand and gravel in the bends of the old riverbed. The Elm Fork of the Trinity River lay on the west end of the property and had done its job of depositing a large amount of ideal material. One half mile to the east of the property was a railroad. The ample supply of material justified the building of a railroad spur that ended near the sand and gravel pit.

The dairy farmer, Francis "Sandy" McLean, saw a golden opportunity to get paid for the material and have a nice sandy-lake water supply left in the resulting gravel pit. The topsoil was scraped back. Mules pulled contraptions called Fresno scrapers, which scooped up about one-third of a cubic yard of material and hauled it to a wash platform.

4

There, the soil was washed to remove the "fines" or silt before it was dropped into a rail car. The leftover silt created the hill on which the Sandy Lake Miniature Golf Course was built. When the "Pretzel" ride was built in 1983, part of the hill was excavated. We found several railroad spikes and two "tie plates," square pieces of iron with four holes for the spikes that rested between the rail and the ties. The golf course has several pecan trees and over the years a couple of trees have died on top of the hill. When we removed the dead trees, we counted the growth rings, and sure enough, they were the correct age to match the story.

During World War II, steel was at a premium price, and the property owner was an admitted alcoholic. The rail spur had been abandoned, and that's where supply met demand. According to at least one source, Mister McLean would occasionally cut a length of rail that he could load into an old truck, take the valuable steel down on Harry Hines Boulevard, and sell it to a scrap dealer. The money was then used to buy whiskey from a bootlegger for his recurring binges. It may well be the only occasion in history were someone "drank up a railroad," according to the man who spun the tale.

Next, problems with urban sprawl cropped up. The edge of town was way down in the Oak Lawn area of present-day Dallas. Carrollton was a whistle stop on the railroad line, and outside of the everyday life of a few hundred people, the most exciting thing to happen in this area was when the Trinity River occasionally overflowed its banks or when news of Bonnie & Clyde crackled over an old tube radio. The Perry, Center, and Gravley families and a few hundred other people called this "wide spot in a narrow road" home. The kids from Dallas discovered a sandy swimming hole, and began to come out on the weekends to swim, picnic, party, and spoon. Not to mention that swimming attire was becoming more provocative by the decade.

Mister McLean was milking cows, and the noisy young hellions were driving fast cars and creating a ruckus. Being a kindly old gentleman, he had a dilemma. He didn't want to be rude and run the kids off, but he feared the possible ruination of his dairy production. A possible solution was to charge a small amount to discourage them. His plan backfired faster than a Model T Ford. First, attendance picked up, and second, it wasn't long before he was making more money from swimmers than from milking, and he sure didn't have to get up as early. By design or by accident, the pool started to be successful, so bring on the swimmers.

The property was also home to Sandy Lake Lodge after World War II. This was advertised as a place for the recovery and rehabilitation of alcoholics. Mister McLean had served in the armed forces and, as with many of his veteran friends, heavy drinking to forget the horrors of the war led to alcoholism. There was a huge two-story ranch house, along with several other frame buildings, where the "Lodge" was headquartered. As one can see from the advertisement, this was considered a country estate. The proximity to Dallas and several military bases no doubt gave Mister McLean an idea. He could help the clients "dry out," and in exchange for their therapy, he "let" them occupy their days in recovery by working and improving the property. Trees were trimmed

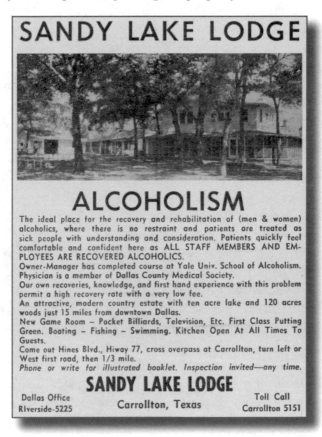

SANDY LAKE LODGE

ALCOHOLISM

The ideal place for the recovery and rehabilitation of (men & women) alcoholics, where there is no restraint and patients are treated as sick people with understanding and consideration. Patients quickly feel comfortable and confident here as ALL STAFF MEMBERS AND EMPLOYEES ARE RECOVERED ALCOHOLICS.

Owner-Manager has completed course at Yale Univ. School of Alcoholism. Physician is a member of Dallas County Medical Society.

Our own recoveries, knowledge, and first hand experience with this problem permit a high recovery rate with a very low fee.

An attractive, modern country estate with ten acre lake and 120 acres woods just 15 miles from downtown Dallas.

New Game Room – Pocket Billiards, Television, Etc. First Class Putting Green. Boating – Fishing – Swimming. Kitchen Open At All Times To Guests.

Come out Hines Blvd., Hiway 77, cross overpass at Carrollton, turn left or West first road, then 1/3 mile.

Phone or write for illustrated booklet. Inspection invited—any time.

SANDY LAKE LODGE

Dallas Office
RIverside-5225

Carrollton, Texas

Toll Call
Carrollton 5151

Advertisements for Sandy Lake Lodge in the early days of the park.
C. 1948, 1952

with care and the grounds cleared and mowed. The place began to look more like a park.

Again, Mister McLean's instinctive eye for commerce focused out of the fog. A suggestion to his jittery clients that the path down through the bushes to the pool was slippery made concrete steps for the swimmers seem like a good idea. However, progress didn't stop there. The edge of the pool, the walls, diving platforms, and seating areas were being improved and looking better every year. Improvements included fencing, a bathhouse, rest rooms, and big gravity-flow sand filters to make the water cleaner. Food stands started bringing in a profit, and Sandy Lake Pool was born over a long period of time.

With success came new problems. Rumors about snakes, man-eating catfish, and alligators began as a joke. Or was it? It probably began as a ploy for the young men to appear protective and heroic with the young ladies. While it was great for impressing a date, it did have some drawbacks. Or did it? Rumors grew, and the resulting publicity was just threatening enough to bring the curious, but unlikely enough not to discourage a dip in the cool water. Business thrived and Sandy Lake Park took its place as a local landmark with Vickery Park on Greenville Avenue and Berger's Lake near Carswell Air Force Base in Ft. Worth. No doubt, a reptile visited the pool on occasion, but the man-eating catfish and the alligator were mythical. Or were they?

Part of the pool today still reflects the shape of the original haphazard designs. These were, no doubt, just blueprints in minds influenced by alcohol, and constructed by hands more particular about the whims of the moment than the concepts of level, square, or plumb.

7

A view of the Sandy Lake Pool prior to 1971.

Our family was living in Arlington in 1969. Dad, Tom, and I obtained our real estate licenses and worked for G. C. Walters Real Estate Auction Company in Dallas. Dad had been to Oklahoma City on business and on his way back to Arlington on I-35, he missed the Highway 121 turnoff in Lewisville. The next exit to the right was Sandy Lake Road. He took a turn that changed all our lives forever. He saw a Sandy Lake Park sign, which reminded him of old Craterville Park in Oklahoma. Dad recalled how he pulled up to the gate and asked for the owner. The gatekeeper told him where Mister McLean was, and if he wanted to talk to him it would be fifty cents for admission. Dad always appreciated the fact that people's time was worth money, even if you just wanted fifty cents worth of conversation. A half dollar lighter in his change pocket, Dad got his money's worth with the proprietor. They visited for a couple of hours, and Mister McLean commented that the place was for sale.

Through our real estate dealings, we had come in contact with a man named Jerry Hicks. We knew him as a senior airline pilot for American Airlines; however, he was also looking for investments and a business to open after his retirement. These plans included his son, Ken. Dad had been searching for land for Hicks on which to build a trailer park. Hicks was investing in about anything that looked remotely like a tax shelter. His abundant stock holdings in American Airlines had been sold at a premium, and he was flush with cash. He liked the Sandy Lake property and thought the land would be a good investment. McLean accepted his one million dollar offer with a substantial down payment and personally carried the note on the balance.

During the seasons of 1969 and 1970, Jerry and Ken owned and operated the Park. There had been a racial incident. The *Dallas Times Herald* ran a picture and a story on a group of black people who had protested at the front entrance of the Park a few years earlier. To say the least, the incident had hurt business. Not only that, the place had a reputation for drinking and wild parties. Mister Hicks' investment sense had been mistimed. Sandy Lake wasn't necessarily a bad investment, but Hicks' other dealings went sour, and he admitted to Dad he knew nothing about running the Park. McLean got the property back when Hicks defaulted on his note.

McLean got mad. I was told his mind was slipping, and he had other medical problems that had taken their toll as well. It was difficult for him to realize he had received over half of the sale price as payment only two years earlier, and he still owned the valuable property. He was irate when Dad called on him to try to list the property again. He slammed the door in Dad's face after cursing him at length.

Dad met Beck James, a well-known Carrollton realtor. Her office was just south of the square in Carrollton, and she had some rapport with McLean. Dad and I met with her to see if she could convince the old gentleman to consider another sale. She knew of McLean's ill heath, and she also knew he had a taste for peppermint candy. An ample gift of the tasty treats and casual conversation softened McLean's dislike for real estate salespeople. Beck also told him the next sale would be for cash (no personal notes), and he would never have to worry about getting the property back on another default. The stage was set to market the property again.

2. Pulling Out of the Station in 1971

During the time Dad, Tom, and I worked for the G.C. Walters Real Estate Auction Company, we had a successful sale of a ranch for Robert Folsom, former mayor of Dallas and a substantial real estate investor. We had a good relationship with Mister Folsom because of the land deal, and he had high regard for us. He felt he owed us enough of his valuable time to look at the property.

Late in the afternoon the first week of January 1971, Mister Folsom met us at the Texaco station at I-35 and Sandy Lake Road. He was driving a new, white Cadillac, and wearing an expensive suit. We drove around the property unannounced, and Mister Folsom asked what we had in mind. Dad told him we had enough money to buy rides and clean the place up, but the real estate was out of our budget. Back at the filling station, he asked me to hand him the leather brief case sitting next to me in the back seat. He opened his case and pulled out a checkbook and a Standard Texas Real Estate Sales Contract. He wrote a personal check and filled out the contract with an expiration date of 3 p.m. the following day. We were impressed!

As soon as Beck James turned off her car engine at her office the next morning, we handed her the contract and check. There wasn't time for her car heater to cool off before she was headed out to see McLean. About 10 a.m., she called to report. At first McLean wasn't interested. After some more peppermint candy and fruitless encouragement, she said she finally told him, "Sammy, sign your damn' name on that damn' line, take this damn' check to the damn' bank and move your damn' stuff!"

He said, "Okay."

Now Beck James is a good Christian woman and relied on her friendly manner and knowledgeable sales skills rather than resort to high pressure and profanity to close a deal. She did, however, know when it was time to take appropriate action for the benefit of all. This was a slam-dunk deal, so she slammed and dunked, and the deal was made.

Mister Folsom's check cleared the bank, and while the title work was being done, we went over to his office to say, "Thank you" and sign a lease agreement. After we visited a while and worked out some details, Mister Folsom said, "Men, when you get on your feet, we'll tear up the lease, and I'll sell the property to you. Tell me how much rent you can pay in the meantime, and draw up a lease with Bobby McMillan in the next office. You'll need to bank with Steve Jordan at Central Bank in Farmers Branch, and you'll need a line of credit to get started. I've set you up with Steve already. Now go to work."

Leaving the office in the elevator, we were kinda' quiet. Thinking out loud, Dad said, "I don't know a better man."

During our fourth year of operation, we were out of the woods enough to buy most of the original land from Mister Folsom.

3. The Rush Family Takes a Ride on the Sandy Lake Park Express

The Sandy Lake Park family, except for Jodi, who had not arrived at the time.

Back in 1971, when we started to open the Park, the pool was in very bad condition from years of neglect. The miniature golf course was even worse. There was a par 3, nine-hole golf course located on the east end of the property that was a beautiful little course, but there were few other improvements worth salvaging. Prior to our arrival, a Merry-Go-Round had been installed, but it was never put into operation before it was removed. We were told that Jerry Hicks, the man who owned the Park for two summers, bought the ride. It was run down and had parts missing, so it was inoperable. There were few developed picnic grounds to speak of and no picnic pavilions, just a few tables scattered here and there in the brush. Trash and junk littered the premises.

The building that we now use as an arcade once served as the Park's drive-through entrance. Our refreshment stand currently operates in the room that sold picnic supplies. The miniature golf entrance still serves its same purpose. The pool building had a walk-through snack bar with a broken soft ice cream machine. We could not repair the ice cream machine, but people mentioned the ice cream for years. On the second floor of the pool entrance building, where our offices and Mom and Dad's apartment is today, was a party room. It had a chain link fence around the outside to keep revelers from falling off and a bar at one end, complete with an old rusted out Coca-Cola box. On the short inventory list of equipment that came with the property was a Wurlitzer jukebox. We figured it was the only thing on the place worth stealing because it was nowhere to be found. Six weeks later, we started pumping the winter water out of the pool, and there in a watery grave was the old jukebox.

We needed office space and a place to live. Mom and Dad, Tom, Suzy, and Little Tom lived on Baird's Farm Road in Arlington. Vickie, David, and I had an apartment on Randal Mill Road in Arlington. We had been there since we had moved to Texas to do the Wild West Show at Six Flags. Driving to and from Arlington was not easy, and we had all our eggs in one basket, so to speak, at Sandy Lake Park. The temporary office at the golf house wasn't working out, either.

Dad called Red Robinson, a carpenter friend of ours from Oklahoma, and he came down with his tools. Rick Farrah, from Corsicana, was a Hispanic man who showed up looking for work, and he had some good

Mexican men to help him. The old party room up the ramp over the pool entrance was chosen as a site for the office because Dad said we would be close to the action and could see what was going on around the Park. The offices, apartments and storage room were built under the original second-story roof, and we moved in. We used a yellow picnic table for family meals and shared the other "facilities." Between Red and Rick, things happened fast. We enclosed the old entrance building and made an arcade room. Buildings for the ride refreshment stand, ticket booth, train depot, bumper cars, and four picnic pavilions were erected.

Between early February and Easter of 1971, Dad got a chance to live his dream of building another amusement park to replace Craterville in Oklahoma. Dad was in hog heaven directing the activity. Mom was getting the tickets ordered and the change boxes ready while she cooked, kept house, and worried about the bills. Suzy, Vickie, Tom, and I did anything and everything else.

Vickie and I started calling companies and booking a few picnics. When the phone started ringing for group events, we realized there was an untapped market. Joe Mosley, the one-time barbecue king of Dallas, catered an event Dad had attended. Dad kept his business card and called him to see if he would be interested in subcontracting the catering for our bookings. Mosley agreed and started catering his delicious beef and ham, potato salad, beans, cole slaw, and all the trimmings. Dad asked him to serve "all-you-can-eat" as part of their agreement. Again Mosley agreed, but second servings were slim pickings, and he would leave the party too soon after the first serving.

Mom and Dad went up Belt Line Road to eat dinner one evening in July. Dad noticed Moore's Barbecue Restaurant. They ate dinner there, and the food was excellent. He introduced himself to the owner, Bo Moore, and asked on the spot if he would smoke the meat we needed. They shook hands, and Bo still works with us today. I am pleased to say Bo has been another blessing for our business. We have never had one cross word to each other in thirty-five years, and his masterful ability to cook our meat has been the foundation of our catering business.

On August 4, 1971, we booked Pizza Hut for a catered meal. Mister Mosley had been dismissed, but we continued to serve the same menu, only more of it. I had never used a twelve-inch long slicing knife, but Dad said he could slice the meat. The problem was that Dad, Mom, Tom, and Suzy had tickets to a Dallas Cowboys pre-season game that afternoon. Dad told me to slice, and off they went. I was mad and scared. Fortunately, I didn't cut myself, and I remember the meat was not sliced thin and neat on the plate as it should have been, but we got the job done.

Our catering improved quickly after we stopped subcontracting the food. The quality of the meat, which Bo Moore prepared, was much better, as were the other items on the menu. Our food presentation and the courtesy with which we served our customers began to help build the reputation of the Park.

Our meat-slicing skills improved as well. Vickie not only became proficient at slicing, she has taught several of our employees how to slice with skill. Over the years, some of those employees have gone on to other jobs in restaurants.

On Labor Day, our first year, we booked Local 100, the Plumbers and Steamfitters Union, for a thousand people. We put up a tent at Pavilion #1 with four catering lines and, man, did we work. We charged $3.00 a plate, including the fifty-cent Park admission. That was a lot of money in 1971, and we needed it. By the next year, we added more catering trucks and expanded our equipment to handle several parties a day.

There was a big ranch house, which served as the home of the previous owners, a two-room duplex, a machine shop, and a couple of other run-down sheds just southwest of the pool. Hicks had poured a concrete slab just west of the pool. It was about ninety by sixty feet, complete with plumbing stubs. He intended the building to be used as an office, warehouse, and apartment for himself. The walls were made of concrete blocks but only completed to a height of four feet. Inside the floor was littered with junk: old boards, wire, pipe, and things he was going to use for improvement of the property. Most of it had little value, but we did make use of some of the supplies.

The ranch house was two stories tall and thousands of stories old. Filth, roaches, and termites had taken their toll. We considered turning it into a restaurant, but we were more interested in running the Park.

The old house was so near to collapsing on its own that we decided to tear it down. Hitchcock House Moving Company was about the only business on Sandy Lake Road in Coppell. Mister Hitchcock told us the house couldn't be moved because the interstate underpass was too low, and the Sandy Lake Road bridge over the Trinity River was too narrow. Dad told him to tear the house down. Hitchcock had a heavy log chain, one hundred, fifty feet long. He weaved the chain in the front door, out the side window, through the side door, out the kitchen window, in and out the back though the bedroom windows and back out the front door. He hooked the chain up to his bulldozer and backed up. The house imploded in a cloud of dust.

In 1975, we poured an additional porch on the concrete slab and built a roof over the whole thing. We called it the "Ranch House

The old ranch house was about to collapse in a cloud of dust in early 1971.

Pavilion" in tribute to the old owner's house, and it seats about five hundred people. Through the years, we have hosted hundreds of picnic groups in that location.

On the east end of the property, the Par 3 golf course had lights for night golf and the small lake that lies there served as a water hazard for Holes 6 and 7. The greens had special tiff grass, and a sprinkler system had been installed. Jerry Hicks had installed light poles and lights for a driving range in the northeast corner of the property, but it was never used for the purpose intended. The "Pro Shop" at the golf course also served as our office for the first few months. The Par 3 was in decent shape and made about $35 a day. A Lady's Professional Golf Association pro, Gloria Ehert, came by and said she wanted to offer golf lessons. We were pleased with the fact that we actually had our own golf pro on staff. We watered, fertilized and aerated the course the next year, and it still made $35 a day. The third year we didn't do anything to the grass except mow, and it still made $35 a day. The following year, we installed softball fields and built picnic pavilions on the ground. The resulting change was much more profitable.

Our first year, 1971, was the most difficult. The Park had a worse reputation than we had known. People wouldn't let their kids come out to play or apply for jobs. Jerry Hicks owed a lot of people in Carrollton money on past-due bills accumulated from his ownership during 1969 and 1970. I walked into Gravley Hardware on the square downtown one day to buy some nails and tools. Milburn Gravley ran a splendid hardware store. He had anything you needed, and if he didn't, he would order it and have it available the next day. I made my purchase, and tried to give him a check from our new checkbook. I think the number on the check was 0006. He looked at it and said, "Cash only from Sandy Lake Park." Mister Gravley became the closest of friends with our family over the next few decades, but even after he set us up on credit, I wouldn't let him forget our first encounter.

On the occasion of Dad and Mom's sixty-fifth wedding anniversary, September 2, 1998, Mayor Gravley honored them with special recognition and presented them with the only "Key to the City" that he ever presented while he was in office.

One of our first newspaper ads about the Par 3
golf course and Gloria Ehert, our golf pro.

SPECIAL RECOGNITION

GENELLE and FRANK RUSH
In Honor of their 65th Wedding Anniversary

WHEREAS, Genelle and Frank met in 1928 at the tender age of 13 while roller skating at the Rush family-owned Craterville Park in Cache, Oklahoma, and began their lifetime partnership on September 2, 1933; and

WHEREAS, their union produced one daughter, Suzy and one son, Frank Jr. Their family now includes son-in-law Tom Self and daughter-in-law Vickie Rush; grandsons Tom F. Self and his wife Annesa, David Rush and his wife Tori, and granddaughter Jodi Rush; and great-grandson Tom F. Self, Jr.; and

WHEREAS, in 1970, Genelle & Frank, and the Rush family, began operating the Sandy Lake Amusement Park in Carrollton, Texas and have continued to play a major role in the success of our community.

NOW, THEREFORE, I, Milburn R. Gravley, Mayor of the City of Carrollton, Texas, do hereby recognize and commend Genelle & Frank for staying active in our community, and working hard to provide an environment where families can enjoy being together. I furthermore commemorate their commitment to the City of Carrollton by presenting them with a Key to the City.

IN WITNESS WHEREOF, I have hereunto set my hand and caused the Seal of the City of Carrollton, Texas to be affixed this 2nd day of September, 1998.

Milburn R. Gravley

Milburn R. Gravley, Mayor

The "Key to the City of Carrollton" and the proclamation declaring September 2, 1998 as Frank and Genelle Rush Day on the occasion of their 65th wedding anniversary.

In addition to the improvements on the swimming pool and minia-ture golf range, we purchased fifteen new bumper cars and a new C. P. Huntington train, #89, from Mac Duce, a well-known ride dealer for Chance Manufacturing in Wichita, Kansas. Mister W. A. Schafer of Schafer Shows sold us a two-abreast Merry-Go-Round, a kiddy boat ride and a Midge-O-Racer ride. Joy Land Park in Wichita, Kansas, sold us the Rock-O-Plane high ride. We purchased six aluminum pon-toon paddleboats for the lake. We had a horse-drawn stagecoach ride; Shetland ponies were used on a pony sweep to round out the attractions the first year.

The next year we bought a Fly-O-Plane from Chicago and four more kiddy rides from a closed park on Forest Lane in Garland. Our Tilt-A-Whirl came from Myrtle Beach, South Carolina, along with a cable-driven Paratrooper. Over the years, we traded up to newer and better rides including a Zumur, Space Shuttle, rim-drive Paratrooper, Little Dipper Coaster, Round-Up, Scrambler, Spider, Rock-N-Roll, Trabant, and Dragon Wagon.

Mister Schafer's mother passed away a few years later, and left a three-abreast Merry-Go-Round that was stored in a truck van. It was in excellent condition, so we bought it, and Mister Shafer gave us our money back on the two-abreast Merry-Go-Round he had sold us ear-lier. The newer ride was manufactured by the Alan Herschel Company, and also was considered a family treasure by the Schafers. When we unloaded the ride, Mister Schafer was shedding a tear or two and asked Dad to promise to never sell the ride to anyone who might not "treat it right."

A few years later, Dad wanted to buy a new Dragon Wagon ride from Wisdom Rides in Colorado. We had a family meeting and voted five to one against Dad. Anyway, when they delivered the ride we were out of good locations, so Dad had it set up in the middle of the road where it still operates today. He was proud of the new addition to our ride family and wanted to make sure he proved us wrong on the purchase.

Over the years, we have bought five new C. P. Huntington trains from Chance Manufacturing for use at Sandy Lake Park. Dad also owned one C. P. Huntington (#8) while in Oklahoma, bringing the total to six. Manufacturer Harold Chance acknowledges that Dad has bought more trains from his company's production of about three hundred and fifty numbered trains than any other single customer. The Chance trains are considered by most people in the industry to be the best 24-gauge trains ever built. We have owned and operated trains #8, 89, 165, 217, 253, and 315 in succession. An interesting fact about the train Dad owned in Oklahoma (Huntington #8) recently came to light. Huntington #8 was purchased by City Park New Orleans. The floodwaters of hurricane Katrina covered that park and the train in eight to ten feet of water in September 2005.

The trains shown display their distinctive numbers and each has been part of our ride ensemble at Sandy Lake Park over the years.

The Shetland pony ride has been a favorite attraction since we opened. In the '70s, Dad bought ponies for $75, tried them out and sold them for $75 if they had a problem or a bad habit. Now days, good ride pony prospects cost several hundred dollars and are difficult to find. The fondness for horsemeat in France and Japan creates premium prices and has taken a lot of horses out of the market. (Don't tell the kids!)

The problems with good ride ponies are numerous. First, they have to be the right size with more bone and flesh than show ponies. Geldings are fine, but most mares and studs aren't reliable. It is a challenge to find one that doesn't have a bad habit such as kicking, lying

down, sulking, biting or rubbing. They have to be sound and healthy without any scars or blemishes. Each one has to be attractive, preferably a paint or at least with great color like buckskin or solid black. Two good eyes and ears and a pretty mane and tail are necessities.

Dad always saw to it that a farrier trimmed their feet; they were treated for parasites and had their teeth floated by a veterinarian. Our ponies work only two days a week about six hours a day. They have a six-month vacation when the Park is closed and get fed the best hay and feed the year round. Dad preferred well-fed ponies, and often quipped, "Well-fed ponies are the prettiest color there is."

The miniature golf course was here when we purchased the Park. Sammy McLean had his alcoholics piece the golf course together much like the construction of the swimming pool. As mentioned, it was built on a hill created from the processing of washing gravel years before. At first, McLean paved the fairways and "greens" with clay or concrete. Later, he started using a fiber material that deteriorated quickly. We replaced the fiber material with synthetic carpet and had to do extensive repairs to the course to get it in operation.

The miniature golf course at Sandy Lake Park.

Come Have Fun

On August 8, 2003, Aline McKenzie, staff writer for the *Dallas Morning News*, surveyed nearly one hundred miniature golf courses in the Metroplex. She picked the most interesting places to take a group of kids to play and rated some of the courses. In the news story, Sandy Lake Miniature Golf was rated #5 on the top-ten list. Some of the fairways are over one hundred feet in length, and the hilly, zigzag design and other "tricks" on each hole keep you guessing where your ball will wind up.

At old Craterville, we had a monkey zoo. It was a chain-link fence and steel-pipe structure that stood two stories tall and covered about two thousand square feet. Dad would keep about thirty Rhesus monkeys in the zoo, and they were quite an oddity. Dad thought the monkey zoo idea would be a hit at Sandy Lake so we built a similar, but smaller, cage where Pavilion #8 now stands. He found five monkeys of various species and had the boys turn them in and padlock the gate. Three of the monkeys were hand-raised by a couple in Garland and were very tame. The other two were sociable but nervous around people. As expected, when people got too close to the fence, the monkeys would steal their personal belongings. Eyeglasses, watches, fountain pens, and combs were the favorite booty for the pickpocket monkeys. Often, we had to unlock the gate, go inside and retrieve the pilfered articles. One of the monkeys had a bad habit of jumping on your back and pulling your hair. When Dad started looking around for an employee to perform the hazardous duty of feeding the animals and cleaning their pen, everyone started trying to be too busy elsewhere. One day a customer reported the monkeys had a large polka-dot bikini bra in the cage. There were plenty of volunteers available to retrieve that article.

We fed the monkeys every day and built a heated blockhouse for them in the winter. A caretaker fed the monkeys one day in January and left his gate key hanging on the fence near the padlock. The next day the key was found on the ground in the open padlock and the monkeys were found to be gone. We trapped two of them nearby the following day, but the other three apparently found the trees along the Trinity River to their liking. I told Dad the monkey cage location would sure make a good spot for a new picnic pavilion, and he agreed, so the conversion was made.

We wanted to have an animal zoo, so we fenced part of the swimming pool area and built a small red barn for decoration. Dad went to First Monday Trade Days at Canton and brought home peacocks, guineas, geese, goats, ducks, and a pair of big white turkeys. Kids loved the Sandy Lake Barnyard, but the odor was a problem for the pool visitors. We moved the barn across the railroad track, fenced in the whole lake, and turned the animals and birds loose in their new home. The train track went by the barnyard and the animals had ample trees for shelter and plenty of water for the waterfowl. The new location proved to be much better.

David loved everything about the barnyard; the animals and the fish and frogs in the lake all kept his attention for hours each day. He took responsibility for the care of the animals before he was ten years old. He and I built a short fish-feeding pier out over the water, and David and his school chums lived like modern day Huckleberry Finns.

The Sandy Lake Pool is, and always has been, the centerpiece of the Park, not only in name but in the eyes of visitors. It originally was three hundred and twenty feet long, one hundred and ten feet wide and ranged in depth down to eleven feet. It held one million, two hundred thousand gallons of water and to the best of our knowledge, was the largest concrete-filtered public pool in the country. Recalling the interesting history of the pool and its evolution to current times brings back memories of countless individuals, families and groups who have enjoyed fun and fellowship in its crystal clear water.

Over the years, the pool changed little, but the old walls started to leak and several layers of pool paint showed a lot of age. In 1998, we decided to make the pool shallow water, no deeper than four feet, to bring it in line with current standards. The sidewalls and the barge in the middle of the pool were in need of repair, and the expense of chemicals and a modern filtration system were factored into our decision. We called on Andrews Gunite Company, our neighbor across the interstate. Mister Dale Andrews came out and gave us some good advice. The deep middle section of the pool was one hundred and twenty feet across and eleven feet deep. He assured us that if we filled it to depth of four feet that a pool slab of that size would crack if we didn't put down piers thirty feet deep and every ten feet in both directions. The cost of the process would be enormous, and he wouldn't guarantee the result. "If you were digging a fresh hole in undisturbed soil and put in stress joints it might work," Mister Andrews noted. Instead, he suggested we fill in the deep section completely, and make more room for decks and sun bathing, so the issue was settled.

Since the existing pool filters will now filter the water according to the new regulations, we have a better pool. One other positive result is that our day care and church youth group business went up because the sponsors weren't afraid of the deep-water section. Also, we have never had a company picnic say our pool isn't big enough. It is still huge!

The down side was that the deep water, high diving tower, and diving boards had to be done away with. "You can't have as much fun as you used to when we were kids," Dad would respond when asked why the diving boards were removed.

Almost every day, someone visiting the office recalls his or her experience as a child or teenager at the pool. They usually remember the diving tower. We have a standing bet when we ask them how tall they think the tower was. Hundreds of people have been challenged with the question, and they almost always guess twenty to forty feet. The actual distance from platform to water level was fourteen feet, four inches. Obviously, to a child standing on the platform and looking down from that height, into eleven feet of water, it seemed to be a lot higher. The ladder side of the platform was on the shallow side of the pool, and a couple of people had jumped feet first into the shallow section over the years. Luckily they were unharmed, but our insurance company was nervous about someone diving head first into the shallow end and being seriously injured. Regretfully, the old tower is no longer around to produce memorable experiences. Like Dad said, "You can't have as much fun as you used to."

The Sandy Lake Park Pool with the high diving tower
and a crowd of happy swimmers.

The Sandy Lake Park Pool as it looks today.

Whistle Stop for Traditional Amusement Parks

Dad always said he never wanted the modern hi-tech look of a theme park. Craterville Park had been known as a dude ranch as much as an amusement park, and Dad liked the image. He also got to know Walter Knott of Knott's Berry Farm in California. We took a family trip in 1956 to meet Mister Knott. Dad and Mister Knott talked at length about how the traditional picnic parks would be around when the new theme parks were in trouble from over-investment. Their vision has proven to be accurate to this day.

While in California, we also went to Disneyland with Bill Wilkerson and saw the Rose Bowl Parade. Bill Wilkerson owned the Indian Store in the Frontier Section at Disney Land. Bill was a full-blood Sioux Indian and bought buffalo skulls and beadwork from Dad for many years; he was anxious to show us Hollywood. Bill had played many roles in western movies. He took us to Paramount Studios, and we got to see the movie set of Gunfight at the OK Corral. *We ate lunch in the actors' cafeteria where there were several stars eating, including Joel Grey and a man named Ronald Reagan. Bill told Dad how much he admired old Craterville and wished he could own a traditional park with a cowboy and Indian theme.*

While we were in California, we also visited with Dad's cousin, Art Rush, who was the personal manager for Roy Rogers and Dale Evans. Art and Roy had a business relationship well-known in Hollywood and a credit to them both. They worked together for forty-nine years and never had a contract or a written agreement. It was also widely known that they never had a business dispute, a relationship of some note in the industry. In Hollywood, the concept of "A man's word is his bond" was a relatively rare idea. At the age of ten, I learned a handshake was as good as a contract, especially if you are Roy Rogers.

Art told Dad that Roy was planning to donate or display his extensive collection of memorabilia in a museum. Since Dad exhibited many of Granddad's keepsakes in the museum as part of the Indian Curio

Store at Craterville, he and Art talked at length about the subject. The idea of a Roy Rogers' amusement park or attraction of some type in which a museum would be the centerpiece was discussed. Art and Dad communicated over the next few years about the concept and the details of such an enterprise. To some degree, those conversations resulted in the construction of the Roy Rogers Museum in Apple Valley, California, which opened in October of 1967.

In January of 1968, Art asked Dad to fly to California to meet with Roy and him to consider a proposal for Dad to manage the museum as well as the inn, restaurant, and horse stables which Roy owned. Roy, Dale, and their family lived nearby, but they were discovering that management of the attractions, and the necessary time commitment to do so, was out of their line of interest.

Dad and I flew to Los Angeles and drove up to the high desert, about one hundred miles to the northeast. We stayed at the Apple Valley Inn as guests of Roy and Dale while the meetings lasted over a three-day period. Dad suggested that additional attractions and amusements in a traditional-style park setting would tie the whole operation together and increase the revenue. Roy was reluctant to make any further capital investment but promised to consider Dad's suggestions. Roy made an offer to Dad to take the management position without any major attraction changes. Dad and I were both impressed with the place, and I think Dad seriously considered the idea of moving to California. The plan never developed, and we stayed in Texas.

Art Rush passed away in 1989. Roy rode off into the sunset on July 6, 1998. The Roy Rogers Museum had been moved to a larger building in nearby Victorville, California, and was renamed the Roy Rogers-Dale Evans Museum in 1976. In 2003, the museum was moved to Branson, Missouri.

During 1968 and 1969, while we were living in Arlington, Dad became acquainted with Mayor Tom Vandergriff. Mayor Tom and Dad occasionally drove around town in the evenings and talked about possible attractions for the city. Mayor Tom was a good listener, and Dad told him about Knott's Berry Farm. The two decided to fly to California and visit Mister Knott. Dad tried to persuade the mayor that a Knott's Berry Farm-style attraction with a western theme would *be a success in Arlington. After their return home, Mayor Tom and the officials considered the option; however, a decision was made to build a water park/aquarium type attraction. The Texas Rangers were getting a new stadium, and Six Flags was on a roll. In a few months, the money was raised for "Seven Seas." The water park/sea life park was successful for the City of Arlington because of the increased tax base and increased employment, not to mention the ripple effect of the economic stimulus. However, the park was not successful on its own and closed after a few seasons of operation, despite the prosperity it had created in the community. Many people finally realized that Arlington was not a good market for a marine park. Dad continued to believe a western theme attraction would have survived in Arlington.*

Mister Knott inspired Dad. He helped Dad have the vision and foresight to realize that a park like Sandy Lake Park had potential in the Dallas area. Dad also never dismissed the idea of old Craterville with its western appeal. The style of Sandy Lake Park and the stagecoach logo that we used reflected his philosophy. Traditional parks are the long-established foundation for the amusement park industry. The historical notion of a day of family fun and diversion in a traditional amusement park is the driving force in park owners like Frank Rush and the Sandy Lake Park family.

4. Laying Track with Special Events

A great many special events Dad had originated at old Craterville Park deserved another try at Sandy Lake Park. Dad had years of promotional experience under his belt, an endless supply of ideas and a traditional amusement park in which to turn his dreams into reality, so he started laying track.

In 1971, there were only four TV stations on the air in Dallas, and two major newspapers, *The Dallas Times Herald* and *The Dallas Morning News*. We purchased advertisement in the media, but Dad also had a masterful ability to promote the Park by offering reporters news items of interest. He said, "Give them a special event for an unusual story, and they will come running."

When we had our Grand Opening in 1971, Dad called the newspapers and TV stations. Roger Staubach had agreed to run a football camp later in the spring and make some personal appearances at the Park. Roger was already famous, but his career with the Dallas Cowboys had not yet come to the full notoriety for which it was destined. Roger's name and face were first-rate endorsements for the Park. Bill Mack, "The Midnight Cowboy" of WBAP radio, was a leading country music disc jockey with a highly-rated radio show. He had worked for Dad in Oklahoma and was glad to come out and make a personal appearance for his old pal, Frank Rush, and talk about the Park to his listening audience. As Dad predicted, the reporters came running. The traffic wasn't exactly bumper-to-bumper to get into the Park, but we were off to a good start.

Grand Opening Day in 1971. Pictured standing from the left: Jay Brown, Dan Coates, Frank Rush holding Tom F Self, Genelle Rush holding David Rush, Frank Rush III, Tom Self, Dr. Jack Payne, Danny Coates, Alie Tennant, Fred Tennant, Suzy Self mounted on horse.
Sitting on stagecoach from left: "The Mid-night Cowboy," Bill Mack, Roger Staubach, Miss Texas 1971 and Vickie Rush.

Flowers were starting to bloom, and so was Dad's promotional appetite. The first Easter Sunday at the Park was coming up, and Dad went to the local TG&Y store on Josey Lane and made a deal with the manager to buy all the left-over candy and Easter baskets. It happened that the manager had over-ordered that year, and he was left with three pickup loads of candy and Easter baskets. The man was tickled when

Dad gave him $125 for dated merchandise, which he couldn't store until the next year. People couldn't believe how much candy we gave away that Easter. We started a tradition that lasted until 2001.

Easter advertisement from 1971.

Easter crowd waiting on the candy eggs dropped
from the helicopter high above in 1971.

An aerial view of the park and Easter crowd from the helicopter in 1993.

While planning for more upcoming events, Dad recalled another idea. Lloyd Cook was the band director at Turner High School; Dad asked him to help get a music festival started on a Saturday in May. Dad contracted Doctor Irving Dreibrodt from SMU to be the judge, and we had eleven bands enter the first FunFest. We had no idea it would grow into what it has become today.

Summer was quickly approaching when Dad went to the Metrocrest Chamber of Commerce and sold them on the idea of having a community-wide event. The chamber's logo was a white cowboy hat, and we had "White Hat Days." We dropped fifteen hundred numbered ping-pong balls out of a helicopter. Each numbered ball was good for a prize from the Park or a chamber merchant.

Newspaper advertisements for
White Hat Day at Sandy Lake Park.

5. Football Camp

From many of Dad's successful promotions, he recalled his football camps at old Craterville. Not all schools in Southwest Oklahoma had football teams, but many of those who did were anxious to bring their teams to training camp in June. Dad hired coaches to help organize and run the camps. There was one individual of note by the name of Darrell Royal. He would later go on to national fame at The University of Texas as the head coach. Coach Royal was the starting quarterback at Oklahoma University in 1950, and noted that the job offer at Craterville was more than welcome. He and OU center, Bob Bodenhamer, along with their wives Edith Royal and Ila Bodenhamer, came to the Park; they recalled what great times they had while coaching the campers and living in the cabins Dad provided as part of the deal. Those camps brought a great deal of publicity to old Craterville and were deemed a success by all involved.

When I was five years old, I asked Mom and Dad to let me spend the night in the dormitory with the coaches and all the big boys at football camp. A thunderstorm started about 2 a.m., and I got scared and wanted to go home. Coach Royal needed to get some sleep, so he was glad to load me up and take me across the Park grounds to our house. I met Coach Royal again many years later when UT was playing in the Cotton Bowl Classic in Dallas. I introduced myself and asked him if he remembered Craterville and taking me home in the middle of the night. He said, "I sure do have fond memories of Craterville, and how is Mister Rush?" He said he didn't remember having to haul me home in the middle of the night, then added, "Don't worry about it though, I had to do that with a lot of college players."

Coach Darrell Royal standing with rope in hand and Coach Bob
Bodenhamer riding shotgun on the stagecoach for a publicity
photo of football camp at old Craterville Park in 1950.

In the late '60s and early '70s, the Dallas Cowboys were playing in the Cotton Bowl at Fair Park, and it was truly the start of the "glory days" for that organization. A football camp at Sandy Lake Park seemed like a winning idea. Roger Staubach had become famous when Dad contacted him about a football camp. Roger was agreeable, and Dad also hired Dallas Cowboy Walt Garrison to co-host the camp. Roger and Walt had free time in June, and so did some of their teammates. Roger would work for $200 a day and the other Cowboy players like Bob Lilly, Walt Garrison, Cliff Harris, and the team kicker Mike Clark, were paid $125 a day.

Roger Staubach and Walt Garrison signing the contract to coach the football camp at Sandy Lake Park in 1971.

Roger Staubach with a group of campers and
overseeing their progress at Sandy Lake Park.

In mid-June, we cleared out the big room of the Par 3 golf course building and started registering young boys at 8 a.m. on Monday. More than two hundred and fifty boys signed up. Roger had 16-millimeter copies of the NFL game films, which were shown while the kids were checking in. We had a full week planned from 8 a.m. until 4 p.m. each day. Each kid got a t-shirt and a Sandy Lake Park cap. Practice started on the golf course lawns at nine o'clock. Groups were formed for offense, defense, and special teams. At 11 a.m., the boys rode the train down to the pool and swam until noon. We served hot dog or sandwich meals for lunch, then more practice, classroom instruction and demonstration, swimming and refreshments. The camp was a very successful, but Roger was in greater demand the next year. The Cowboys had won Super Bowl VI on January 16 and Roger was named the MVP, so Bob Lilly and Walt Garrison ran the camp in 1972 and 1973.

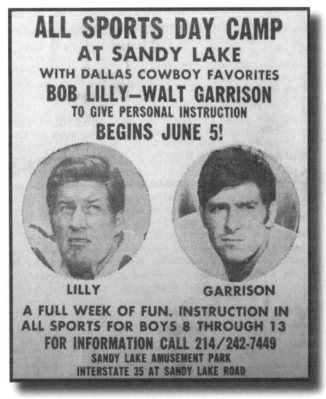

Bob Lilly and Walt Garrison advertisement for football camp in 1972.

Bob Lilly was a larger-than-life hero for everyone. He was good looking and easy to get to know. From the first day of camp, we learned that Bob's stellar reputation on the football field was exceeded by his kind nature and genuine friendliness.

Walt had been a star player for the Oklahoma State University Cowboys before being drafted by Dallas. Vickie and I attended OSU at the same time as Walt, and I knew him casually because we were both into rodeo. The camps were a good experience and helpful for the students, and Walt made them fun for our family. His daily jokes and good nature made the whole thing seem more like play than work.

On the first day of camp in 1972, we were getting the kids registered in the morning, and Bob asked Walt if he brought the footballs. "Yep, I saved a whole sack of 'em," Walt answered. He pulled a big duffle bag full of new-looking footballs out of the bed of his truck. Someone asked where he got them and he said, "Well, when we left the Super Bowl dressing room last January, they had put the footballs we used for warm up in that sack, and I sure didn't see any reason to leave them lying around." The kids never knew how valuable those footballs were as souvenirs, but I did. I still have the one I "inherited" after camp was over.

We expected, and got, an increase in attendance with more than three hundred and fifty students the next year. Mike Clark was the place kicker for the Cowboys, and Bob Lilly asked Dad to hire him as a kicking coach and for additional help. Every day, one or two of the other Cowboys would drop in to visit Garrison or Lilly at camp. Cliff Harris, Charlie Waters, and Jethro Pugh made guest appearances. When Jethro got in my pickup one day to get a ride to the other end of the Park, his knees extended well above the dashboard. I was really impressed with his physical size, and with the fact that Jethro had actually been in my truck. To be sure, there was a "Hall of Fame" full of talent at those camps. As usual, the successful football camps whetted Dad's appetite for more special events.

The next year, 1974, there was a young soccer star named Kyle Rote, Jr., who came by wanting to run a soccer camp at the Park. Kyle's father, Kyle Rote Sr., was a famous football star at Southern Methodist University years earlier. Kyle Jr. was the star player for the

Dallas Tornados, the professional soccer team. He also had just won the "Super Stars" competition. "Super Stars" was a popular televised event that involved top athletes from every professional sport, including auto racing, basketball, track and field, football, and baseball. Contests of various skills were set up to determine the best all-around athlete. The competition was a "number one" television series hit, and everyone was talking about the show and Kyle. The sport of soccer and Kyle, Jr., were popular, and when we signed up boys for soccer camp we had nearly six hundred entries and a two-week camp. We were surprised but pleased that soccer would outdraw football in Dallas.

Kyle Rote Jr. advertisement for soccer camp in 1974.

6. More Special Events

The first year at the Park, Dad knew that the Fourth of July weekend would be busy. We scheduled a fireworks show for the three nights of July 2, 3 and 4, and got ready for big crowds. There were very few other fireworks shows in North Dallas. It didn't cost much to advertise, and fireworks were not as expensive or as sophisticated as they were to become later. Dad hired a man named Jim Longnecker who was an experienced pyrotechnic expert to "shoot the show." We built steel mortars of various sizes to Jim's specifications, and buried them in the ground on the open field that ran along the north boundary of the Park.

As a rule, we didn't stay open after dark because Dad and Uncle Fred Tennant were concerned that if we stayed open late the place might get a reputation as a "hangout." The Independence Day Celebration was an exception. Almost every ride had lights, and we had lights on the miniature golf course, front gate, swimming pool, and the old Par 3 golf course. It was a magical time at Sandy Lake and a throwback to the days when old Craterville stayed open well into the evening all season long. People streamed into the Park all three days with grills and picnic supplies. Every part of the Park was full of cars, and between the shining oasis of the ride lights and the glow of a full moon, people were excited and happy.

We waited till 10:30 p.m. to shoot the fireworks so the rides could operate as long as possible. About 10:15, people started honking their car horns and flashing their headlights, more in fun than in protest.

Aerial fireworks are paper-wrapped chunks of gunpowder imbedded with a mixture of various sulfur-based chemical fireballs that ignite in different colors. The fuse is about thirty inches long and burns in about a second. When the shells are dropped into the mortars, the fuse hangs out over the top and a safety cover is removed. You had to make sure you didn't have your hand or head over the mortar because the powder charge that launched the actual bomb has a nasty habit of igniting without warning. Jim used a traffic flare to light the fuse, then quickly turned away as the bomb took off skyward. Occasionally the device would explode prematurely, only a few feet above the ground. Jim had an assistant whose sole responsibility was to keep a wet tarpaulin covering the boxes of shells waiting to be loaded, just in case a shell misfired.

Modern day fireworks shows are fired remotely with an electronic fuse in a fast-paced barrage of color and noise; however, there was a different feel to the one-shell-at-a-time fireworks show of an earlier era. People studied more closely the detail and beauty of each aerial explosion, and had time to anticipate the next.

There were special effects at the Sandy Lake fireworks shows. We had a fifty-foot telephone pole in a highly visible location. Jim attached a pyrotechnic American flag at the top of the pole. The flag was about eight feet tall and twelve feet wide. When the show started, the lights were dimmed in the ride area. The "Star Spangled Banner" played over the loud speakers as Jim lit the fuse to the big flag. People stood and sang the anthem as the red, white, and blue flag sparkled in the night sky. When the flag went dark and the music was over, there was just time to hug the kids, wipe away a patriotic tear, and settle down on a blanket before the show began. The shows usually lasted about twenty minutes, providing Jim and his assistant did a proper job of controlling things. At the conclusion of the show, they would fire off the finale. Dozens of smaller shells simultaneously filled the air, accompanied by enthusiastic whistles, shouts, and car horns. It usually took about two hours to empty the Park and two days to pick up the trash.

No Park guest was ever injured by the fireworks, but I do have one vivid memory and a scar on my right foot to show for it. One year, Jim Longnecker became very ill on the day of the fireworks show. Even with no professional replacement for him, the show had to go on. Dad decided he and I could perform the task. Everything went perfectly until Dad touched off the finale motors. Three sets of mortar tubes, with each set holding about fifty shells, were touched off, all at the same time. One shell exploded too close to the ground. Luckily Dad was not hurt, and all but one of those little fireballs missed me as well. One fireball went into the top of my tennis shoe and continued to burn at the same temperature as the surface of the sun. I headed for the paddleboat lake, which was nearby, and stepped in. That is when I discovered those little fireballs even burn under water for a few seconds.

We held the annual fireworks shows until the late '80s. New safety regulations required Mister Longnecker to attend school in Austin for two weeks of certification classes, time which he could not schedule. Cities in the area started having "free" fireworks shows at taxpayers' expense. Our expenses went up drastically, and it was a challenge to keep the ride lights operating for only two or three nights of use each

Advertisement for our first July 4th celebration in 1971.

year. It was very dry the final year the show was scheduled, and the fire chief threatened to shut the show down if the wind was high. The show went on as scheduled, but the family decided that the risk was too great to continue in following years.

People had become accustomed to sitting along the roads, in fields near the Park and on rooftops in the surrounding neighborhoods to have a free show, even though thousands still paid to enter the Park.

The first year without fireworks, irate neighbors called to complain. When one woman was told the show would not take place, she said, "Well, when did the Communists take over the Park?" Every year, around the first of July, people continue to call and ask what time the fireworks will start.

Prior to 1971, Dad had seen the Gulf Oil Special Events Sound Truck at a parade in Houston. Gulf Oil provided the truck with its specialized public address system for events they deemed appropriate. Our first year, Dad called Gulf Oil and scheduled the truck to be at the Park on Easter and July Fourth. The truck came free of charge for several years before Gulf Oil ended the promotion. In 1976, Dad called New York to book the truck and found out it was no longer available. He asked a person in the promotion department where the truck was located. The man told Dad there were actually two trucks built by Frazier Sound Company, and when the contract expired, Frazier Sound put the trucks in storage. Dad asked, "Where is Frazier Sound located?" The man replied, "Wherever the hell Farmers Branch, Texas, is." By coincidence, Frazier Sound in Farmers Branch was about four miles south of Sandy Lake Park.

Dad and I went to look at the trucks the next day and found them in a warehouse on Valley View Lane. Mister Frazier told Dad the trucks were marked down to book value of $2,800 each, and that he wanted to sell them both. Dad couldn't get a check out of his pocket fast enough. He paid the man, and I drove one truck home and went back for the other.

Mister Frazier was an innovator and guru of sound systems for big arenas and outdoor stadiums nationwide. The trucks were custom-built with generators, amplifiers and all the necessary equipment to do any outdoor sound job. Sixteen special speakers were mounted in a tower that raises hydraulically from inside the truck and can be tuned and adjusted to cover an area of several blocks.

We kept both trucks for several years and used them for events in the Park. They provided sound for the performance stage and FunFest, and we also booked them for outside commercial sponsors. We had need of only one truck so Dad decided to sell the other one, but he didn't want competition. He ran an ad in Chicago, and a man from Illinois bought it for more money than Dad had paid for both trucks. Chalk another one up to Dad and his "horse trades."

The Sandy Lake Amusement Park Special Events Sound Truck.

At Craterville Park in Oklahoma, one of the main attractions was a sixty-by-sixty foot performance stage built on the infield of the railroad track. Appearances by popular TV and movie stars were held on the stage. Dad also had circus acts and other similar attractions booked almost every weekend. At Sandy Lake Park, Dad wanted to build a stage for special events just like Craterville.

Whistle Stop for Uncle Fred

Years earlier, Fred Tennant had been the manager of the Cotton Bowl, and Dad hired acts and performers through him for personal appearances on the stage at Craterville Park. Uncle Fred, as we called him, knew everyone on the show circuits and when they had an open weekend, he would book them at the Park for a show. Uncle Fred was retired, but he knew Angus Wynne, the founder of Six Flags. When we got the contract to do the Wild West Show at Six Flags in 1967, Uncle Fred was the man who introduced Dad to Mister Wynne and helped formulate the deal. He continued to be our advisor when we opened Sandy Lake, and he showed up every morning to lend his considerable talents in the amusement business. Dad and Uncle Fred went way back, and they were good for each other. Dad was glad to have someone to bounce ideas off of, and Uncle Fred relished the idea of sharing the challenge of opening the Park. Even though he was on volunteer status, he took as much pride in the project as if he were a full partner.

Uncle Fred had contacts at the state fair grounds in Dallas, where they were doing some rebuilding. He knew about our plans for a stage and noticed some huge roof girders that had been taken down from the old livestock building. They were stacked there waiting for a new life in the entertainment field. The girders were sixty feet long and made from extra-heavy treated oak. The fair manager was glad to give them to Uncle Fred and Dad if they would remove them. Mister Hitchcock, the man who had wrecked the ranch house building, knew just what needed to be done. He had an extra-long, flatbed semi truck and a crane. The girders were loaded up and moved to the Park in 1972. Hitchcock set the beams up on bedding blocks, bolted in cross braces and built a deck on top. Presto, the new stage, just like the one at Craterville Park.

Uncle Fred influenced a lot of things at the Park. He told Dad to put a fifty-cent general admission charge on the front gate. "That will keep out the riffraff and give you control on who comes in," he sug-

gested. We still have an admission charge for the same reason today.

Uncle Fred also suggested where the stage should be built. He liked a location close to the rides and right in the middle of the attractions, so that is where it went.

Uncle Fred considered Sandy Lake his second home until he passed away. I remember him standing down by the ticket booth on one crowded July Fourth. He looked around and took it all in with pride and said, "Well, it looks like we will break even today." The Sandy Lake Park Family more than broke even with Uncle Fred.

Uncle Fred Tennant with Tom F Self inspecting his
reserved parking space at Sandy Lake Park.

The second year at the Park, Dad decided we needed a fishing tournament for kids. The State Fish and Game Department would provide five hundred, one-pound catfish if we applied for them. We filled out the paperwork, and a big tanker truck showed up on schedule. The driver told Dad he had three hundred extra fish to get rid of so we gladly took them off his hands. We invited some underprivileged kids and the Boy Scouts to fish free. About a thousand kids showed up, and most of them got to take home a fish.

We discovered the youthful anglers failed to catch about twenty-five fish. The survivors were transported to the paddleboat lake and released. Dad started feeding the fish leftover hot dog buns and fish food. Some of them grew to weigh twenty pounds or more; they would come near the shore and wait for food at the sound of Dad's voice. The offspring of those same fish can still be seen in the paddleboat lake begging for hot dog buns from kids.

In 1975, Dad planned a rodeo school as a special event at the Park, but with a new twist. Mechanical bulls were just coming onto the market and he wanted to use one. A mechanical bull, like the one later featured in Urban Cowboy, is a motor-driven bucking device on which "wannabe" bull riders practice or compete.

Dad had known Freckles Brown for many years. Freckles was in the Army and stationed at Ft. Sill near old Craterville when they became acquainted. Freckles is legendary in the annals of rodeo. He will always be remembered for riding Tornado, the theretofore-unridden bull, at the National Finals Rodeo in 1967. Freckles lived in Hugo, Oklahoma, when Dad hired him to conduct the rodeo school.

Shawn Davis, the World Champion Saddle Bronc Rider in '65, '67, and '68, had met Dad at the NFR in Oklahoma City. Shawn lived in the Carrollton area and had a mechanical bull. Dad made an agreement for Shawn to help teach the rodeo school and provide the electric Toro as part of the deal.

It was easy to sign up student cowboys anxious to receive personal instruction from the likes of Freckles and Shawn. We set the mechanical bull in front of the performance stage and purchased four sets of bleachers to seat the onlookers. Dad notified the newspapers and they ran stories about the event. It was a cold, raw Saturday in May, but a good number of autograph hounds and curious patrons were there to watch. The Park had again received good publicity.

Freckles Brown showing proper riding technique on the mechanical bull with Shawn Davis and a group of bull-riding students looking on.

Advertisement for the bull riding school.

Rusty Wahkinney leading a fast war dance at our first annual Indian Powwow.

Advertisement for the Indian Powwow.

Tito Guizar performing to a standing-room-only crowd.

Window card advertisement for our Mexican fiesta in 1973.

"Fall Harvest Appreciation Weekend"
advertisement held in October of 1971.

Kids Fishing Rodeo held at Sandy Lake Park in 1972.

7. FunFest

SANDY LAKE AMUSEMENT PARK

Again, Dad reached into his bag of tricks and former promotions and recalled band camps at old Craterville where the kids stayed for five days in the big bunkhouse and received daily instructions. At new Craterville, we didn't have a bunkhouse, so he held a marching contest on three Saturdays in the spring.

Colonel L.D. Irons from UT Arlington came to Oklahoma to judge the marching contest at new Craterville. Colonel Irons was a bandmaster with extraordinary knowledge of band music and a reputation to match.

One contest day at new Craterville in 1959 stands out in my mind. Dad had just purchased a new Cadillac, the first car I had seen with electric windows. It was cold and damp and Colonel Irons never got out of Dad's car to judge. With the motor running and heater on high, the old gentleman would roll down the electric window and listen when the band came strutting past the car. The old master needed to hear only a few bars of music to rate the group's ability.

Those two school band promotions at old Craterville and new Craterville would become the foundation and inspiration for what was to come at Sandy Lake Park. Dad knew that if he could get bands and school groups to come, especially on school days when the Park was otherwise closed, those events could be the salvation of the Park.

Dad introduced himself to Lloyd Cook, director of bands at Turner High School in Carrollton. Mister Cook agreed to talk to some other band directors and see if they would be willing to bring their bands out to Sandy Lake. The idea was to have a fun music festival. Someone came up with the name FunFest and it stuck. Mister Cook knew Doctor Irving Dreibrodt, better known as Doctor Dri, at Southern Methodist University and helped Dad get in touch with him about the event. He came out a few weeks ahead of time and talked with Suzy and Dad about the details. We didn't have an area that was appropriate for a marching contest. We were also concerned about weather, so Doctor Dri suggested a concert format with the bands seated under a picnic shelter. Big trophies were ordered, and the event began to take shape. Eleven bands attended the first year. Doctor Dri and Mister Cook judged the event under the shade trees near Pavilion #2, and we were thrilled because about five hundred students and parents were present.

Since Suzy had experience taking entries and keeping books for the rodeos we held in Oklahoma, responsibility for dealing with the FunFest registration fell largely to her. By the next year, the stage had been built and since weather might be a problem, Dad rented a big tent from the Childress Tent Company. The tent completely covered the performance stage and bleachers, in addition to lending a festive air to the event. There were around thirty bands for the Second Annual FunFest, and we started to realize the event had special potential.

The most amazing thing about FunFest is how it has grown each and every year for thirty-six years. More days and weeks were added through the '70s to accommodate the ever-growing numbers. When the groups numbered more than five hundred, we expanded the contest to a three-week event. Everyone thought, "FunFest just can't get much better than this."

The Sandy Lake Park family is presented with
"The Sandy Lake Park March" by composer Jerry Nowak in 1983.

In 1976, we considered adding other types of groups to FunFest. We tried a cheerleading contest. The idea sounded good, but the girls were more interested in putting on makeup and fixing their hair and costumes than they were spending money on the amusements. Also, each group might only have three to five cheerleaders, so there weren't enough students participating to justify expenses.

In 1977, we added a choir division to the contest, and it caught on quickly. Not only did the choirs have lots of students, they could move on and off the stage more quickly because they didn't have instruments to deal with. For the 1978 contest, the orchestra division was added. Orchestras started slow with only one contest day needed at first. The orchestra division currently has more than one hundred and twenty groups and lasts five days.

In 2005, more than one thousand, four hundred and fifty schools and church groups were represented, with attendance in excess of sixty-five thousand students. The contest currently takes forty days over an eight-week period to complete.

Woody Schober of Irving ISD helped us get the choir division started, the circumstances of which he recalled at FunFest 2006 on the thirtieth anniversary of the choir festival. Mister Schober called Dad in 1976 to inquire about supplying several horse-drawn wagons for the Centennial Celebration for the city of Irving to be held at Texas Stadium. Dad told Mister Schober there would be no charge for the wagons if he would help organize a choir festival for FunFest. Mister Schober agreed and was amazed that Dad would make a trade of that nature. "Looking back thirty years, and considering the success of the FunFest choir competition for that length of time, Mister Rush's trade looks better every year," he mused. Judges chosen included Mister Charles Clingman from Southwestern Oklahoma State University in Weatherford, Oklahoma, and Gene Brooks of the American Choral Directors Association. Currently, Doctor Joey Martin of Texas State University; Cecile Johnson, Denton, Texas; Jolyne Antista, Trinidad State College, Colorado; and Ruth Millner, Dallas, Texas; as well as other very talented choir directors/adjudicators serve at FunFest.

FunFest judges John Haynie University of North Texas, Dr. Irving Dreibrodt, Southern Methodist University, Col. Joe T. Hayne of Texas A&M University, and Dr. Bob Foster, University of Kansas take time out for a photo at FunFest 2005.

Weldon Minnick, orchestra director from Mesquite ISD, was our first orchestra coordinator. Under Mister Minnick's guidance, equally knowledgeable judges were brought in for the orchestras. Mister Minnick passed away a few years ago, and Royce Cotney of Lamar High School in Arlington took over the coordinator's position at FunFest.

The rides create a certain amount of noise, but that doesn't disturb the bands and choirs on the stage. The orchestras need a quieter environment. The Ranch House Pavilion provided an enclosed place away from the action. Sandy Lake has enough bus parking area to allow for the choir and orchestra festivals to be held on the same days. There are five days on which there are fifty or more choirs and twenty-five or more orchestras competing at the same time. The Park really gets busy, and we keep saying, "FunFest just can't get any better than this."

Whistle Stop for Dr. Dri and the Other Bandmasters

Known as the "Best Dressed Band in the Land," the Southern Methodist University marching band is famous worldwide for the many flashy costume changes. Doctor Dreibrodt was responsible for bringing costume design and flexibility into a new era at SMU and across the nation. He is a flamboyant dresser himself, and he wanted his bands to shine like new money. He is a showman extraordinaire when it comes to presenting a half-time show.

Doctor Dri has guided Suzy and FunFest every step of the way. He suggested many of the rules for the event, and has been responsible for bringing in most of the adjudicators who have been the cornerstone of our continued success. When Suzy has a situation come up that might be problematical, she often relies on Doctor Dri for guidance. His quiet assurance, knowledge of music, and sense of fairness always keeps the FunFest train on the track.

For thirty-six years, Doctor Dri has been an adjudicator for one, two, or three weeks during the band festival. He has never missed a year. He is a member of both the Texas Bandmasters' Hall of Fame and the American Bandmasters' Hall of Fame. He is a blessing in trumps for our family and for FunFest.

Dad told Doctor Dri early on that we didn't know how to select band judges, but he asked Doctor Dri to recommend judges who were positive in their approach and comments. As a result, many of the most famous bandmasters in the nation have graced our judges' platform, including Colonel Joe T. Haney, Director Emeritus of the Fightin' Texas Aggie Band at Texas A&M University, who has been a FunFest adjudicator since 1981. Colonel Haney is the originator of the A&M Corps' unusual and famous marching style. The Joe T. Haney Drill Field, on the campus of Texas A&M University is named in his honor. He was inducted into the Texas Bandmasters' Hall of Fame in 1999.

Joe Frank has been in music education for forty-five years, and a FunFest adjudicator for twenty. Mister Frank is one of the most influential band directors in Texas, serving as Texas Music Educators' Association State Band Chairman and also State Orchestra Chairman for TMEA. He served in music education and as Conductor of Wind Ensemble at SMU during his career. He was honored as the Texas Orchestra Director of the Year in 1991 and is a member of The Bandmasters' Hall of Fame.

Doctor Robert Foster is the Director of Bands at the University of Kansas. He has served as President of the National Bandmasters' Association and the American Bandmasters' Association. He is a member of the board of directors of the John Philip Sousa Foundation. His KU bands have won many honors, including the Marching Band of the Year. Doctor Foster is an annual adjudicator at FunFest.

John Edmondson, from Sunrise, Florida, has arranged an extraordinary amount of music for bands, with more than seven hundred publications to his credit. His arrangements and compositions have comprised a significant portion of the music performed by bands throughout the nation and at FunFest. John has been an adjudicator at FunFest nineteen years.

Jerry Nowack is from Flemington, New Jersey, and authored the "Sandy Lake March" in honor of the festival. He was with FunFest for many years and added a great deal of notoriety on those occasions.

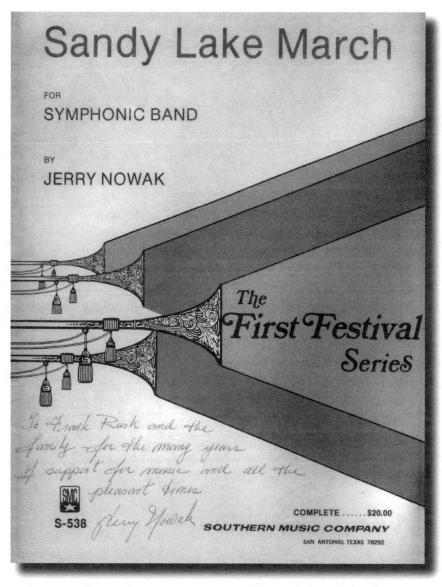

The front cover of the "Sandy Lake March," by Jerry Nowak.

The "Sandy Lake Park March" original score.

Bill Moffit from Purdue University was at FunFest for a number of years. While at Purdue, he annually upheld the tradition of leading his band down the brickyard at the Indy 500 while playing "Back Home Again In Indiana." He was also director of the National Future Farmers of America Band.

John Haynie from the University of North Texas in Denton, Texas, is known internationally as an educator and is considered one of the finest trumpet players of all time. John's reputation as a trumpet virtuoso is legendary and his ability as a performer, teacher, and researcher are unexcelled. His new book, The Haynie Legacy: Lessons in Trumpet, Lessons in Life, *is now in print.*

Doctor Royce Lumpkin is Chairman and Professor of the Music Education Department at the University of North Carolina at Charlotte. For many years, Doctor Lumpkin was Professor of Music at North Texas State University. He has served as President of the International Trombone Association. Since 1989, we have been privileged to have this very gifted man as an adjudicator at FunFest.

Eddie Galvin is a retired Associate Professor of Music at Texas A&M University—Corpus Christi. He is the past president of the Texas Bandmasters' Association and was elected to the Texas Bandmasters' Hall of Fame in 1972. He was honored as the Bandmaster of the Year in 1996. Eddie is a widely-sought clinician and adjudicator and to date has served at FunFest for fourteen years.

Doctor Francis McBeth retired in 1996 as Professor of Music and Chairman of the Theory-Composition Department at Ouachita Baptist University in Arkadelphia, Arkansas. Since 1977, Doctor McBeth has adjudicated bands at FunFest. He served as conductor of the Arkansas Symphony Orchestra in Little Rock and was appointed Composer Laureate of the State of Arkansas. He is past president of the American Bandmasters' Association. Doctor McBeth shares Dad's love and interest in American Indian lore, due in part to his distant kinship with Chief Quanah Parker.

Colonel Truman Crawford adjudicated for two years at FunFest prior to his untimely death in 2002. Colonel Crawford was for many years the director of the U.S. Marine Drum and Bugle Corps stationed in Washington, DC. He served eight presidents and traveled the world representing our country. His reputation and experience is unsurpassed, and we miss him greatly.

The other band adjudicators whom we have been privileged to have at FunFest are equally talented and famous, each in their own right. By no means do we forget their contributions and the prestige they have brought to our festival. Such people as Don Hanna, retired director of Bands at Hardin Simmons University in Abilene, Texas; Wendell Evanson from Henderson State University, Arkadelphia, Arkansas; Doctor Ken Van Winkle from New Mexico State University in Las Cruces; Doctor Robert Bailey from Northeastern State University in Tahlequah, Oklahoma; Doctor Gary Barrow of Arkansas Tech University in Russellville, Arkansas; Lieutenant Colonel Jay Brewer from Texas A&M University in College Station; and David Ritter of West Texas A&M University, Canyon, Texas; have all been outstanding adjudicators at FunFest.

The choir and orchestra adjudicators do not take a back seat to anyone as far the extraordinary talent and extensive contributions they have made to various fields in music education and FunFest as well.

There is little doubt that the primary reason that FunFest has enjoyed such a fantastic tenure is due in large part to the fine gentlemen and ladies who come to help us adjudicate the contest each year. To each of them, we owe a special debt of gratitude for their service.

Many of the band, choir and orchestra directors who bring their groups to FunFest have become close friends to the Sandy Lake family. Their loyalty to our contest is not only essential to our success, our friendships are mutually fulfilling. The directors' annual visits give us a chance to catch up on news from their hometowns and renew our acquaintances.

During FunFest, the Park staff includes our family, regular employees, and other seasonal personnel as well. Suzy does a tremendous amount of work with all aspects of the event year round. The office secretaries have been challenged by helping with the mailing list, entries, daily schedules, and details of putting hundreds of groups in order. Big Tom is responsible for keeping things organized at the stage and keeping groups moving in the fast-paced schedule. The rest of us see to our normal duties in the operation of the Park and help out with bus parking, the extra load of business at the concession stands and rides, and fill in wherever we are needed to keep things running smoothly.

Suzy's college friend, Patricia Kitchens from Lawton, Oklahoma, comes to help her check in the groups and run FunFest Headquarters at the front gate.

Allison Snyder of Carrollton, Texas, is an extremely talented musician and one of our special FunFest helpers. Years ago, as the festival grew, Suzy needed a capable person on stage to assist the adjudicators and directors, keep the sheet music organized, operate the sound console, keep the things moving, introduce the groups, and announce their selections. Allison fit the bill, and he has one other vital skill: he can accompany any choir that needs a pianist. Most choirs bring recorded music or their own pianist for accompaniment, but some also rely on Allison. It is often amusing to have an unknowing choir director discover Allison. One of them might say, "My pianist is not here yet, and its time for us to perform! What can I do?" Suzy simply tells them to give their music to Allison when they get on stage, and he will handle it. They may walk onto the stage with reservations about what might happen in an unrehearsed performance. Not to worry. Allison on keyboard is as solid as they come. A good many choir directors have shaken hands with him after a performance and told him their choir never sounded so good. Allison has been on stage all day, every day, at FunFest for twenty-five years.

Allison was Doctor Dri's student at SMU. Doctor Dri and all the adjudicators have the highest regard for Allison and his professional skill. We came to know him when he was the choir director at First United Methodist Church in Carrollton. Listening to him on a church organ or piano is a religious experience in itself. He is a good Christian man and a blessing to all who come in contact with him.

8. Fun Facts

When a band performs, each director receives hand-written comment sheets from the judges. When directors return home with a beautiful trophy, constructive comment sheets from nationally known adjudicators, and happy kids, they have something to show for their efforts. While it may be a fun-oriented contest, any director who has been to FunFest will tell you they performed for judges who deserve the highest degree of respect and credibility in the school music field. At FunFest, everyone is a winner!

FunFest draws groups from Oklahoma, New Mexico, Arkansas, Louisiana, and, of course, Texas. The majority of groups come from North Texas. Usually they travel to and from the contest in one day. Many other groups charter buses and spend a couple of days in the Metroplex. If the students get to see Dallas for the first time, shop at the Galleria or North Park Malls, see the historical Fifth Floor Museum where President Kennedy was assassinated, and attend a Texas Rangers game or other area attractions, it can be an educational and memorable trip.

FunFest fills many hotel rooms and restaurants, and filling stations benefit from fuel sales as well. The economic impact of the festival in the community has been largely overlooked. We do not overlook the impact on the Park, however. We are open and busy on days in April and May when we would otherwise be closed. Our Park would be successful otherwise, but not to the extent we are with FunFest.

The festival impacts music score sales, band instrument purchases, enrollment in band programs, bus charters, and all the jobs that go hand-in-hand with those related businesses. We require directors to purchase original scores, not photocopies, of sheet music for the adjudicators. Band students purchase band instruments worth millions of dollars and bring them to FunFest. When Suzy puts out bids for more than fifteen hundred, thirty-four-inch engraved trophies each year, the dealers clamor for the business.

There have been troublesome issues over the years. The Robin Hood legislation that Texas enacted years ago was a concern because we felt that many school districts would not have the finances to allow some groups to attend. Robin Hood is a law that takes a portion of the tax funds from more affluent districts and transfers the money to the lower income districts. We feel some effect, but band booster clubs pick up the slack in most cases and see to it that their bands come.

The "no pass/no play" rule has had a much larger impact. This legislation restricts students from participating in extracurricular activities when they fail a subject. This has been a hotly-debated issue since its inception. For most students, it is an encouragement for them to pass every subject. For the students who cannot pass every subject, it may have a detrimental effect. They may be discouraged to the point of dropping out of school, or if they stay in school and continue to fail, they may lose interest in extracurricular activities. As to the effect on FunFest, the group may attend anyway but be several members short.

A substantial positive impact is made on individual school programs, according to music directors. They say it serves as an incentive for most students to make passing grades so that they can participate.

Awards time at FunFest is the best time of all. The judges are recognized and division placing and trophy presentation is greeted with applause and ear shattering shouts of excitement. Suzy presents the trophies and comment sheets, and I announce the division placing. On many occasions, Mom and Dad sat side by side under the shade trees nearby and observed it all with satisfaction.

Our adjudicators have told us that FunFest is the largest privately-operated school music festival in the nation. Other promoters and parks have tried to copy FunFest, but a few unique circumstances and the blessing of many fine people have made it work beyond our wildest dreams. FunFest is a winner all the way around.

Dad's success at Sandy Lake Park will be measured in many different ways. His legacy to the Park, to the community, to school music programs, and to the hundreds of thousands of people FunFest has touched, speaks for itself.

Congratulations, Dad! FunFest is a hit!

9. High Diving Mules, Security Lions, and Trained Buffalo

Johnny Rivers was the showman who had the diving mules on the Boardwalk in Atlantic City, New Jersey. The animals he used were truly horse-size mules, and they dived off the pier into the Atlantic Ocean. The act was so unique and unusual that it became a huge drawing card for the beach and the Boardwalk for many years.

After training and presenting circus acts across the nation, Johnny hit on the idea of training smaller donkeys or miniature mules to dive into a portable swimming pool. Johnny worked for Dad at old Craterville, so Dad called him for a booking at Sandy Lake. We purchased advertising space in local newspapers, and the diving mule show garnered a lot of free publicity for the Park. A large crowd of people showed up, and the act was booked for repeat performances for two more seasons.

The donkeys were trained to be turned loose and voluntarily walk up a ramp to a diving platform. They began their training at ground level with the promise of a carrot for a reward. After gradually raising the ramp to greater heights, they would learn to dive, head first, into the tank about nine feet deep and twenty feet in diameter. Another short ramp allowed the animal to climb out over the edge of the tank and back to the ground.

People laughed, applauded, and couldn't believe their eyes. One miniature donkey wore a saddle and had a monkey jockey. A trained dog, supposedly from the audience, got loose, ran past a protesting Mister Rivers and made a dive just to cool off. After twenty-five years, people who visit the Park still talk about the high-diving mules.

A July 4th advertisement featuring fireworks
and Johnny Rivers' High Diving Mules.

One of the mules showing good form in mid dive.

A high wire walker, known as the "Crowned Prince of the Air," was booked for a show at the Park. He stretched a three-hundred-foot-long cable between two, eighty-foot-high scaffolds high above the swimming pool. He was very daring, but he also had some personal issues. We wondered if he was trying to kill himself and wanted an audience as a witness. He never became fully suicidal and finished the job, but the cable in his mind started to unwind, so to speak. After three weeks of his scheduled five-week engagement, Dad had to let him go.

Jerry Olson, from Nebraska, was noted for his rodeo specialty acts for the Professional Rodeo Cowboys Association. Dad had met Jerry at the National Finals Rodeo in Oklahoma City and told him if he was in Texas during the summer and had an open weekend, to let him know. As it turned out, Jerry was available for one weekend the following summer. Jerry had an extraordinary trained buffalo. It is very difficult to train a buffalo to ride and do tricks, and Jerry was the first person in the rodeo business to be successful in the endeavor. The animal was unusual and very talented. He had a nose ring and reins for a bridle and worked like a trained quarter horse. Figure eights with lead changes, spins, back-up and walk, trot, and canter were all part of the animal's repertoire. In addition, he would lie down, roll over, and sit up. For a finale, Jerry would ride the buffalo up a ramp onto his custom-built horse trailer and do a salute to the "End of the Trail" painting. Granddad Rush would have loved the act, and so did the audience.

L.V. Sanders was an animal trainer from Arkansas. Dad had seen an advertisement about him in the *Amusement Business* magazine, so he contacted him. While L.V. was a talented animal trainer, he was not able to book many shows. He had the entire summer open, so Dad invited him to live at the Park while he was looking for work. L.V. showed up a week later with five dogs, two goats, a llama, a miniature musk ox, twelve chickens, a roller-skating horse, and a lion, all of which were part of his act in one way or another. He had an old trailer and a camper on a pickup. He camped out under the shade trees in the pony pasture where water and electricity were available. Every weekend, he did shows in a circus ring in front of the stage. Almost all the animals in his menagerie were in the show, and there was no end to the variety of tricks they performed.

After a while, we wondered what the chickens did to earn a position with the troop. L.V. finally confessed that the lion had a fondness for fresh poultry, and he had a fondness for eggs. After three weeks, the supply of live chickens had to be replenished.

We were having fireworks on the Fourth of July while L.V. stayed at the Park. For added entertainment, L.V. performed three different animal acts during the afternoon. We had a huge crowd all day, and the fireworks were over by 11 p.m. It took about two hours to clear the Park.

About 1 a.m., we were checking to make sure everyone was gone. In a grove of trees, hidden mostly from view, I could hear soul music blasting away. I drove over and told the group of about twenty people that we were closed, and it was time for them to leave the Park. They were all driving tricked out Monte Carlos, and they told me they would leave in an hour or so. There were too many of them to argue with, so I drove away. Several of the employees, including L.V., were gathered at the front of the Park talking about the big day. We thought about ganging up and tossing the group out, but L.V. had a better idea. We took a flatbed golf cart with a big headlight down to his camp and loaded up the sleepy lion. When we pulled up to the group in question, L.V. got the lion's leash, told him to unload, and led the lion between the big headlight and the revelers. On cue, the lion let out a loud roar.

Luckily the windows on the Monte Carlos were rolled down because the owners didn't bother to open the doors. They all jumped in, rolled up the windows, and the dust flew as they drove down the road and out the gate. The next day, two guys showed up asking if they could get the beer and picnic coolers they left on some tables down in the trees. One man said, "They turned a guard lion loose on us last night, and we had to leave in a hurry!" We told them we didn't know anything about a guard lion, and they probably just had too much beer the night before.

The lion had a new job description, complete with an official title. We used the guard lion several times during the remainder of the season to help close the Park; however, the lion departed with L.V. in the fall.

While L.V. was at the Park, David took a shine to him. David liked the trained dogs and was working daily with L.V. to learn how to put them through their paces. Suzy took an interest to one of the trained goats and delighted in giving him treats in return for doing his stunts. Before L.V. left, Dad traded for the dogs, goat, and related circus props. Dad didn't think we needed the guard lion for security duty, or he would have bought the lion as well.

The following year, we were wishing the guard lion were still around. Willard "The Wiz" Mason worked in our catering department, and was known park-wide as a free spirit and a clown. As a joke, we started putting a collar and leash on Willard, and driving him around the Park on a golf cart at closing time. When Willard's leash was jerked, he would roar like the lion and act like a wild man. While he was not as intimidating as the real lion, people usually left the Park on time, and had something to laugh about on their way out.

A cartoon by park employee and artist Roxanna Posey
showing park employee Willard "The Wiz" Mason
acting as our wild man security guard.

10. The Family Circus

Following L.V.'s departure, Dad was anxious to keep doing free shows the next year. We built a circus ring and assembled it in front of the stage. Outdoor carpet was added to floor the ring; some flags for decoration and four large sets of bleachers surrounding it gave the site a circus feel. We advertised "The Family Circus" free show for day care and church youth groups on Tuesday and Thursday each week and company picnic groups on the weekends.

David had the trained dogs, Jodi had a trained horse named Sandy, Tom F was becoming an expert trick roper, and Suzy had the trained goat, so planning got underway.

Whistle Stop for Sandy

Dad found Jodi a trick horse advertised in the want ads, and, wow, what a horse. Mister Bell from Duncanville, Texas, had trained the horse. He said the animal was a soured show-horse, and was headed to the soap plant when he found him. Mister Bell claimed when he looked in the horse's eye, he knew right away he was going to save his life, and teach him to do tricks for the children who visited his stable.

Mister Bell came out to the Park and worked with Jodi and her new horse regularly throughout the winter and spring. Dad gave the horse his new show business name, "Sandy." Jodi was only eleven years of age, but both Mister Bell and Sandy were impressed with her horsemanship. He showed Jodi the cues for Sandy's tricks, and Sandy responded eagerly for her.

Most trained horses, or "high school horses" as they are known, can learn five or six tricks or "responses." Add a few variations of a learned response, and you have enough for a professional act. Sandy knew more than forty-five separate and distinct tricks. We soon realized that in this one animal there was a mother lode of ability and talent that was difficult to comprehend.

Mom owned and performed with a high school horse at old Craterville named "Ace of Spades." Mom understood what she was witnessing and was so amazed, she began making a written list of responses and the appropriate cues so Jodi wouldn't forget. A partial list of Sandy's tricks include counting, smiling, yes and no, untying a handkerchief from any leg with his mouth, dancing front or rear, rearing up, lying down, stealing the covers, drinking from a bottle, kneeling, praying (or double kneel), sitting up, and rearing. He would kick, paw, and charge with teeth bared and ears laid back, but only on cue. When Jodi was mounted, Sandy would perform dressage moves, including a standing gallop, side pass, and five different gaits. His most impressive trick is known as an "Airs Above the Ground." This is a move associated with the Lipizzaner breed where a horse jumps straight up with all four feet, and at the top of the jump, the animal

85

kicks its hind feet backwards and paws the air with its front feet. This is supposed to be the most difficult response a horse can learn, but it is also wearing on the animal's body. Sandy could do this move with ease and grace.

We sadly came to discover that Sandy had been "force broken" during his training time with Mister Bell. We should have suspected as much, since Mister Bell didn't believe in awarding treats as a training aid. In May, it was getting closer to show time. One day when Mister Bell was watching Jodi put Sandy through his paces in practice, Sandy failed to do a response fast enough to satisfy his former owner. Suddenly, Mister Bell broke out a buggy whip and began beating the animal fiercely. Dad and I quickly intervened, but by that time Jodi was in hysterics. Dad told Mister Bell to leave and not come back. Tricks or no tricks, when we all calmed down, we promised Jodi and Sandy that he would never receive another whipping.

Sandy was truly a remarkable and pleasant animal. After Sandy retired, he lived to a ripe old age with Dad feeding him green alfalfa and sweet feed daily. I always figured Sandy was saved from a bad fate at least twice.

Jodi and Sandy were favored by many as the hit of the show. What little girl in the audience wouldn't love to have a horse like Sandy? Jodi dressed either as a cowgirl or in English riding attire for her performances. Each time Jodi showed Sandy, it was a different routine. She wanted Sandy to demonstrate all his tricks, but there wasn't enough time in a single show. Every once in a while, Sandy would surprise Jodi and show a trick that Mother hadn't put on the list, one that Jodi didn't realize that he knew. The experience taught Jodi much of her considerable knowledge about horses, which she still uses on a daily basis.

L.V. had sold us the necessary props for the dog show and worked out a routine with David for his act. David wore a cowboy hat and a red satin shirt, and the dogs wore bandanas around their necks to add color. Each of the dogs had special talents, including doggie leapfrog, hurdles, balancing, or hoop jumping. A dog, Silly, was the clown of the team and deliberately fouled up his tricks to the joy and laughter of the crowd. The final trick was performed by Corky, a sweet little Heinz 57 mutt. Corky was trained to climb up a twelve-foot ladder and jump into a pillow in David's arms.

Tom F was a cowboy from birth. Big Tom had some "spot cord" trick ropes left over from our days at Six Flags and when Tom F got big enough to swing one, he started learning his craft. By the time Tom F was a teenager, he had taken lessons from the trick-roping master, J.W. Stoker, of Weatherford, Texas. Stoker is a life-long friend of the family and has performed trick roping around the world for decades. Big Tom and Suzy would drive to Stoker's house at every opportunity so Tom F could have a lesson.

Tom F had won the Will Rogers World Champion Junior Trick Roper title at the National Cowboy Hall of Fame a few months earlier. Stoker won the senior division title the same year. Dad purchased a beautiful palomino roping horse, Chiquita, for Tom F. The horse had a golden color and a milky white mane and tail. Chiquita's disposition was one of gentle calmness: perfect for crowds and trick roping. Tom F looked like a young western movie star from an earlier time; when he roped, people would clap and yell. Trick roping is not a talent that everyone can learn. The hand/eye coordination required is akin to the most difficult of skills. The trick is to make it look easy and smooth, and Tom F learned from the best. His "Texas Skip" and "Cowboy's Wedding Ring" were the highlights of his act, and he seldom dropped a loop.

The three-act show opened with recorded music. I announced the action, and Vickie and Big Tom backed the kids' performances behind the scenes. We even had a warm-up act: Suzy and her goat. While the kids and sponsors were settling into the stands, the two of them would get the crowd fired up by doing the only four tricks the goat knew: bowing, rearing, jumping on a box, and eating candy treats. When the show was over, the kids were invited to pet the horses, the dogs, and the goat while "Happy Trails To You" was played for the "sell out."

Often, more than five hundred youngsters would catch the Tuesday and Thursday shows, and on weekends the crowds would double or triple that number. On July the 4th, when the Park was full of people coming to see the fireworks, a few thousand people made up the audience.

Prior to the third year of the show, David had dog trouble. First one thing then another had cut the trick dog population from five to two. David needed a new act. David's lifelong friend, Scotty Schoonmaker, was having dinner with us one evening when he recalled a stunt he had done as a Boy Scout. It was called the shrinking box. The trick was to put a large object in one end of a box then pull an identical, but much smaller, object from the other end of the box. The shrinking box idea grew to maturity before Vickie served dessert.

We had an old electric golf cart that could be made to run, and with the addition of plywood sides, paint, gauges, whistles, bells and levers, we visualized "Doctor Dave's Incredible Shrinking Machine." The construction got underway with David, Scotty, and me making plans as we built.

Once the shrinking machine was complete, we found a regula-tion-sized basketball, which David would place into the intake door. The machine would shake; bells, lights, and whistles would go off and out the back came a fist-sized basketball. A cat named Sylvester, was safely reduced to a very similar kitten. Next, one of Dad's female bird dogs was loaded in the contraption, and after the job was completed, out came her look-a-like puppy. A chicken from the Sandy Lake Barnyard was inserted next, but when the machine got hold of the chicken, alarms went off, sirens blew, and smoke began to pour out of every opening. What had gone wrong? Doctor Dave was frantic and about that time, an explosion propelled a plucked rubber chicken out the top of the machine and into the crowd. The audience went wild. It seemed very unfortunate that the inventive doctor's machine had mal-functioned. Doctor Dave came to the rescue with an oversized monkey wrench, but he had to crawl up into the dangerous intake door to make the necessary repair.

David wore a big black stovepipe hat, a doctor's smock and bright pink tennis shoes for his show costume. At that time, Scotty was the same age as David, but a good fourteen inches shorter. Scotty was hid-den inside the machine all along, doing all the control work, including the rubber chicken throwing.

Doctor Dave would attempt to repair the machine so the show could continue, but he was in for an amusing fate. It appeared that he had been caught in the gear works and unwillingly pulled into the intake door, body and all, except for one pink tennis shoe. The machine smoked and rattled and out the back came the much shorter version of Doctor Dave (Scotty) with the oversized hat hiding his face, the oversized lab coat dragging the ground, wearing one pink tennis shoe and carrying a much smaller monkey wrench. The diminutive Doctor Dave ran off into a waiting vehicle, and was driven away.

Doctor Dave's Incredible Shrinking Machine, Jodi's trick horse, and Tom F's trick roping were classic hits that summer. In a few months, Scotty started growing up to David's size. Rodeo for Tom F and Jodi, cattle showing for David, and school for all four cast members caused the show to fold before the next year. Besides, Doctor Dave was out of short friends, the bird dog puppy and kitten grew up, and the once-tame barnyard chicken left for calmer climes.

"The Family Circus" cast from left included Jodi Rush mounted on Sandy, Scotty Schoonmaker, "Dr." David Rush and trick roper Tom F Self.

Jodi Rush performing a "side pass" on Sandy.

Tom F Self trick roping on the Dr Pepper stage
while his horse Chiquita looks on.

"Doctor Dave" is about to shrink a live chicken
in his incredible shrinking machine.

11. The Show Goes On

Henry Castro and his family had a breath-taking high wire act. Dad hired Henry to bring his act to the Park, and Sophie Sanchez, our long time employee, caught his eye. He kept hanging around because of Sophie and because the crowds loved his act. It was remarkable in the respect that the only other similar act was done by the famous "Flying Wallendas." There were four walkers on the lower level of a high wire, thirty-five feet above the ground. Between the first and second walker was a rigid bar supported by shoulder hooks. The same was true between walkers three and four. Two more balancing family members stood atop the rigid bars with a third rigid bar between them. Now that six people were in place, a seventh person stood even higher on the third tier. After the group was in place on the wire, the whole bunch moved cautiously forward across the high wire in a seven-person pyramid.

Henry also had a "Globe of Death" act that he set up on the performance stage. Four riders on four motorcycles would enter the fourteen-foot metal mesh globe via a trap door. Once the door was closed and the motorcycles fired up, they would spin round and round and up and down in criss-cross patterns. It was very exciting, and drew good crowds every Saturday and Sunday for a couple of years.

Oh yes, Henry and Sophie wound up happily married and continued to work at the Park.

Dad would often advertise a "Free Pony Give Away." Because most kids would love to have a live pony of their own, large crowds would show up. Since some people didn't really have a good place to keep a horse, Dad would offer to buy the pony back if the winning family wanted. More often than not, the winning child, thrilled beyond belief, would take the new pet home.

Henry Castro (bottom row, second fro left) and family
performing their seven-person high wire walk at Sandy Lake Park.

"The Globe of Death" motorcycle globe
set up on the Pepsi Stage at Sandy Lake Park.

A Teddy Bear picnic, pig races, armadillo races, semi-truck rodeo, pony races with monkey jockeys, a dog and cat costume show, and a fancy bicycle contest all drew the interest of patrons of the Park. The special events and shows were big attractions, but the company picnic business and FunFest were taking up more of our time than ever. As the years went by, more emphasis and effort went into the development of group events.

12. Company Picnics

We started the first year with four picnic pavilions and added more shelters as we grew. Currently there are twenty-five pavilions of different sizes, and each one has its own advantages, even though each has shade trees, parking, and plenty of room for games. Groups often want the same pavilion year after year, and we try to accommodate them.

Pavilion #6 was the site of an old Super Slide that the former owners had attempted to open prior to our arrival. The slide was about forty-five feet tall and had nine sliding lanes down to a landing pad. The whole contraption was junked out and too dangerous to restore, so it was dismantled. The four-inch steel poles that supported the structure were the only part of the slide that could be salvaged, and they were lined up just right to build a pavilion. The only problem was that the poles were four feet tall on one end and thirty feet tall on the other. We cut the tall poles off twelve feet high, welded the excess on the short poles, added metal rafters and a tin roof and called it Pavilion #6. There have been hundreds of thousands of catered meals served under #6, thanks in part to the old Super Slide.

When we came to the Park, it did not take long to realize that the market for company picnics was blossoming, just as we had hoped. The first year we booked about fifty different companies; considering the Metroplex's size in 1971, that seemed to be a good start. We placed a forty-person minimum on catering and allowed smaller groups to bring in home-cooked food or to grill food at the Park.

Our catering continued to increase each year. Bo Moore's meat preparation was excellent every time we sliced a brisket or ham. Bo used two huge rotisserie hickory wood ovens to smoke the meat and it was more flavorful than meat cooked in ovens with shelves fixed in place. As the meat cooks slowly for about fourteen hours, the shelves and meat continually rotate to self baste each brisket. Also, the turning action keeps an even temperature throughout the oven. Bo trained good "block men" or people who knew how to slice the brisket thin and across the grain so it would be tender. We also continued the policy of having a person slice the meat in the catering line as the plates were assembled. Slicing the meat ahead of time would otherwise allow it to dry and lose quality. Thanks in large part to Bo's ability to prepare the meat, we got rave reviews from our customers. Our reputation for great barbecue grew quickly and remains one of our best selling points.

Our name for good food and a variety of entertainment in the Park began to get the attention of picnic committees. Heritage Press and U.S. Gypsum, Inc. were among the companies to book dates the first year. Darrell Wood personally booked the Heritage Press picnic for twenty-five years. U.S. Gypsum, Inc. continued to hold its annual picnic with us every year until 2001. Fox Electric Company holds the record at thirty-five years and counting, having never missed a year since 1972.

The largest single group we have served to date is the Bell Helicopter Union picnic with five thousand, one hundred people attending. The largest number of separate catered groups in one day stands at nineteen. The most combined meals served in one weekend is about eight thousand, four hundred. For eight thousand, four hundred people you must prepare a lot of food. The approximate needs are:
- 320 briskets
- 90 hams
- 300 gallons of beans
- 2,100 pounds of potato salad
- 1,700 pounds of cole-slaw
- 450 gallons of tea
- plus bread, pickles, jalapeno peppers, and dessert.

The companies that have visited the Park over the years number in the thousands and cover every imaginable type of business. One thing they have in common is the enjoyment of visiting a place that has a variety of entertainment, great food, and a relaxed atmosphere. The main reason that companies plan a picnic is the fellowship. Getting away from the office and meeting their co-workers' families pays dividends many times over for the company. Nothing gives us more pleasure than to finish the day and realize that we had a Park full of happy people.

In 1980, a group of five hundred men came to a convention in Dallas, and the convention committee wanted a western party with steaks as the entrée. They had an unlimited budget, and every Western amenity we could think of was acceptable to them. We had Indian dancers from Oklahoma in a tepee village, trick ropers, bullwhip artists, trick riders, gunfighters, and several mounted riders to add more "color." We gave stagecoach and horse-drawn hayrides. Covered wagons, chuck wagons and anything that looked Western was used as a prop.

When the group arrived in chartered buses at 4 p.m., cowgirls tied red bandannas around each of the city slicker's necks and fitted them with new straw cowboy hats. We found out in a hurry that very few men in the group spoke English. We learned that our guests were the executives of a big international banking firm from all over the world. After a couple of hours of Texas style entertainment, it was time for dinner.

We had asked them what their budget was for the meal they said they didn't care as long as the "steaks were big, really big." Dad and Bo had found some porterhouse steaks that were as big as a steer can grow, and we cut them one and a half inches thick. Each steak weighed about twenty-six ounces, and they were Prime USDA corn-fed beef.

We had built a cement block firebox about forty feet long, four feet high, and six feet wide. Dad designed and had a welder build eight four-by-six feet steel frames, each with an expanded metal cooking surface. They had handles on each end so they could be picked up by four men and moved along on top of the firebox.

Earlier in the afternoon, the firebox had been loaded with mesquite wood and set ablaze. When dinnertime neared, the cowboy cooks set to work. The bed of hot coals and half-burned mesquite logs were ideal for the task at hand. Two cooks loaded each steel frame with forty steaks. The frames were steadily moved forward along the fire pit while another frame of uncooked meat was made ready to follow. At mid-point, Dad and Bo used long-handled pitchforks to turn the meat as it was moved forward. By the time each frame reached the end of the line, the steaks were cooked to perfection. At the chuck wagon near the end of the fire pit, we again used pitchforks to heft the steaks onto fourteen-inch platters. When a steak was placed on a platter, it reached all four sides. Another large platter held baked potatoes, fresh corn on the cob, and fresh garden salad with special Texas ranch dressing.

The dudes were impressed with everything, including the fact that it took "two plates to eat like a cowboy." A cowboy band sang Western music during the meal and groups of square dancers stirred up the dust nearby. The Dr Pepper Company provided soft drinks for the Park, and even though we had iced tea and beer for beverages, we also set up a fountain for soft drinks. The men only sipped samples of the strange beverage at first, but before the evening was over, they had used more than eighty gallons of Dr Pepper. We had lots of tea and "long necks" remaining after the party.

Frank Rush serving a Texas-sized steak to a convention guest.

The convention committee was thrilled beyond its wildest expectations. We were thrilled to an even greater degree when we got the payment for the event. We did host a few Western events from time to time, but never one that paid or played better. The phrase "Chuck Wagon Dinner" stuck, and we still use the title on our printed tickets.

13. They've Been Working on the Railroad

Over the years, we have employed hundreds of teenagers and adults. A great many of them have gone on to school or other jobs but remain close friends of our family. Some of them come back to help us, even though they now have full time jobs or businesses. It is a pleasure to have a human resources person call for a reference and inquire about an employee. A few were fired, but most just grew up and moved on in life. Some have been with us so long that they are part of the family and have been individual blessings in one way or another.

Gene Canalizo showed up at the Park the first few days we were here in 1971. Gene had worked at the Park when he was in high school. He and his wife, Zondra, had lived at the Park when they were married, and Gene started Pool Kare, a business for servicing pools like the YMCA and larger city pools. He introduced himself to us, and we got along like we had known him for years. He started taking care of the pool preparation, filters, and general maintenance and continues to do so to this day.

Big Tom had been a lifeguard in high school, and was a good diver and swimmer, so he took over the pool management duties and hired the lifeguards. With Gene's help, the future for the old swimmin' hole looked good.

Gene is a Cajun. He never misses an opportunity to hear or tell a good joke. Zondra and Suzy are both "married" to Elvis. Gene and Zondra's kids worked and hung out at the Park when they were growing up. Gene is a remarkable person with his hands and tools. He can fix anything mechanical, electrical, or otherwise. He started helping with other maintenance chores around the Park. He has been a blessing to our family both personally and professionally.

Tommy Davis was a lifeguard for Mister Hicks the year before we came to the Park. Tommy and a couple of his co-workers showed up in May 1971 looking for a job with us as new owners. Big Tom hired them on the spot and a close relationship developed. Tommy lives and works in Round Rock, Texas. Every six months or so when we phone each other, we just begin talking without introductions, as close friends often do. Tommy, Big Tom, and I had a lot of fun together, pulling practical jokes and horsing around. Tommy is the only person who ever took a dare and jumped off of the roof of the office building into the swimming pool. He came up unharmed, but he said he thought he would never get down to the water. We enjoyed hunting dove together. Tommy's Granddad Davis had a farm near the Hebron Baptist Church, about nine miles northeast of the Park. On September 1, 1971, when dove season opened, the three of us loaded our shotguns after we went under I-35 and road-hunted all the way to Granddad Davis's farm. There were only a few farmhouses along the way. Today every acre has been developed into the city of Carrollton.

Greg Williams was a co-worker with Tommy for years. He now works for Park Place Lexus in Dallas. He was humorous every day and saw things with the same twisted mind that I did. On June 20 of 1977, he and I were at the pool one day, and I said, "Just nineteen more days." He looked at me with a puzzled look for a few seconds and then smiled. He said "Yep, just nineteen more days." We counted down the days and no one else could figure out what we were secretly looking forward to. Finally, the day arrived accompanied by much celebration from Greg and me. It was July 7, 1977, in other words, 7-7-77.

We made plans to be together on 8-8-88 and Tommy and Greg showed up on cue. I didn't see Greg for several years, but 9-9-99 was coming up and Vickie said, "Aren't you going to call Greg?" I said, "No need, he'll show up." About nine that morning, Greg and Tommy walked in with special T-shirts for the four of us with the number 9999 printed over the Park logo.

Willie West, at age thirteen, started working for Dad in 1971. Willie now owns a successful air-conditioning business and still does all of our A/C work. Suzy and Willie pick on each other at every opportunity. He says she is short. She says he has lost his mind. They are both correct to some degree. Willie has the dubious honor of earning the first "Burned Bean Award" for infamous deeds by Park employees. Dad bought a new riding lawn mower and trusted Willie, at his young age, to mow with it. Willie proceeded to drive the mower into the barnyard lake. Willie said he did a lot of growing up when, "Mister Rush let me have both barrels." Willie's children also worked at the Park as teenagers, and at nearly fifty, he has started another family. His daughters will probably follow in the footprints of their dad and half-sisters someday.

The two Meaux sisters, Janet and Sharon, and their brother Joe worked in the Park. The girls babysat our kids and Joe was a ride operator. They tell stories about the excitement of their first job and how much they were afraid of Dad. Dad never did a thing to harm them, but he was the boss and his blustery commands kept them hopping. They are all married with children, and one daughter has worked in the office.

Van Vaux lived on Belt Line Road in Carrollton, and started helping Big Tom at the pool checkstand at thirteen years of age. Van is brilliant with computers. He eventually attended Texas A&M and was an engineering student. He would come home from College Station to work at the pool every summer. Dad asked him about his grades every time he showed up. He was very shy but finally confessed he didn't know his actual grades because he scored one hundred on every test. Thus his college instructors were dumfounded about how to grade him. Van said, "My classmates are all mad at me because I ruined the curve, and my instructors couldn't really test me because I make a hundred on everything." Van has gone on to manage the main computer bank for The Associates and other equally hi-tech jobs.

Richard Flemming was a strong, handsome lad when Dad hired him. He was Dad's right-hand man at the rides for years. He could and would do anything Dad asked of him, and they became close. Richard finished high school while working at the Park and was ready for college. He didn't really know where to go or in what to major. Dad wanted him to get an education, and Richard needed guidance, so Dad called his friend, Don Davis, president of Cameron College in Lawton, Oklahoma. He told Mister Davis, "Richard is one fine football player and makes straight A's." Before Mister Davis had a chance to explain the process for enrollment, Dad said, "I'm sending him up there to see you. You take care of him for me," and hung up the phone. Richard went to Cameron on a scholarship, and was a starting player on the Cameron's National Championship Junior College Football Team. Dad never cared that Richard is black and Richard never cared that Dad is white. They had a father/son relationship closer than many blood kin.

Ramon Mireles was an alien worker who came to work with Rick the carpenter. He didn't speak a word of English, but he understood work. He picked up trash with care, drove the train with pride, and anything else Dad ever asked of him was finished with a smile. He came to love Dad, and the affection was returned. Dad bought him clothes and food and saw to it that his needs were tended to. Ramon cut off the end of his finger one day while tying up one of our horses. Dad took it harder than Ramon. Dad had a missionary friend named Walter Gomez who lived in Pharr, Texas, and did work in Mexico. They found a lawyer in Del Rio who would help get Ramon and his family citizenship papers. The legal work involved took years and was very difficult to complete. After years of work and waiting, Ramon became a naturalized citizen. All of his kids lived with him and his wife up on Old Denton Road. They were able to purchased a nice home with their wages from the Park. All of his children got American educations, and have good jobs to show for their efforts. Three of Ramon's sons, Hector, Rudy, and Troy, still work for us at the Park.

The three Buckholt sisters lived in Farmers Branch, and between them, they performed every job in the Park. Babysitting to selling tickets, cleaning rest rooms and answering the telephone, running rides or catering was done with ease by Diane, Ramona, and Susan. Diane "worked" even before we could put her on the payroll with her older sisters. She was skilled at organization, years beyond her age. As soon as she turned fourteen, she was officially hired. Later she learned to slice barbecue, and kept the kitchen and the employees running smoothly. She and her husband teach school as adults, and have a beautiful daughter, Lanie. When the telephone rings, and her happy voice says "Hi, Mom," or Hi, Dad," we know it's Diane.

Roxanna Posey started working for us in the early '80s. She was assigned child-sitting duties with the kids, and they all kept busy with chores in the Park. Roxanna loves horses. She and our children drove the stagecoach ride in the Park on weekends. She is talented in drawing cartoons, so she kept a notebook with humorous drawings of things that happened in the Park. When her mother moved to Canton, Texas, she

A Roxanna Posey cartoon depicting herself as the train driver who thinned out some of the park's resident Canadian geese.

got a job as a riding instructor in a facility for troubled teens. She was inspired by the changes she could make in a young person's life, while her clients were learning to ride and care for horses. She completed her degree and still teaches at the facility.

Jay Ross, Kent Welch, and Lauren Moss all started working at the park in 1972. Kent is now a successful insurance salesman in East Texas. Lauren was, and is, drop-dead gorgeous and became a Dallas Cowboy Cheerleader. She now lives nearby with her husband and children. Jay, Kent, and Lauren, along with Vickie and me, had great times together and became life-long friends.

Jay Ross met his wife, Melanie, while they both worked at the Park one summer, and they have two beautiful teenage daughters who work for us. Jay is president of two North Star Banks in Denton, Texas, and remains one of our closest friends. He still slices barbecue for catering jobs at the Park.

Like Greg Williams, Jay and I find humor in the same things. When Jay worked at the Park full-time, there was another employee in the catering department named Wayne Webb. Jay and Wayne are both very intelligent, but they played the "dumb and dumber" game with each other. To their credit, they got really good at it. They kept us laughing, each trying to say or do a more boneheaded thing than the other. Wayne was a perfect look-alike of The Fonz on the television show, *Happy Days*. One day Jay and I were sitting on a table near the kitchen, and Wayne came walking across the parking lot doing his best Fonzy impression. I commented, "You know, Jay, Wayne is about two eggs short of a dozen." Jay let Wayne get closer and said, "Wayne, you should hear what Frankie just said about you." "What? What? What did he say?" asked Wayne. Jay's masterpiece reply was, "You only got nine eggs."

In 1979, Sophie Sanchez was working at Farmers Market in Dallas when Dad stopped to buy some fruit. He always had his eye open for help and asked Sophie if she wanted a job at the Park. She came out, went to work, and has been a blessing for us ever since. She did everything. She worked her concession stand at the rides and kept things organized and clean all over the Park. Her husband, Henry, and daughters worked with us also. Dad and Mom came to love and depend on Sophie from breakfast to closing time. She became as much a part of the family as any of us. Sophie had a contagious laugh and smile for anyone who crossed her path. Sadly, Sophie passed away after a brief illness on November 6, 2004.

Danny Arias came to work in March of 1983. He had work-visa papers, but like Ramon Mireles, wanted to get his full citizenship so he could bring his family from Mexico. It seemed to take forever, but Danny is today a naturalized citizen. His wife and older kids work part-time at the Park. Danny can do anything there is to be done in the Park. He loves to mow and keep the Park looking neat. He has always helped Vickie and me in the kitchen, so Bo Moore started teaching him to slice and smoke the meat a few years ago. Now that Bo has slowed down with the daily cooking duties, Danny has taken charge. Bo likes to tell how many good cooks he trained in his restaurant over the years, and says that Danny is likely the best of the bunch. Danny has management skills and finds things to repair or improve that we overlook. He is a blessing for sure and "Mi Amigo."

Georgie Vaughn came to work for us after Dad met her and some of her friends who were working at the State Fair of Texas. There were three other ladies including Jean Ferdick, now deceased; Francis Landers, who runs Cedar Canyon Dude Ranch in Lancaster, Texas; and Betty Young, who lives in East Texas. We called them the "Golden Girls" because they matched perfectly the actresses on the popular TV show. They could serve more food and have more fun in a refreshment stand than any other set of four women. It was always like a TV situation comedy with their daily antics. Benny Marshall joined Georgie a few years ago and runs the souvenir and hat shop during FunFest. In March 2004, Georgie moved to the Park to stay with Mom after Dad had his injury. By the way, Georgie keeps us supplied with world-class cream pies.

Dad and David have had several men work at the rides who have been with us for years. Many of them are Hispanic, and they work from late winter through the summer. They also help us close in the fall and winterize the Park. Jeff Harlan runs the Pretzel ride and keeps everyone entertained with his scary masks. Bob Bryce drives the miniature train and makes the trip even more enjoyable for Park guests with his tall Texas tales. Both Jeff and Bob take special care to help Park guests enjoy their day. Big Tom has employed many young adults as lifeguards in the pool. One of many who have gone on to successful careers is Doctor Jeff Cantrell. We could tell that even as a young man,

Jeff had potential. He is now a very competent surgeon in Lewisville, Texas.

Suzy has had especially good help in the office and at the front gate. Vickie and I have watched kids start their first job in catering and go on to successful careers. We hire semi-retired people who help us during the open season. They enjoy remaining active and have a special fondness for being around our younger guests. Each person who works at the Park has memorable stories and individual experiences they like to recall. For most, the joy of working in a fun environment around families is rewarding. For all, we have provided a job that supports them and their families or is extra income to add to their regular job.

Family businesses are the most common form of ownership in America. In 1971, when Mom, Dad, Suzy, Big Tom, Vickie, and I started our ownership of the Park, we were and are six equal partners. At the time, Tom F was two years old and David Frank was one. Vickie gave birth to Jodi on July 6, 1972. Vickie's mother, Genevra Foster, came down from Oklahoma to help during FunFest for several years. It has been a blessing to have our personal family and our employee family to operate the Park.

David, Jodi, and Tom F grew up playing and working in the Park. They drove the stagecoach and for several years, had a three-act, free show for youth groups on Tuesday and Thursday all summer, along with many other duties. David has always been interested in the field of park administration and attended Texas A&M University with that vocation in mind. Dad hired David in 1993 to be our ride operations manager after he graduated, a job for which he is ideally suited. He oversees the training, maintenance, and operation of the rides and does a fantastic job. Tom F is responsible for the ticket booth and payroll. Jodi and our daughter-in-law Tori are both excellent in office duties and group sales.

When Tom F married Annessa (Musil), she started helping out as well. The same was true when David married Tori (West) and Jodi married Frank (Cuccurullo). The next generation including TJ Self, Whitney Rush, and Taylor Cuccurullo haven't gotten quite old enough to work yet, but frankly, they are already running the place.

We each have our special areas of responsibility, but we all help each other daily and fill in when there are outside obligations or illness.

It is very rewarding to have previous employees come back to visit the Park and say, "I learned to work at Sandy Lake Park." They talk about how Dad "cracked the whip" and kept them on their toes, and about how they later came to realize learning to work changed their lives and helps them every day. It is always a pleasure to see how they have been successful in school or their chosen field and realize they took something home besides a paycheck.

14. Steep Grades and Rough Track Along the Line

We struggled the first few years to make ends meet. Mom, Dad, Suzy, Big Tom, Vickie, and I sat up at night wondering how we were going to have enough money to pay the electric bill. The Lord, hard work, and a lot of luck got us over the humps, but on a few occasions, the going got difficult.

In the late '70s, a local Hispanic radio station approached us with a deal to host a station promotion at the Park. They booked three popular mariachi bands from Mexico for a special concert appearance. We agreed to hold the event on a slow Sunday in August. If people went by the station and picked up a station bumper sticker for their car, they would to be admitted free. The station paid for the entertainment and related expenses. It seemed like a winning deal because we wouldn't be out anything, and we got to keep all the receipts from the amusement and food sales.

On the Wednesday ahead of the event, the station manager called to ask how many cars we could park. We estimated five thousand cars, maximum. He said, "Well, we ran out of the first ten thousand bumper stickers, and ordered ten thousand more stickers of which seven thousand have been given out."

Panic!

The bands were among the most popular groups in Mexico, and everyone in the Hispanic community was eager to see them.

We prepared as best we could, but by 8 a.m., the cars were backing up onto the I-35 exit ramps. By 10 a.m., all of the major feeder roads within four miles of the Park were blocked. At 11 a.m., we closed the front gate because we couldn't park any more cars. Only one of the big buses with the band aboard was able to get into the Park, and the other two bands were nowhere to be seen. Police sirens wailed. The fire department and police reserves were called out, and it started getting ugly. Thousands of people parked along side roads or in the yards of houses more than two miles from the Park.

There were a few thousand people standing along Sandy Lake Road in front of the Park. When the band started playing on the stage, the overflow crowd stormed the eight-foot chain link fence. The fence fell under the pressure and the throng walked into the Park. The station manager was on the PA system pleading for calm, and he did a great job under the circumstances.

We all thought it just couldn't get any worse, but at 2 p.m., it clouded up and rained two inches in forty-five minutes. The employees and our family were scared to death. Lightning flashed and thunder rolled, and the crowd started to file out. By dark it was over. The crowds had dispersed, and peace and mud had settled onto the Park grounds.

The City of Carrollton quickly passed a city ordinance addressing the need to have adequate traffic control at any major event in the city. We learned a costly lesson about outside promotions. Thankfully, no one was injured and the Park recovered.

The last days of April and the first couple of days in May of 1990 brought record rainfall to the watersheds north of Dallas. Lake Ray Roberts had been built and was filled to capacity two years ahead of schedule. On May first and second, a slow moving and intense rain storm moved from Weatherford toward Gainesville and deposited as much as nineteen inches of rain on the already saturated soil. On May third, the weather cleared and the sun came out in daytime, and a full moon shone at night. May fourth was a scheduled FunFest day, and the Park was ready for a big crowd.

An employee who was helping us during our busy FunFest season had his RV plugged in near our storage barn at the northwest corner of the Park. Around 2 a.m. May fourth, he awoke to the sound of running water, and when he peered outside, he noticed a fast moving stream nearby. He stepped out into the moonlight and became alarmed.

Since the Park is enclosed by chain link fence, it was unusual to hear anyone knocking frantically on the door of my house in the middle of the night. Eddie, the employee, explained that I'd better come have a look. What had been high water on the Trinity River had turned into overflow. Water backed up onto the normal floodway and was still rising. It was a beautiful night with no clouds in sight, but it had taken two days for the flood water to come down the estuaries of the Trinity River to our property.

I woke Tom and Dad and called Gene Canalizo at home and asked him to "come quick."

We immediately started gathering the horses, moving vehicles, and working to save what we could. The water flowed into the paddleboat lake, filled it to overflowing within a few minutes, and crested into the swimming pool. More water flowed in to fill the barnyard lake and when that was full, the water began to overflow into the ride area and rise around the stage. Culverts under Sandy Lake Road were inadequate and only handled a small portion of the deluge. The Sandy Lake roadbed began to act as a dam, and the water kept rising. By sunrise, water began to rise around the amusement rides. Gene was turning off electricity and dismounting the electric ride motors.

Many of our employees arrived around 4 a.m., sensing that the situation needed their best efforts. In a few hours, we accomplished many tasks that would save a tremendous amount of expense and equipment. Luckily, our homes at the Park were spared because they were on slightly higher ground. When the water spilled over Sandy Lake Road, it continued to rise two more feet. By 7 a.m., news helicopters were overhead, and we had been completely flooded.

All of our draft horses, along with Tom F and Jodi's rodeo horses, were loaded into our horse trailers by dawn. My friend Mike Boyd from Rowlett, Texas arrived with an extra trailer and to oversee evacuation of the horses.

About a dozen Shetland ponies for the pony ride had been driven to the top of a hill in their pasture by the water. We put a big, round bale of hay on the hill, and knowing they would be above water level, left them to enjoy the hay. News helicopters spotted them and moved in for close-up pictures. This disturbance made them stampede into the shallow water and toward the river. They soon became stranded in water deep enough to cover all but their backs, necks, and heads. The fire department had a rescue boat, so two firemen and I motored west toward the river and the swimming ponies. We were able to catch and halter two ponies and felt like we could lead one on either side of the boat back to dry land. Off we went ferrying the first two ponies, and to our surprise the other ten ponies followed, half swimming, half walking back to safety. The news helicopters circled overhead taping the rescue. Luckily their loud rotors kept them from hearing what those two firemen and I were saying about them.

The schools coming to FunFest that day were unaware of the situation. Suzy and Vickie began calling schools across North Texas and telling them to stay home. They would ask, "Why? It's a beautiful day." Thursday, Friday, and Saturday FunFest days were canceled, but many groups agreed to reschedule the following week if we could reopen.

By mid-afternoon, the water finally crested, but the damage was done. The pool was full of muddy water and the wooden barge in the middle of the pool had floated loose. Silt and floodwater covered almost everything.

At that time, Dallas Water Utilities was installing an eight-foot diameter pipe along an easement just beyond the north boundary of our property. The construction had caused a breach in the natural dike or barrier, which probably would have kept the Park from flooding at all. While there were other unusual circumstances, DWU officials realized that they were largely at fault, and they admitted they did not know how to rectify the problem quickly. In the meantime, water continued to inundate the Park.

Mom's brother, Royce Walker, lived in Phoenix, Arizona, and was an expert with heavy equipment and soil placement for construction projects. Dad called him on Thursday evening, and he was on the next flight, arriving in Dallas before noon on Friday. Dad called the DWU foreman and arranged a meeting near the point of the water breach at 1 p.m. After a few minutes of discussion with the DWU foreman, Uncle Royce told Dad to go home. He would handle the problem. He also assured Dad that by dark that day no more water would be flowing into the Park.

There were two big bucket loaders and an even bigger bulldozer parked near a mountain of construction soil close by. Uncle Royce began directing the loaders to dump soil near one end of the breach, and he directed the bulldozer driver to start pushing the soil into the rushing water and compacting the soil at the same time. The whole team moved forward all afternoon and by dark, as promised, a three-hundred-foot-long dam was in place and stopped the incoming water. The DWU foreman was highly impressed with Uncle Royce's ability to quickly solve the problem. He assured us later that no one who worked for him could have done the job. Uncle Royce hopped a plane back to Phoenix the next day, taking our love and gratitude with him. He was, and always will be, our hero.

With the source of the flood diverted, the water began to recede, and we went to work. Before the silt had a chance to dry, we washed down the roads, rides, and buildings. The picnic tables, which had floated down to the fence near Sandy Lake Road, were put back in place and cleaned even before the ground dried under the pavilions. Four big oil-field water pumps were brought in from Wichita Falls to pump the muddy water out of the pool and paddle boat lakes. Everyone worked twenty-hour days, and by the next Tuesday, May ninth, the Park reopened for FunFest as scheduled.

Those big pumps continued to run noisily as they brought the lake back down to its normal level. They had to be placed near the Ranch House Pavilion where the orchestra contest is held. When the first orchestra warmed up on Tuesday, we shut down the pumps. After awards time in the late afternoon, the pumps roared back to life until their job was complete.

The flood of 1990 was a challenge, but because of the efforts by all, a minimum of disruption occurred. Many things have changed since then to help prevent a reoccurrence. Now, we all have an acute understanding of the trauma that anyone suffers when his or her home or business is flooded. If I ever get a chance to be the "Uncle Royce" to anyone in the same situation, I pledge to do my best to follow in his footsteps.

15. The Rail Yard Keeps Getting Smaller

Originally, the Park property consisted of about one hundred and eighteen acres of land. In 1974, Mister Folsom was ready to sell the Park property to us as previously agreed. The east nineteen acres of the property bordering I-35 was in a separate tract. He priced those nineteen acres a lot higher than the rest of the acreage, and we didn't feel that we could afford it all. We did need ten acres because we had picnic pavilions, the shop and maintenance building and part of the train track on that tract. He divided off the ten acres we needed, and sold the rest to Horace Ardinger, a real estate investor. Those ten acres, plus the rest of the property gave us a total of one hundred and nine acres of land. Mister Folsom came out smelling like a rose. He sold us one hundred and nine acres for considerably more than he originally paid for the whole tract, and made an additional sum on the nine acres he sold Ardinger. The old saying, "It takes money to make money," is true.

Three acres of the property were on a separate tract farther down Sandy Lake Road and next to our neighbor Curtis Tabor, who owns Southwest Landscaping. Curtis wanted the land for expansion, so we sold it to him in the late '70s.

In 1982, the City of Carrollton wanted to widen Sandy Lake Road. We finally made a deal but had to give up some road frontage amounting to a little more than one acre of ground. The city wanted us to give it the needed right of way, but since Sandy Lake Road was a thoroughfare, by law, the city had to pay for it. Dad was ready to horse-trade again. He told the city we wanted a new chain link fence, a turn lane into the front gates and some trees replaced. The contractor was to work on the road only when the Park was closed for the winter, and the city needed to fix a drainage problem. Runoff backed onto our property when rainwater came from the east side of I-35. Dad also asked them to include a paragraph in the contract stating the road could never be raised more than four inches. This was the thickness of an additional asphalt overlay. All the conditions were agreed to, so we donated the land to the city. The city council was elated. The city was short of cash for the project and gladly signed the agreement knowing it needed to address most of the issues anyway. Several council members told Dad he had done the city a big favor. Dad felt like we would receive more benefit to our property and goodwill in a trade than we would for a cash sale.

After the road construction was finished, Dad bought four hundred red climbing rose bushes and had our employees set them out along the fence facing Sandy Lake Road and throughout the Park. We rigged a water tank with a water hose in the back of a pickup. For years, the roses thrived and were a sight of beauty each summer. The city was required to mow the right of way, but because of the deep ditch their mowers were usually unable to keep the weeds in check. Someone from the street maintenance department decided to kill the weeds with chemicals. We didn't realize it immediately, but the over-spray also killed most of the roses.

Next, the City of Dallas Water Utilities Department wanted to buy some land to put a lift station on our northwest corner next to the Trinity River. Their easement along our north property line was two hundred feet wide. Several ninety-six-inch water mains lay within the easement. They were expanding the DWU water plant from one hundred million gallons of filtration to three hundred and ten million gallons of filtration per day. Dad, as usual, was in the mood to horse-trade. Their value on the land they needed from us was low. Also, by survey, our land extended into the middle of the Trinity River. He couldn't see that land in the middle of the river was ever going to be of much use to us, so he told them he would trade. We were not anxious to enlighten DWU that part of our train track actually extended about four feet onto their property. Rather than get in a court battle over the land value, Dad told them we would swap the 1.5 acres they needed for a twenty-foot strip of land along the north border of our property. They agreed, and the deal was made. Not only was Dad's thirst to trade quenched for the moment, he took great satisfaction in the fact that he traded land under the muddy waters of the Trinity River for land that was high and dry. In addition, the train track placement issue was resolved.

In 1989, we started noticing water standing on the west end of our property next to the river. In fact, it got so bad trees began to die after a few years. There were some particularly wet years during the early '90s, and water was consistently about knee-deep where it had previously never stood for any length of time. There were thousands of ducks dipping down in the shallow water to get acorns from the big oak trees. It became a haven for them because there was little human traffic to disturb them.

We had been long-time friends with our neighbor, Curtis Tabor. He was growing more landscape shrubs than ever and selling them to grace the landscapes of thousands of homes and businesses in North Texas. He started building up his property southwest of our property, and putting in more plants. Curtis had unintentionally dammed up drainage in the process. I went down to talk to him about the problem, and to his credit, he didn't throw me out. We just had a good talk about the issue. He sure wasn't going to admit any wrongdoing, and I didn't blame him. It was obvious that a problem had been created. Trees were dying, and we couldn't stand by and have our property damaged by standing water.

Our request was for Curtis to provide a channel across his property to provide relief. I am sure he knew we had a good case, and I am also sure he didn't want to get in a court fight. Dad, Tom, and I didn't need a court fight either, especially with a good neighbor. He called me back in a few days with a suggestion. He said, "Frank Jr., why don't I just buy the property you're worried about, and then there won't be an issue." I told him it wasn't my intention to force a sale. In fact, we hadn't even considered a sale until he made the suggestion. He needed the land for more trees and shrubs, so we gave him a price for the fourteen acres. He hollered about the price but took the deal. He told me years later that he sure put the land to good use, and he was glad he owned it. I told him if he wanted his money back, I'd give it to him. He smiled and said, "No thanks."

The result of various land transactions has been that our property has gotten a bit smaller over time, but more ominous threats occasionally arose.

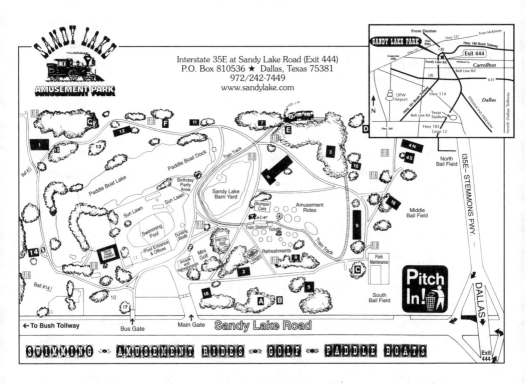

Interstate 35E at Sandy Lake Road (Exit 444)
P.O. Box 810536 ★ Dallas, Texas 75381
972/242-7449
www.sandylake.com

16. Side-Tracked on the Interstate

Another issue came up in the early 1990s. The city council wanted to clean up the I-35 corridor, and in the process, bring in more businesses, which would add to the city's tax base. A "Freeway Zone" was created. We received a map showing the footprint of properties involved. The original map included only a small pie-shaped piece of our land at our northeast corner. This was only a thirty-five by one hundred foot tract, but it placed most of the picnic grounds and ride area in the Freeway Zone because it was under the same legal description as the small sliver of property. We were not aware of that fact at the time and disregarded the paper. Later, all hell broke loose when fifty or more longtime businesses and homes were going to be shut down and have their Certificates of Occupancy revoked. Like everyone else, we were shocked to find we would be closed down. Business firms like Lee Jarmon Ford and Beaver Chevrolet were included. Mom and pop businesses up and down both sides of I-35 were to be displaced. Jimmy Logan, a local tire and auto repair business owner, started a recall petition, and we signed it. Recalls for elected officials are common but rarely are they successful. If enough voters sign the petition, an election is held prior to the end of the elected officials regular term. News reports and public protest began to take root with the bad news. Soon Logan had more than enough legal signatures to demand a recall election. Six of the seven city council members were successfully voted out of office.

There were a lot of hard feelings over the issue. It was very divisive for the city. The efforts of a lot of people, especially Logan, proved the power of the vote is the strongest medicine when elected officials lose sight of reality. The Freeway Zone still stands, but the new city council members later made the Freeway Zone a tool for progress, without closing long-time businesses. I rest assured that supply and demand in the real estate market should dictate progress, not the whims of a few misguided councilmen.

17. Nearly Derailed by the Bush Tollway

For many years there had been plans for a new highway around Dallas. Originally this was known as Loop 9. Later the parts of the road were Highways 190, 161, and our part was later named Section IV or the "Super Connector" for the President George Bush Tollway. Section IV connects the I-35/Bush Tollway interchange to the LBJ/I-635 intersection. The cities of Carrollton and Farmers Branch, the County of Dallas, and all the landowners thought they knew about where the road would be constructed. Anticipating the alignment, the City of Carrollton left a four-hundred-foot-wide portion of a landfill unfilled so the road could be built.

The North Texas Tollway Authority was the builder, and they had the formidable job of planning, designing, and acquiring the right-of-way. At least eleven government agencies were required to sign off on the NTTA plans. The Environmental Protection Agency, Wildlife Department, and Corps of Engineers had problematic issues with the design and location of the road. The original route was chosen, but then the EPA told NTTA to go back and study all possible routes along Section IV. The EPA had a major issue with a pistol range located north of Belt Line Road and directly in the proposed route. A grid of thirty-five various combinations was laid out by the NTTA engineering and design contractor. Seven of these routes came through the heart of the Park rather than the assumed western route. The swimming pool, office building, and main gate were dead center in the crosshairs, and we would be out of business if any of those seven routes were chosen. No one thought much about it and most figured the study was just to satisfy the EPA. A few weeks later, I went to a meeting and learned all but five routes had been eliminated, yet two proposals still crossed the heart of the Park. We continued to feel there was little reason for concern.

When the final decision was made, we were devastated that the tollway rerouting selection would close the Park. Back in 1957, Dad and Mom had our Park confiscated in Oklahoma by the Ft. Sill land grab, and old Craterville was taken away from them. Like Yogi Berra said, "It was de-ja-vu all over again," as far as our family was concerned.

We hired two condemnation attorneys in downtown Dallas and got ready for a fight. They worked for us three weeks, stirred up the NTTA attorneys, and charged us $25,000 before they got out of the starting blocks. We needed help fast and decided to call on Bobby McMillan, our friend who had worked with Robert Folsom when we bought the property. He came out and agreed to look into the issue. Bobby had been on similar boards, knew most of the NTTA board members, had extensive knowledge of real estate negotiations and knew our family personally. Bobby was a blessing from that point on. The wall of mistrust with the NTTA disappeared instantly. Their lawyers no longer had to talk to our lawyers, and the talking points were laid out and addressed. Not that it was easy, but things turned out better in the long run.

A short time after the decision was announced, a NTTA public hearing was held at a big hotel on the LBJ Freeway. We contacted the newspapers and TV stations and expressed our concerns. We arranged for some people to speak on behalf of the Park rather than leave public input to chance. Dad was at his best when he spoke, and how he kept his composure was remarkable after all he had been through. He spoke about his love for the Park business and about our family history for five generations. He repeated one of his favorite lines about why he was in the entertainment business and had no desire to be a doctor or lawyer. "If you're a doctor or a lawyer, everyone who comes in the door has a problem. In the amusement park business, everyone who comes in the door is looking to have fun."

Representing our company picnic business was Donna Springer of Fox Electric. Fox had held its annual picnic with us for thirty-two years. Speaking for the church groups was Mark Beaman from the DFW Church of Christ. They send small groups to the Park, and occasionally have three thousand people for a church-wide picnic.

Mark noted how few places there were where church groups could go and be comfortable. Doctor Irving Dreibrodt, Director Emeritus from Southern Methodist University, explained how FunFest, our spring school music contest, was attended by over one thousand, four hundred bands, choirs, and orchestras annually and was the largest private music contest in the nation. John Schoenthaler, who brings his Discover and Share Day Care kids to the Park several times each summer, represented the commercial day care centers that visit the Park on weekdays during summer vacation. A man unexpectedly spoke from the Hispanic Chamber of Commerce on behalf of the Hispanic community. He mentioned our Easter Sunday celebration, and told how Sandy Lake Park is an economical place where families of all races meet for a day of fun and fellowship.

That day there wasn't a lot in the news. There were no big stories to bump us out of airtime. The media was impressed by the standing-room-only crowd that showed up in our support. The meeting was delayed to open up a partition and bring in more chairs. It seemed to go our way, but protests don't always sway progress.

That evening, at six and ten, and the next morning on the news, the story got aired on Channels 4, 5, 8 and 11. *The Dallas Morning News*, *Ft. Worth Star Telegram*, *El Sol* newspaper, and WBAP radio reported the meeting.

The next day, our office phone lit up like a Jerry Lewis Telethon. People by the hundreds were calling in our support. We didn't want to start a petition, but we did prepare a list of the names, address, telephone numbers, and e-mail addresses of the NTTA board members; Jerry Hiebert, the NTTA manager; Kenny Marchant, our state representative; and then Governor George W. Bush. We spent the next few weeks sending out the list and thanking people for their support. The NTTA board was inundated by public protests, and quickly realized that the closing of Sandy Lake Park would be a battle that they would not want to join.

Months later, after the deal was settled, Bobby McMillan was in Jerry Hiebert's office at the NTTA, waiting on some papers. He asked a loaded question when he inquired if there had been a lot of mail about the Park. Mister Hiebert ushered Bobby into an office down the hall and pointed to a file cabinet. He said, "That's full of letters, e-mail and door-to-door petitions youth groups did on their own."

We all get to do our jobs and forget at times why we work. It was very uplifting for us to be reminded people in the community realize a place like Sandy Lake Park is needed. It's just good that there is a park at which people have built fond memories over the decades, and they can come back with their kids or grandkids and have another memorable day.

The county and cities of Carrollton and Farmers Branch spent considerable time and effort proving the economic impact and construction cost of the selected route were ill-advised. Their efforts also had considerable influence with NTTA.

Between the uproar about the Park and the realization that the best route was mostly along the original alignment, the NTTA reconsidered and chose most of the original tollway alignment. They did, however, bypass the pistol range near Luna Road and Belt Line Road.

The exact footprint across our property took away part of our back lot area, and a portion of our big red storage barn had to be removed. The tollway is elevated some twenty-five feet where it crosses our former property; however, access will enhance our property and relieve traffic congestion in the area.

Very early in the planning stages, five white government cars pulled into the Park one morning, and one man said they were inspecting the proposed right of way. We took them over to the general area, and they got out of their cars with note pads, maps, and cameras ready. They looked around and asked if there were any historic structures or graves on the property. What about hazardous materials? What about water, gas or oil flowing out of the ground? What about endangered wildlife species? Half as a joke and half in truth Big Tom said, "Well, there is a pair of red-tailed hawks that roost in the big cottonwood tree way down there." The lady who had asked the question jumped to action. She took a roll of film and made several pages of notes on the tree.

Later in the process, we learned someone, probably the same lady, had taken a picture of an endangered bird on the right of way two miles south of the Park. NTTA was trying to get the "Record of Decision" (ROD) from all the government agencies. The ROD was necessary before the project could get under way. The bird picture caused a snag with the Wildlife Department whose attorney was in Atlanta, Georgia, and he was in no hurry to make a decision. It took several months and created a delay until the Wildlife Department finally gave the okay. There is no telling how much money the picture of one bird cost NTTA, not to mention the fact that the much-needed tollway was put on hold for several months.

In the spring of 2003, after construction was started, a different hawk was seen nesting in a tree near Belt Line Road. Some animal rights people got wind of the fact and demanded the tree not be removed until the baby birds were out of the nest. News helicopters and reporters buzzed around and got their stories. Safety fences were erected a respectful distance around the tree, but construction continued. The hawk probably wondered what all the fuss was about.

The NTTA settled fairly with us and were great neighbors to work with during construction. Granite Construction Company was awarded the contract for the section of road over former Park property and was great to work with as well.

The City of Carrollton was responsible for obtaining the right of way necessary for the Sandy Lake Road access to the tollway. We had to give up another acre of land from our bus gate west to the tollway for the turn lane. In 2003, we reached an agreement with the city after some tough issues were resolved. The tollway opened for business on September 9, 2005, but it seems our property, the rail yard as we call it, gets smaller by the year.

Jodi Rush Cuccurullo, with daughter Taylor and mounted on Foxy, check out the President George Bush Freeway and the Sandy Lake Road exit sign a few days prior to opening in September of 2005.

18. Trees Along the Track

During 2000, the City of Carrollton adopted a Tree Preservation Ordinance. When one city gets a new idea on something to regulate, other cities often follow suit. Several cities in the area were adopting new tree protection codes but without much forethought to the negative effect on the development and growth they wanted. The idea that trees are a natural resource and construction and development may deplete that resource to some degree seems like a worthy issue. After the City of Carrollton had bulldozed some trees on city property, the council was looking for some way to get back in the good graces of the tree huggers. The idea of passing a Tree Preservation Ordinance would appease the upset constituency and make it clear that the city fathers were attempting to advance city development at the same time.

There were some public meetings and discussions aimed at pacifying everyone concerned. The Tree Ordinance was adopted in spite of at least two oversights on the part of the city. First, the city already has landscaping codes in place, but very little recognition of the existing codes was considered. The second, and more substantial implication of the Tree Ordinance, relates to the enormous expense incurred in complying with new law. There was a notable absence of consideration or discussion presented about the impact that the added expense would have on development costs.

The trees in our Park are a vital part of our business. Without trees, we would be on a vacant lot. Based on Dad's life-long love of trees, he understood this. His earliest public accomplishment ranges back to his boyhood days when he came up with the idea of planting a tree on the state capitol grounds in Oklahoma. Dad had read the poem "Trees" by Joyce Kilmer, who had died at Flanders in World War I. He asked Granddad if he could plant a tree in Kilmer's honor. A newspaper story relates the event. The seed planted in Dad's mind about doing unusual things in a big way and getting a little news coverage didn't hurt either.

Dad also had a habit of bringing home a trailer full of trees to be planted at Sandy Lake almost every year. The natural variety of trees that came with the Park was greatly increased by Dad's foresight.

In 1980, I asked Sandy Rose, an arborist friend, to inspect a huge pecan tree on our property. "How old do you think this tree is?" I asked. He estimated over one hundred, forty years, then added, "I can tell you one thing, Indians camped under it sometime." Dad wanted to know

E. Frank Rush (Dad), with shovel, planting a tree in honor of Joyce Kilmer
on the grounds of the Oklahoma State Capitol in 1925.
Also pictured are a troop of Boy Scouts, the Governor of Oklahoma
in the dark suit (center) and Frank S. Rush (Granddad) in the white cowboy hat.

Oklahoma Mountain Boy Plants Fir, Joyce Kilmer, War Poet, Memorial

EVERYONE knows Frank Rush, Oklahoma's beloved naturalist who lives at Craterville in the Wichita mountain range. This introduces his son, Frank Rush jr. who is headed in the direction that his father has followed.

A few days ago young Frank was reading a book. Looking up he said:

"Father I'd like to plant a tree for this boy. I'd like to plant it at the capital."

"This boy," referred to Joyce Kilmer, war poet who gave his life in Flanders.

"That's a fine idea," Frank sr. told his son. "We'll just do that."

Then followed a search for the tree. At last a small evergreen was chosen. Carefully it was dug up with a generous quantity of its native soil clinging to its roots.

With the tree, Frank sr. and Frank jr. drove to Oklahoma City to set it out.

"We thought that all there would be to it would be just to ask for a place to plant it," Frank sr. said Thursday. "But bless me they ordered out the boy scouts, and the governor and everybody."

So Wednesday young Frank took a spade and dug a hole for the "Joyce Kilmer Memorial tree," on the sweeping capitol lawn. A troop of boy scouts presented the colors. The governor appeared, tall, bareheaded.

And now a fresh young evergreen tree, from the Wichita mountains grows on the capitol lawn, pressing its mouth against the "earth's sweet flowing breast," the tribute of young Frank Rush to a war immortal who knew and loved the trees.

Frank Rush jr.

"TREES"

I think that I shall never see,
A poem lovely as a tree.
A tree whose hungry mouth is prest
Against the earth's sweet flowing breast,
A tree that looks at God all day
And lifts her leafy arms to pray,
A tree that may in summer wear
A nest of robins in her hair,
Upon whose bosom snow has lain
Who intimately lives with rain.
Poems are made by fools like me,
But only God can make a tree.
                    JOYCE KILMER.
(Who gave his life in France)

A picture and headlines from a news story about the tree planting.

129

which tribe.

All facts aside about the family's experience with tree preservation, we are concerned that this issue affects future economic development in Carrollton. In the public hearing in June of 2000, I asked for a variance for the Park from the city's Tree Ordinance. City Director John Webb said the city staff would work with us on our predicament of being "heavily forested." Hopefully, Mister Webb's statement will be upheld in the future. At any rate, with the Ordinance in force, it remains to be seen what the full effect could be in the future of Carrollton, but it has already started to take a toll. We love and appreciate trees and have an obligation to protect them, but the trees we have always considered an asset are now a liability.

19. Birds on the Track

During a Tree Ordinance meeting in June of 2000, City Director Webb stated, "It's no secret why we are here tonight. It is because a mistake was made on city property." Mister Webb was referring to the bulldozing of the trees in a Snowy Egret nesting site on city property a few months earlier.

The old Josey Ranch property on Whitlock Lane had a huge number of Snowy Egrets nesting in a rookery in the trees. Thousands of birds called the timbered tract home. Neighbors were complaining about the smell, the danger of disease, and the bird droppings on their homes, cars, and kids. The city was getting a lot of calls, and the birds were creating a mess, so one Sunday morning about 4 a.m., a city bulldozer was dispatched to level the trees. By daylight, the birds were swarming and squawking with alarm. Baby birds were dead or dying, but the deed was done.

The animal rights activists were appalled, and the media was more than eager to make a report. Marches on city hall were organized, and the size of the crowd at the city council meeting rivaled a local Friday night football game. Protest signs were prepared, and protesters picketed on the sidewalks outside. Resignations were demanded while the rescue of hundreds of birds was still underway, and the TV cameras kept rolling.

Someone at city hall assumed if the trees were gone, the birds would leave. Not only was it a total miscalculation, it turns out that Snowy Egrets are a migratory bird and are protected under Federal law. Criminal charges were discussed and fingers pointed in every direction. The council and staff had egg on their face for a long time.

Eventually the storm blew over, mostly as a result of the city passing the Tree Preservation Ordinance. John Webb's statement about "the mistake" (at the June, 2000 tree meeting) was a public admission of fault on the city's part. It was also a clear directive to all that the Tree

Preservation Ordinance, good or bad, was a peace offering to the irate environmentalists. It is possible that the Ordinance, which our family considers detrimental, would have never passed in absence of "the mistake." The sequence of events and the resulting paradox of this issue should serve as a reminder that too much governmental intervention, on any level, can be misguided.

On a lighter note, I have this mental picture of a meeting in some city office prior to the fateful event. Staffers are drinking coffee and scratching their heads or some other part of their anatomy wondering what to do about the messy birds. Someone says, "Why not just send Bubba down there with that big ol' city bulldozer and push them trees over." Someone else says, "Great idea, and if we do it at night no one will know what happened."

20. Famous Passengers on this Train

Famous visitors come to the Park from time to time. The Dallas Cowboys and Kyle Rote Jr., who ran our football and soccer camps, came back often with their families to visit or ride the rides. Other people of note often show up unannounced to enjoy the Park.

Mister Don Carter owned the Home Interiors Company and later became more widely known when he owned the Dallas Mavericks National Basketball Association franchise and many other enterprises. Mister C., as his friends know him, and his family, including his wife Linda and his sons Joey and Ronnie, lived in nearby Coppell. We got to know them when we took Dad's horse-drawn Santa's sleighs to their house for rides around their property for Christmas parties. Joey and Ronnie drove to the Park to swim before they had drivers' licenses and while Sandy Lake Road was still a back road. Mister C. also thought Bo Moore was the only person in the country who knew how to cook good barbecue. For many years, he held the Home Interiors corporate picnic with us, and always made sure Bo was here to cook the meat. Mister and Mrs. C. have become special friends of our family and a joy to know.

Charley Pride, the country singer, showed up for his family reunion for a few years, and Vickie, as a special fan, would always make it a point to give him a big hug.

Fritz Von Eric and his famous family of professional wrestlers were regular customers for many years. They enjoyed being out of the spotlight and packing a picnic for visits to the Park. Although Fritz and all of his sons, except one, have passed away, we still remember his warm smile and his wonderful kids and grandkids when they visited the Park.

The Dallas Cowboys have their practice field in nearby Valley Ranch. Over the years, almost every famous Cowboy, along with his family, has visited the Park. They show up unannounced and always seem to enjoy the amusements and special times with their families.

Deion Sanders loved to fish at least as much as he enjoyed playing professional football and baseball. He came to work for the Dallas Cowboys and was in the spotlight on and off of the field. Our friend, Jeff Bennet, was in the top echelons of marketing for Pepsi at the time and was largely responsible for Deion's endorsement of Pepsi Cola. Jeff also was responsible for Sandy Lake Park's exclusive contract to sell Pepsi for a few years. Deion and Jeff worked together professionally. Since Deion was always looking for a private place to fish, Jeff asked Dad if Deion could come to the Park on the evenings after the Park closed. Dad said, "Anytime."

Deion showed up in a couple of days pulling a small bassbuster boat. Dad told Deion that David would show him where the fish were. He stayed until after dark catching and releasing bass with David. When Deion pulled his truck back by the office building, he and Dad started talking. Near midnight, the conversation finally broke up. Deion told Dad he had a great time talking, and he was happy that the conversation had been about something besides football.

We extended Deion a standing invitation to come back, and he did on a regular basis while he played football in Dallas. He pulled up in the parking lot unannounced one afternoon and stopped to tell me that he would be on the lake fishing. He knew the gate combination, and could let himself in and out if nobody was around. I asked him how the fishing was in Florida where he was raised. He said, "Mister Frankie, (he called me Mister Frankie) you can have a flat tire on any road in Florida, throw a hook in the bar ditch while you change the tire, and catch a mess of fish."

Deion liked the fishing and the fact that no one took advantage of his celebrity status while he was here. He still has a standing invitation to fish anytime he chooses.

Deion pulled in the gate one day pulling his golf cart on a trailer behind his truck. Dad greeted him and Deion said, "Mister Rush, you've got a nice golf cart, but I'd like for you to drive mine for a few

Frank and Genelle driving Deion Sanders'
golf cart at Sandy Lake Park in 1998.

Deion Sanders and Frank Rush enjoying fish stories at Sandy Lake Park

weeks to keep the batteries up while I'm on a trip." Dad was like a kid in a candy store and took Deion up on his offer. Dad and Mom sported around on the custom-made cart and did plenty of showing off until Deion came back in town.

International visitors have attended the Park as well. The City of Carrollton has a sister city: Yung Ho, Taiwan. Brad Mink, Director of Economic Development for the city, called one day to see if the visiting mayor and his entourage could have a picture made with our stage-coach. He explained that it was not necessary to have the horses hooked up, but he thought a stagecoach picture would make a great souvenir for the Taiwanese mayor. Dad never missed an opportunity to do more than necessary to help anyone, so he planned a more elaborate recep-tion than was requested. We had the stagecoach horses hooked up for rides around the Park. Dad's big Longhorn steer "Tumbleweed" was saddled for pictures as well.

The Yung Ho, Taiwan, mayor and his wife pose with Frank and Genelle Rush on their visit to Sandy Lake Park. The mayor was treated to a ride on "Tumbleweed," Dad's longhorn steer, and he and his party posed for pictures on the Sandy Lake stagecoach in front of the main gate to the park.

Jodi and Tom F dressed in their rodeo clothes, and were mounted on their horses to welcome the group to the Park. Wagons from Dad's collection, including a covered wagon, a buckboard, a chuck wagon, and a Park wagon were on display. Mister Mink and party arrived, and the visiting mayor was thrilled when we dressed him up in a big Stetson, bandana, boots, and chaps.

The group took several rolls of film rather than just one picture. We were told later that those pictures grace the mayor's office in Yung Ho. Mister Mink wrote Dad a letter stating that his visit to the Park had been the highlight of the dignitaries' trip to America.

We filmed two episodes of "Walker, Texas Ranger" at the Park. Series star Chuck Norris was a pleasant person while he was here with the film crew. He came back with his family a couple of times to relax at the Park.

The Dallas Stars won the Stanley Cup in 1999. Eddie Belfour, the popular goalie for the Stars, was in a TV commercial that was to be produced and filmed at the Park. It is a long-standing tradition to allow the players on the winning team to keep the beautiful Stanley Cup trophy for a couple of days for their private enjoyment. The commercial's story line was for Eddie to take the trophy out for a picnic at an amusement park. The film crew and Eddie showed up with the celebrated trophy, and they rode the rides while the film crew shot the necessary footage. Eddie didn't need any security guards with him, but two big tough-looking trophy sitters never let the Stanley Cup out of their sight.

The Dixie Chicks performed for an American Airlines party just about the time they had their first number-one album. Later they became more famous and had more number-one hits.

Zig Zigler has been to several group functions. Doctor Kenneth Cooper of the world-famous Cooper Clinic held a picnic at the Park. Other CEO's visiting the Park with their groups include Jerry Thompson of Southland Corp and 7-11 Stores; Bob Minyard, owner of Minyard's Food Store; and Vernon Baird, patriarch and owner of Mrs. Baird's Bakeries.

Former Dallas Cowboy superstar, Pettis Norman, holds his PNI company picnic with us every year; and he always has a special guest star show up in a big limousine to perform for his employees.

The Stanley Cup takes a ride on the Sandy Lake Park Tilt-a-Whirl
during the filming of a commercial ad at the park.

Michael Jackson, M.C. Hammer, and Tina Turner have all graced the
stage at the PNI picnic. The PNI employees know it is Pettis, dressed
in costume and pantomiming music of the famous stars, but they love
it. There is also a $500 reward each year for anyone that can guess in
advance whom Pettis will impersonate. So far, no one has collected.

Dad's rodeo friends often drop in unannounced to check on the family and hear a Frank Rush story. Jimmy Smith, owner of Smith Brothers Roping Supply in Denton, never missed a chance to "call on Grampy and pick up a little cheer," as he put it. Professional cowboys from across the country stop by the Park when they're on the rodeo circuit to rest their horses and call on Dad.

Roy Cooper, holder of seven rodeo world championships, was a regular visitor both in person and on the phone. Roy's longstanding friendship with Dad was highlighted by an unusual gift and a public expression of his respect. In 2000, at the National Finals Rodeo in Las Vegas after Roy roped his final calf in the closing performance, he removed the rope from his saddle horn and rode to the arena fence, where he presented Dad with the rope. Roy received a standing ovation as he left the NFR arena for the final time; the gesture of friendship from Roy was a cherished moment for Dad.

World Champion Cowboy Roy Cooper presents his rope to Frank Rush after he tied his last calf at the National Finals Rodeo in Las Vegas in 2000. Insets show Dad's hands holding the rope shortly after the presentation.

21. Frank Rush Productions

Dad's collection of parade wagons and horses has been operated under the name of Frank Rush Productions since before we moved to Texas. On many occasions, we booked our Western equipment and cowboy personnel for events outside of the Park.

One time, we did a full Wild West Show in the Dallas Convention Center for a packed house full of convention delegates. Dad hired Red Stegall, the famous Western singer, with his band The Coleman County Cowboys. The event went well, but is was an odd feeling doing a Wild West Show in the huge building.

Just a note: Big Tom, Suzy, Vickie, and I had spent a lot of nights dancing to Red's special brand of Western swing. We were acquainted with him on a casual basis, but that one gig cemented our friendship with Red.

Don Carter, our Coppell neighbor, hired us to help entertain at Home Interiors' "HI" annual convention inside Reunion Arena near downtown Dallas. Mister C. also hired Neal Gay, producer of the long-lived Mesquite Rodeo Company to put on an exhibition rodeo, and Crystal Gayle performed on the stage. All we had to do was parade the top fifty saleswomen, one from each state, into the arena on our stage-coach and in five other horse-drawn wagons. Soil had to be trucked in and spread on the arena floor, and a full set of rodeo pens and a perfor-mance stage were erected at great expense. Rehearsal went well, but when the ladies were loaded on to the wagons and introduced to a full house, all seventeen thousand co-workers started cheering as we drove the wagons into the arena. There was one big unforeseen problem: draft horses listen to the driver for their cues. On my wagon, and the others as well, it was so loud the horses couldn't hear a command of any sort. I remember being aware that no matter how loud I whistled and yelled, I literally could not hear my own voice. The wagons were stopped in the arena by pulling on the lines to the bits in the horses mouths, but when it came time to "giddie-up," the horses just stood there in the bright lights and the din of noise. When we hollered for help, Neil Gay's cowboys, waiting behind the chutes to start the rodeo, couldn't hear us either. Neil finally realized what was happening and sent the mounted rodeo pickup men to our rescue by leading our teams out of the arena. Mister C. was not happy because we had held up the show, but later when he realized the problem was unintentional, we all had a chuckle.

We provided much the same entertainment for the Cattle Barons' Ball at Bunker Hunt's ranch west of Grapevine, Texas.

Frank Rush introducing Caroline and Bunker Hunt to Gus Palmer at the Cattle Barons Ball. Gus Palmer was often hired by Dad to bring Indian dancers to Frank Rush Productions shows.

On yet another occasion at the Hunt Ranch, when the Reverend Pat Robinson was running for President of the United States, we delivered him to the center of the fund raising festivities on Dad's stagecoach. Bob Hope was the host for the evening, and lots of other celebrities were there. When Reverend Robertson arrived atop the coach and waved a big Stetson that we had loaned him, the cheering throng went wild.

Dad took this photo of his friends Linda and Don Carter with Dixon and George Palmer at the reception for Pat Robertson at the Hunt Ranch in 1984.

The Southwestern Exposition and Livestock Show in Fort Worth is home of the first and longest running indoor rodeo. Each January since we moved to Texas in 1965, Dad booked his wagons in the opening day parade. The parade is billed as the world's largest all-horse parade. There is a rule that no motor-driven floats or vehicles are allowed. There are usually around five thousand horses in the parade along with one hundred and fifty other commercially sponsored wagons, stage-coaches, and buggies.

We have taken between six and eleven wagons to Fort Worth annually for forty years for corporate sponsors. It is always a major project to get all the rigs, horses, harness, signs, and drivers to the staging area for the parade. Our corporate sponsors love exposure to crowds that number from fifty thousand to one hundred thousand onlookers. In addition, local television stations cover the event for home viewers.

The Sandy Lake Park Special Events Sound Truck provides the public address system and background music for the parade marshaling area. Wrangler Jeans and Western Wear sponsor the truck, and Cowtown music fills the air as the announcer calls the order of the lineup.

The Texas Christian University Horned Frog Marching Band and mounted color guard leads the parade followed by two of our wagons with members of the Stock Show Board of Directors on board. Our other wagons, riding clubs, and various parade units are assigned positions, and it is as much fun to drive or ride in the parade as it is to watch it from street-side. The parade stretches for miles and takes nearly three hours to pass in review. If you like horses of every shape and color, and love parades, the Fort Worth Stock Show Parade is a must-see event.

144

Ft. Worth Livestock Show Parade scenes include Frank Rush Productions hitch wagon driven by Tom F Self with Rev. Barry Bailey of First United Methodist Church of Ft. Worth riding beside him.

Jodi and Frank Cuccurullo are bundled up on
the colorful Toys R Us parade wagon in 2001.

Frank Rush III driving the Wrangler-sponsored
Director's Wagon at the 2001 Ft. Worth parade with stock
show director Judge Byron Mathews in the white hat.

Menzo Yearian managing the lines on a pair of Dad's
paint draft horses and pulling his authentic Dr Pepper
delivery wagon in the Ft. Worth parade in 1986.

Dad bought season tickets when the National Finals Rodeo (NFR)
was moved to Oklahoma City in 1965. Since we were in Oklahoma
City at the same time working the Santa Claus sleighs for TG&Y
stores, we attended every performance of the rodeo. Dad knew the general manager of the Professional Rodeo Cowboys Association, Clem
McSpadden. Dad suggested to Clem that during each performance
of the NFR, the various corporate sponsors could be introduced on
his stagecoach. Clem liked the idea. We had a four-horse team of red
and white paint stagecoach horses, and Big Tom drove the stagecoach
around the arena with the VIPs on board. The introduction was unique
and a big hit at the rodeos.

When the NFR moved to Las Vegas, Dad offered to take the coach,
but the PRCA got a better offer. Mister Benny Binion, owner of the
Horseshoe Casino in Las Vegas, had attended the NFR in Oklahoma
City. Not only was he instrumental in getting the NFR moved to Las

Vegas, he owned a stagecoach pulled by six matched black horses. Scott Smith of Weatherford, Texas, was Binion's stagecoach driver and a friend of ours as well. Mister Binion volunteered the use of his stagecoach to the NFR for free, and since the casino name was on the coach, he got publicity and recognition. The PRCA got a freebie instead of paying Dad, but the tradition that Dad started still takes place at each NFR performance in December.

Tom Self driving the Frank Rush Productions stagecoach in the National Finals Rodeo. World champion bull rider Freckles Brown is riding shotgun and contestants for the Miss Rodeo America contest greet the audience in the State Fair Coliseum in Oklahoma City.

Whistle Stop for Mr. Binion

There have been several books written about Mister Binion and his colorful and storied life. His reputation and tales about his involvement with the Dallas mafia and other questionable aspects of his life would depict him as an unsavory character in most social circles. By the time Dad got to know him, he had settled into life as a successful casino owner, rancher, and benefactor for rodeo cowboys. The mystique of Benny Binion was nonetheless compelling. An excellent book, Benny Binion, *written by Jim Gatewood, was published by Mullaney Corporation in 2002.*

Dad was introduced to Mister Binion in Oklahoma City in 1965 at the National Finals Rodeo. Mister Binion, Dad, and others were eating breakfast together at the NFR host hotel one morning. I went over to the table to sit next to Dad and was introduced to the group. I was nineteen years old and didn't fully understand who Mister Binion was. He reached in his pocket and gave me a $5 Binion's Horseshoe Casino gaming chip with his picture embossed on one side and said to me, "Frankie, when you get old enough, you bring that chip out to Las Vegas and see my place." I was really impressed that anyone would give away money, especially money with his picture on it. I have taken Mister Binion up on his invitation, and he got back a good bit more than his original investment, but I still have that same chip.

We were visiting Dan Coates in Ft. Worth one day, and Dan asked Dad, Big Tom, and me to ride out to a ranch on the west side of town. A horse trainer had just received a load of black horses that had been purchased to pull Mister Binion's stagecoach. A group of cowboys was attempting to hook them up to the stagecoach for the first time. It was a hot, dry summer afternoon as we neared the barn where the action was taking place. A big cloud of dust showed where the cowboys and the new horses were working. The men were fitting the harness and trying to get the animals into position in front of a stagecoach. The horses were more than a little wild, since they had not been harnessed before, and someone noted it would be just as easy to harness a covey

of quail. Eventually, the horses were successfully broken, and Mister
Binion kept them on the road for many years. By the time Scott Smith
took on the job of driving the horses a few years later, the horses were
seasoned and well-behaved.

When we attended the NFR in Las Vegas, Scott would invite our
whole family downstairs to the Binion's Horseshoe Steak House for
dinner. Mister Binion would sit at the head of the table and hold court
for a different group of cowboys and VIP's each night after the rodeo.
Dad wanted to pay for our steaks, but Mister Binion wouldn't hear of
it. He told Dad, "Frank, any one of those blackjack tables upstairs
will pay for all the steaks we'll eat tonight. Put your money away."
Dad obliged, and the rest of us went upstairs to gamble at one of those
blackjack tables.

In 1984, we were hired by the U.S. Olympic Committee to provide
a show for the Olympians when they visited Dallas. Cloyce Box had
agreed to host the U.S. team, local VIPs, and dignitaries for an evening
of Texas entertainment at his famous ranch. The Cloyce Box Ranch,
east of Frisco, was the original South Fork set for the TV series Dallas.
At the time, J. R. and the rest of the Ewing clan had the number-one-
rated show. The event was the first stop on a two-month-long victory
tour for the athletes, and the local "movers and shakers" wanted to
see and be seen with them. We gathered up everyone and everything
Western to use for props and greeted the medal winners and their entourage with plenty of Wild West entertainment. Gold Medal winner and
gymnast, Mary Lou Retton, was the super-star of the event, but all of
the other athletes were enjoying their newly-found celebrity status, too.
We, along with the other entertainers, enjoyed the evening as much as
the honored guests.

In 1988, Errol McKoy took over as president of the State Fair of
Texas. He was making big strides in the corporate sponsorship department. He asked if we could provide some of our horse-drawn wagons
for the twilight parade that takes place each evening of the twenty-four
day fair. I called our old friend and neighbor Don Carter, and he agreed
to let Home Interiors sponsor the stagecoach. Bill McNutt, owner of
Collin Street Bakeries of Corsicana, had been sponsoring one of our

Frank Rush Productions stagecoach and outriders wait for the Olympians to arrive at the Cloyce Box Ranch near Frisco, Texas in 1984.

Gold medal gymnast Mary Lou Retton sits on Chiquita, owned by Tom F Self, and holds hands with her fellow Olympian on Buckshot, owned by Jodi Rush.

original bakery wagons in parades for years, and they also signed up to be a sponsor. Both of the business owners liked the timing of the fair. It runs from late September through mid-October, and would help the Christmas sales of their companies.

The following year we added Kool-Aid and Justin Boots as sponsors for two more wagons. Each year, we added more units until we had as many as seven wagons with seven sponsors. Over the years we had wagons sponsored by Pepsi Cola, Mrs. Baird's Bakeries, James Woods Motors, Schepps Dairy, Dr Pepper, and many other businesses.

A single horse draws some wagons, while two-horse teams pull others. We decorate each wagon to reflect the theme of the parade, and all wagons must be trimmed with lights. Since the parade takes place after dark, the effect is beautiful.

The parade is led by the U.S. Marine Drum and Bugle Corps from Washington, DC. There are ten colorful themed-and-lighted motor-driven floats. The Budweiser Clydesdale Wagon and the Hella Temple Band are highlights of the parade. The parade winds over a two-mile route through the fairgrounds, and it ranks second only to the automobile show as the most-seen event at the fair. Twenty-four parades each year, times an average of five wagons per parade over a sixteen-year period, adds up to more than nineteen-hundred accident-free trips around the fair grounds by our horses and wagons.

Frank Rush Productions horse-drawn wagons add to
the Twilight Parade at the State Fair of Texas.
Here wagons sponsored by Pepsi, Mrs. Baird's Bakery, and Collin
Street Bakery are enjoyed by some of the 3.5 million annual fair visitors.

Lights twinkle from one of Frank Rush Production's
stagecoaches at the State Fair of Texas.

Milkman driver David Rush waves from the Schepps Dairy
wagon in front of Cotton Bowl Plaza.

When not hitched up for the parade at the State Fair of Texas, the wagons are on display for state fair visitors in the livestock barn.

Frank Rush Productions wagons have been seen by tens of millions of visitors at the state fair and countless other parades across Texas and Oklahoma over the years. For Dad, his collection of pretty horses and beautiful wagons were as much of a joy to him as to those who smiled and waved as the wagons passed in review.

22. Hunting with Dad and His South Dakota Connection

Dad's main hobby was work, but he loved to hunt nearly as much. He always kept three or four good bird dogs and spent a lot of time in the field. Hunting trips with Dad were memorable.

Shawn Davis, the world champion cowboy and our long time friend, knew another cowboy who owned The Hole In The Wall Ranch near Kaycee, Wyoming. John "Witch" Holman was the owner of the ranch and a champion saddle bronc rider at the NFR as well. Shawn introduced Dad to Witch, and he invited us up to Kaycee to hunt mule deer and antelope. Big Tom, Dad, and I accepted the invitation and packed our hunting gear in the fall of 1973.

The Hole In The Wall Ranch was famous as the place where the real Butch Cassidy and The Sundance Kid hid stolen cattle during their rustling days. The neighbors owned the historic Triple T Ranch, and the two ranches shared hunting rights with each other. The best mule deer hunting was on the Holman ranch, and the antelope hunting was on the Triple T.

Dad was especially interested in the Triple T because he was aware of a federal test case over the right to kill eagles between the government and the family that owned the ranch. The issue arose when the eagles were killing and eating newborn lambs in the sheep herd. The result of the case found that if a rancher's livelihood depended on protecting his livestock from predators, the government had no claim. However, there were strict rules that made it a crime to touch or use any part of an eagle, including their feathers, for any purpose, after the bird had been killed. American Indian representatives took issue with the law because they were using eagles and eagle feathers centuries before white men's laws.

Dad recalled conversations with his Indian friends about the case. He had followed the case involving the Triple T with interest, but outside of it being a topic of conversation, it was nothing more than coincidence that he went hunting on the Triple T.

When we arrived at the Hole In The Wall Ranch to hunt, Witch Holman met us; and we bunked down in a big, log hunting lodge. The next day, Witch was understandably cautious about our hunting knowledge and concerned about the possibility of one of us getting lost. By noon the first day, John realized that Big Tom and I were capable of hunting on our own. Since we had guided and hunted all our lives, he figured we would take care of ourselves. Dad stuck with John in his truck, and they spent the afternoon antelope hunting. Dad got a nice antelope buck.

The next day, Big Tom and I wanted to hunt the backcountry alone. With some instructions from Witch, we set out on our own before daylight. Early that morning, Dad filled his deer tag with a giant buck that was grazing goodies in a melon patch near a creek bottom. By noon, he was ready to head for Texas, while Big Tom and I were in the backcountry trying to figure out which way was north.

Witch and Dad met us at a designated location after sundown. They were pleased to see that we finally had succeeded in getting our two mule deer bucks and had them field-dressed and ready to load. Dad was still ready to head for Texas. With his deer and antelope in the bag, he ribbed Tom and me that "the old man could still hunt faster, shoot straighter, and get home earlier" than we could.

The following day, Witch took Big Tom and me to the Triple T to hunt antelope. We pulled into the pasture gate on the Triple T about sunrise. Each pasture had three to four thousand acres under fence, and sagebrush covered low rolling hills as far as the eye could see. Witch pulled his old truck up on some high ground and began glassing the country. Witch was a man on the move. The idea of spending two days on foot, stalking game, and trying to get close enough for a sportsmanlike shot, wasn't in his time schedule. In addition to being a skilled saddle bronc rider, rancher and hunter, Witch was a master of profanity. He used cuss words to start and stop every sentence, just as sure as the first word in a sentence is capitalized and there is a period at the end. For Big Tom and me, his habit was educational and contagious. "There are four good herds of ^#(*+'n antelope out there, but the biggest %$&+ buck I've seen usually stays in that @!~* south valley over there," he noted.

Witch also had one more bad habit. He drove fast. Real fast. Off we went at full speed down a cow trail, while Witch looked out the side window rather than at the terrain ahead and the sagebrush rapidly disappearing under the front bumper of the truck. He slammed on the brakes, looked closer for a moment, then shouted, "Hang on #%+=!" Big Tom and I had anticipated his instruction early on, but we tightened our grips anyway.

We rounded a hill, came to a sliding stop and Witch said, "Here the ^#@`s come. Get ready to warm them #>`~'s up." Several does and some young bucks started racing by in the distance, seemingly out of range, but Witch instructed Big Tom to hold fire because the big bucks always trail the herd. That gave Big Tom time to ask me, "How ^$+* away are they?" I said, "#!)| if I know, I can hardly see them at this distance, but I would guess five hundred ^@)-'n yards."

As Witch had predicted, a huge buck came flying along at full speed, trailing the herd. Big Tom fired from a standing position. I saw a puff of dust hit about thirty feet behind the speeding animal, and suggested that Big Tom lead the animal by the same distance for his next shot. When he shot the second time, the big old antelope rolled like a tumbleweed. Witch hollered, "Whoowee! You %@*^_'s from Texas shore know how to shoot the &#(@'s." Big Tom and I were as surprised as anyone. Big Tom accepted Witch's compliment without reply, then he turned to me and said, "How the <'*# did I do that?"

After we loaded Big Tom's trophy in the old truck, we raced off in pursuit of my buck. We were flying low when all of a sudden, Witch yelled, "Look out @#$%^&*()_+>~!" Ahead loomed a ditch about five feet wide, five feet deep and way too near the speeding truck to stop. We braced for the impact, but rather than feel the brakes engage, I remember the sound of the truck motor revving up. Witch floored it, and we jumped the ditch as smoothly as Witch could string together profanity. An hour later, I was still shaking so bad, I missed an easy shot at an antelope standing less than one hundred yards away. Witch made some comment like, "You don't shoot as good as your #%^< brother-in-law!" Being a novice at my newly-acquired habit of profanity, the absolute best reply I could think of was, "Kiss my keister, Witch."

I finally bagged a smaller buck. We met Dad at camp and headed back to Texas.

A few years later, my high school buddy, Donnie Jordan of Elk City, Oklahoma, and I were planning a hunting trip to New Mexico in early November. Dad knew an Indian hunting guide in Costilla, New Mexico, and suggested that he could get us in some prime mule deer country; but Dad would have to go with us. Donnie and I agreed, in light of the fact that Dad offered to buy the gas and groceries.

Dad and I met Donnie in Hammon, Oklahoma, got into his old Bronco truck, and away we went. From the start, Dad continually ragged on Donnie about slowing down so he wouldn't get a speeding ticket. By the time we crossed the Texas panhandle and into New Mexico, Donnie and I were rethinking our deal with Dad.

We bunked down in the local motel in nearby Questa, then drove up the road to meet our hunting guide. We spent the afternoon just looking over the country. The next morning, Donnie and I told the guide we wanted to hunt the backcountry, just like Big Tom and I had done in Wyoming. Dad stuck with the guide, and about sunup the first day, he shot a real trophy-sized mule deer near the town's garbage dump. Again, Dad was ready to head for Texas. Donnie and I hunted for two more days without success. Well, so much for the backcountry.

We headed home. Before we went twenty miles, Donnie rounded a curve and a large mule deer buck was standing in the middle of the road. We narrowly missed the buck and the rocks on the shoulder of the road. Not only did Dad laugh long and hard about Donnie trying to kill a buck with his truck, he told Donnie to slow down.

We were pulling into Abbott, New Mexico, about 1 a.m. when Dad said, "Donnie, you better slow down. There'll be a cop in this town." About thirty seconds later, red lights flashed behind the Bronco. While the officer approached the truck, Dad was slapping his knee and giggling. Donnie produced his driver's license and signed for his speeding ticket.

Dad went wild, laughing at Donnie and bragging, "I told you so." When we got near Clayton, Dad said, "There will be another cop in this town, too. That cop in Abbot has called this cop to tell him you're coming so he can get some more of your money." Donnie said, "They'll never take me alive." Sure as shootin', the Clayton police pulled Donnie over near the first city limit sign! Donnie was mad. He jumped out of the Bronco asking, "What's the problem, I sure as hell wasn't speeding." The officer replied, "No, but the police department in Abbot called and reported your license plates don't match the truck you're driving. Is this truck stolen?" He also told Donnie to keep his hands in plain sight and to assume the position on the front of his squad car. At that point, Dad decided to go to Donnie's defense. The officer did not take kindly to the idea of two men in hunting clothes coming at him and told Dad, "Sir, unless you want me to handcuff you and put you in jail, I suggest you shut up and get back in the truck." Thank heavens, for once in his life, Dad quit talking and got back in the Bronco. After an hour or so, and a phone call to Donnie's wife, Beverly, it was discovered that the local kids had switched the license tags on his Bronco with the tags on Beverly's car as a Halloween prank. We finally got out of Clayton around 4 a.m., with Dad warning Donnie to watch out for the cops in Dalhart.

Just after World War II, Dad and some friends in Lawton went pheasant hunting in South Dakota. Since gasoline, tires, and shotgun shells were scarce after the war, not many out-of-state people drove that far to hunt. Dad's doctor friend could get the rationed gas stamps, and his buddy who worked at Fort Sill could get shells. Dad had a car, so the three of them were in good shape to travel and hunt. Dad and his friends wound up in Winner, a town in the south central part of the state.

In a field near Hamill, South Dakota, a farmer named Joe Harrington was working on a windmill. They helped Joe fix the pump, and then asked if they could hunt. In a thick German accent, he said, "Just shoot all 'dem blamed pheasants, 'dere eating up my corn." They had no trouble filling their limit with the corn-fed birds. That meeting resulted in a friendship with Joe and his wife, Ida, that lasted until the old couple passed away in the mid-'70s. Dad took various friends to hunt on the Harrington place. Later, I got old enough to hunt with him.

I learned to share Dad's love for the sport and the country, and those were very special hunting trips for us.

There was a family by the name of Fott who lived nearby, and Joe had introduced Dad to them during their last hunt together. Granddad Fott and family owned about thirty-two thousand acres of South Dakota's finest grass and farmland. There were two sons and one daughter: Joey, Lawrence, and Adeline Hight, who were closer to Dad's age. The brothers lived on the ranch at Hamill, and Adeline's husband, Don Hight, is a rancher who lived near White River, South Dakota. Don owned well over a thousand buffalo cows, which he pastured on his ranch. Because of Granddad Rush's involvement with saving the buffalo from extinction, Dad instantly founded an interesting relationship with Don and Adeline. Dad also developed close friendships with the Fott family, primarily because they were wonderful people, but it didn't disappoint Dad that they had fantastic pheasant-hunting land.

From 1977 until 1982, Dad, Big Tom, and I hunted deer and pheasant with Don and his son, Dan Hight, on their buffalo ranch at White River. We enjoyed successful hunts, but the real treat was the experience of seeing the picturesque ranch and buffalo herd. Dad loved everything about the trips: the game, the country, the livestock, the history of the ranch, and the nearby Rosebud Indian Reservation. Don and Dad were cut from similar cloth. They were visionaries, enjoying unusual life styles, and thriving on horse trades and bull sessions. The two of them could have been business partners or brothers.

Dan and Don were cowboys in the truest sense of the word, with one exception. They didn't ride horses to work the buffalo. Horses would have been less effective than the methods they used. Dan flew an old Piper Cub airplane to check pastures and livestock from the air. The plane was baling-wired together and not very airworthy. If Dan got in trouble flying, he would just land on top of a big flat mesa, and walk home for more fuel or baling wire.

When roundup time came, the buffalo were lured with hay into small pastures. From there, they could be enticed into the extensive and strong working pens with corn and water. No saddle horses were needed. Trucks then delivered shelled corn. One half of a semi-load of corn was fed each day, and the buffalo became fat and content. When the animals were ready for market, the various jobs associated with sorting and weaning could be done in the massive corrals with heavy sorting gates and crowding chutes.

The buffalo were shipped to market at a small packing plant and meat market in Sturgis, South Dakota, a hundred miles to the west. The meat was then sold to individuals, restaurants, and grocery store chains. Dad always went to Sturgis to buy the buffalo tenderloin, and those corn-fed buffalo steaks were without question the best meat we ever ate.

Big Tom and I helped work the buffalo on our visits, and even though we were comfortable with range cattle, the buffalo were considerably more imposing. We took the advice of Don and Dan to stay on top of the fences and work the gates with long swing ropes. Dan appreciated the extra help, and we enjoyed the work. Don and Dad seldom let the activity interrupt their conversations.

Once, when Adeline was helping her husband and son, a big buffalo bull accidentally ran headfirst into a steel fence post and dropped dead on the spot. Not wanting to waste the meat, Don quickly cut the buffalo's throat to drain the animal's blood. He then told Adeline to drive her big one-ton pickup close to the animal. He said, "We can't sell this one on the market, but we can sure put the meat in our freezer." He loaded the animal with a tractor/loader and told Adeline to drive the carcass to Sturgis for processing. She headed north on Highway 83 to Murdo, then turned west down I-90 with the buffalo resting in the bed of her truck.

It was close to noon and Adeline had forgotten to take the lunch box out of her truck, so Dan and Don headed to Murdo for lunch at an Interstate 90 truck stop. They were served their meal about the time two truckers walked in. Trucker #1 said, "Did you see what I saw back up the road?" Trucker #2 said, "That was the damnedest thing. That little lady was driving ninety miles an hour with a bloody buffalo standing up in the back of her pickup!"

Don and Dan stopped eating in mid-hamburger and panicked. Apparently the old buffalo bull was not as dead as he should have been. Don ran to the pay phone, called the slaughterhouse and alerted them that his wife was on the way, and they'd better be ready. Adeline arrived with the bloody animal still standing in the bed of the truck. Apparently the bull was in shock from loss of blood, but being the sturdy animal a buffalo is, the old fellow still had the strength to stand. Thanks to the butcher, the animal was quickly dispatched with a .30-30 rifle, and all was well. Well, not everything was well. Adeline reported that she had thoughts of borrowing the .30-30 to use on her husband and son. She eventually calmed down, and, in the best tradition of a buffalo rancher's wife, laughed about the experience later.

In later years, Dad and Mom traveled to the Fott ranch near Hamill, South Dakota, for their annual hunting trip. They took their beloved black Labrador retriever, Bear, and the trips became more about visiting close friends than hunting, even though Dad and Mom never failed to get their limit of pheasant. After Granddad and Grandmother Fott passed away, Lawrence and Bonnie Fott and their son Richard adopted Dad and Mom as part of their family.

Dad was never asked to pay for any of his hunting privileges even though hunting is big business in South Dakota. He got even with eternal friendship, regular weekly phone calls, and gifts. He took work boots, winter coats, flashlights, knives, and anything else he thought would be handy on a farm and gave them, wrapped in love, to his friends. He and Mom donated Bibles for all the kids in the small Lutheran Church in Hamill, an act that endeared them to the whole community. Dad learned the U.S. Post Office in Hamill was in danger of closing because of the low volume in stamp sales. He came home and told Suzy and Vickie to start buying all of the stamps for Sandy Lake Park from Elvera King, the postmaster in Hamill. The annual purchase of about $10,000 in postage, to this day, has been instrumental in saving the post office for the community.

Dad also became friends with other ranchers on the White River. The Larsons and the Fotts owned two of the largest ranches in Tripp County, so there was even more country to enjoy. The South Dakota State Department of Game, Fish and Parks VIPs hunted on the Larson Ranch with Dad. His friendship with Chuck Post and Richard Barringson became close over the years. They loved to hear Dad's tales about Granddad Rush's Game Warden days in the Wichitas, and Dad thought it was interesting to know and hunt with these fine gentlemen.

Big Tom, Little Tom, David, and I have taken turns going with Dad on his trips to Hamill. In 1987, when Little Tom went along for the trip, Dad was deer hunting with Darrell Larson. Like Dad, Darrell preferred to park his truck on a high hill and visit as they glassed the area for deer. One morning, an impressive mule deer buck appeared in a valley on the driver's side of the pickup. Darrell told Dad to quietly open his door and stand in front of the truck so he could use the hood for a shooting rest. Dad could see the buck clearly in the cross hairs of his scope and squeezed off a shot. To his surprise, the buck just stood there. To Darrell's surprise, the report of the rifle made a very unusual noise. Dad readjusted his position and fired a second shot, successfully killing the deer. Only after Darrell stepped out of the truck did they discover the reason for the first missed shot. A rifle's scope is about an inch above the muzzle of the gun, and, while Dad had an unobstructed view of his target, his gun muzzle, though only slightly lower, was pointed directly at the edge of truck's hood. The result was a nice round hole in the truck fender and an extremely red face on Dad.

Hearing of the mishap and knowing Dad could take some good-natured ribbing, Mister Post and Mister Barringson presented Dad with a special "Trophy Hunter's Award" for bagging a 1987 blue Chevy pickup with one horn.

Dad always insisted on safe hunting by himself or anyone with him. The accident was embarrassing, but thanks to the good-natured ribbing and understanding from his host and friends, he got over the incident.

Dad's South Dakota Trophy Hunter award issued in jest by
Richard Barringson of the South Dakota Department of Game, Fish and Parks.

23. Unwinding with Dad and Santa Claus

In the off-season, from October to mid March, the Park is closed. During that time, especially after New Year's Day, there are company picnics to book, FunFest entries to schedule and lots of wintertime maintenance to be completed. We all get anxious to close in the fall, and even more anxious to open in the spring, but we do enjoy the peacefulness of the Park when it is closed.

Dad was never one to "unwind" for any extended period of time, so he always found plenty to keep us occupied. Some people would simply rest during November and December when Park activity was slowest. Dad considered doing anything other than Park-related business as rest, so he took advantage of holiday season opportunities.

I cannot enumerate the events since moving to Sandy Lake in 1971 without recalling our earlier years in Oklahoma. Thinking back to Oklahoma reminds us of how much our heritage still influences the many people Dad touched.

Around 1958, Dad got the idea of building a Santa Claus sleigh big enough to be pulled by horses and carry about forty people. He called on Jesse Robertson, who worked for Larrance Steel Company in Lawton, with a drawing scratched out on a notebook page. Jesse could design and build anything out of wood or steel. He made a few calculations on the same sheet of notebook paper and set to work. A frame was built, the steel was shaped, and the welders took special interest in the novel project. Shortly, Jesse rolled out Dad's dream, ready for a paint job.

Dad called Eddie Poindexter, a talented artist who had painted the rides and decorations at Craterville. Eddie was also inspired when he set to work on the project. Eddie's artwork was beautiful, and while it has been freshly repainted several times, his colorful creations remain much the same today. Eddie did have one rather unusual problem for a painter. His hands shook. I don't mean a little, I mean he couldn't fill a coffee cup more than half full or a mop was needed. I was a young boy and relished the hours watching Eddie paint. He never used a brace rod. He never used a straight edge. He could, however, paint a line, a letter, or a word with edges that were crisp and unwavering. I remember asking him how he could use a paint brush so well when his hands shook so violently. He said, "I hold still and let the brush do the work."

Dad started booking the Santa's sleighs to shopping centers as a pre-Christmas attraction. The center's merchants or property owners would pay Dad, then advertise to their customers, "Free Rides on Santa's Sleigh." Eventually, Dad met a man named Hugh Wiersig, head of marketing with the TG&Y stores based in Oklahoma City. TG&Y had dozens of stores across Oklahoma and North Texas. Hugh told Dad to plan on working every day from the weekend before Thanksgiving until Christmas Eve. Each store along the route would host the sleighs for three or four days.

The beautiful, big sleigh pulled by draft horses was an instant hit. Eventually, Dad had Jesse build another sleigh to cover more TG&Y store bookings. When we moved to Arlington, Texas, Dad built the third sleigh with the theme "Santa's Candy Kitchen." After we moved to Sandy Lake Park, we built a larger sleigh that would hold about eighty people. More and more bookings were coming in, and four sleighs could not keep up with the demand.

For variety, we built a "1776 Freedom Express" trackless train with a caboose for the bicentennial celebration in 1976. The train could hold about thirty people and had a gasoline engine. We used it as an amusement ride in the Park during the summer. In the fall, we repainted the train with a Christmas theme and put it on the road with the sleighs. A different paint scheme would allow us to use the train for various parades.

We owned two stagecoaches, so we started decorating the coaches for Christmas and booking them as "Santa's Stagecoach." In Texas, it seemed perfectly normal that Santa would have a stagecoach.

For several years, we had seven different rigs on the road from Thanksgiving to Christmas Eve. That translated into about two hundred and forty-five working days each year, twelve head of horses, seven trucks, and seven drivers. It also became a very successful venture from a financial standpoint. Mister Wiersig recalls how literally hundreds of thousands of adults and children were attracted to TG&Y stores just to ride the sleighs each year. He not only appreciated the economic impact this had on the stores, but how customers felt good about a big corporate store bringing a holiday highlight to their neighborhood.

We still have the Santa's sleighs and use them for a few Christmas bookings around North Dallas. Many people remember the joyful childhood experience of riding one of Dad's Christmas wagons around some parking lot and petting the giant draft horses. This is not nearly the only way Dad's enterprises have brought joy and entertainment into the lives of millions of people, but if it were his only legacy, it would be a worthy one typical of him.

Frank Rush Productions fleet of Santa's sleighs at work.

24. Sandy Lake Park Christmas

The National Finals Rodeo was coming to the State Fairgrounds Coliseum in Oklahoma City in 1965. Dad bought six season tickets at arenaside for the event. Since we were in Oklahoma City with the Santa's Sleighs, it was perfect timing. We all loved rodeo, and many friends were contestants or involved in the operation of the year-end championship event. Big Tom and I drove the sleighs in the daytime. Dad saw to the other drivers and sleighs, helping them move from store to store and keeping everything running smoothly. In the evening, we would go to the NFR and see the top cowboys of the day compete for the world champion titles. Dad and Mom did not miss a single performance of the NFR from 1965 to 2002 in Oklahoma City or after the event was moved to Las Vegas.

It is always fun to be together and witness the best of the rodeo world's performances, and the family tradition of going to the NFR each year continues. Driving the Santa's sleighs in Oklahoma City and seeing all of the extra decorations in Las Vegas always gets us in the Christmas spirit, but coming home to be with our families and loved ones is the best time of all.

"It's Christmas Time at Sandy Lake Park"

When Christmas comes to a summer resort,
It seems it would be a bleak place to be,
So I thought I should write a little report,
'Cause the world should all see what us "parkies" all see.

Now, of course, most people would build a fire and stay warm,
But we think of last summer and the smiles on the faces,
And our hearts fill with gladness to hold out the storm,
Some good memories make parks the happiest places.

Think with me for a moment about using
Merry-go-round horses to pull Santa's sleigh,
Bumper car shopping,
And packages bulging with free rides for the day.

We'll use our giant pool to slide on and skate,
And have turkey and dressing and gravy and corn sticks,
But the kids have to wait,
Packages come after picnics.

After dinner, it's down to the rides.
The Rock-O-Plane is where all the action will be.
We'll turn on the lights and sing our Yuletides,
It's a "parkies" own vision of a real Christmas tree.

Use left over popcorn to trim it up right.
Fire up the train and ring its loud bell,
Throw Sno-Cones as ammo for a Christmas day fight,
And turn on the loud speakers and sing a Noel.

For Jesus Christ's birthday, we'll all thank the Lord.
We'll light happy candles to fill up the dark.
And for children of all ages, let no one be bored,
'Cause its Christmas time at Sandy Lake Park.

– Frank Rush III

25. The Reason We Own the Train

Anyone who brings a child to ride the ponies, the train or the merry-go-round, does so because it will add to that child's experience and enjoyment. The vast majority of us whom God has blessed with the gift of a child, will work, sacrifice, and provide for our kids. While there may have been other motives for my grandparents, my parents, Big Tom, Suzy, Vickie, and me to chose to work in and own this business, above all, the number one reason we own the train is our children and grandchildren.

Tom F and David were born shortly before we moved to Sandy Lake Park in 1971. Jodi was conceived and born soon after we arrived. The three of them grew to adulthood on the property. Grampy and Grammy, as Dad and Mom came to be called by our family, were fortunate grandparents to have the three grandchildren nearby. They reveled in their accomplishments and taught them a work ethic at a young age. In return, Mom and Dad are filled with years of cherished memories.

Tom F is not only an accomplished trick roper, he is a professional team roper. He competed in the National Finals Rodeo in Las Vegas in 1989 and 1990. He also showed champion quarter horses and paint horses in the American Quarter Horse Association and the Paint Horse Association World Championships. He has traveled the nation as a member of the Professional Rodeo Cowboys Association, competing with the top pros. He is also an occasional golfer, and I've heard people talk about his ability to make long and straight drives on the golf course. Tom F commutes from his home in Valley View, Texas, to work at the Park. He has responsibilities with the ticket booth in the ride area, payroll, and employment records. He keeps an eye on our draft horses and a herd of Longhorn cattle that he and his parents own.

Tom F's wife, Annesa, is an accomplished rider as well. She barrel races professionally in the Women's Professional Rodeo Association

Tom F Self, Jodi Rush, and David Rush
driving the stagecoach at Sandy Lake Park in 1978.

and was the National Collegiate Champion Barrel Racer in 1990. Both Tom F and Annesa have done their share of riding and winning at the sport of rodeo and they keep on the go with TJ.

David now works full-time at the Park as the Ride Operations Manager. He was active in Vocational Agriculture in high school and served as President of R.L. Turner Future Farmers of America. His Vo. Ag. project involved raising registered Simmental cattle. He showed winning heifers and steers at fairs in Dallas, Fort Worth, San Antonio, and Houston, and has trophies as well as a wonderful education to show for it. After high school, he sold his Simmental herd and used the money to attend Texas Tech University for one year, then finished his degree at Texas A&M. He graduated with a Bachelor of Science degree in Recreation, Park, and Tourism Sciences. After David apprenticed as a ride foreman at Fiesta Texas in San Antonio for a year, Dad asked him to come home and learn more about the business here. David attends safety seminars, hires and trains our ride operators, and manages the ride maintenance and records. David is a real pro and has the park business in his blood. He also likes to hunt and bass fish every chance he gets.

David's wife, Tori, is a beautiful southern gal from Mississippi. She attended Ol' Miss and graduated from the University of North Texas with a degree in education. She taught school in Garland for one year after she and David were married and moved to the Park. Tori works part-time in the office with group sales and accounting and substitute teaches at Prince of Peace Christian School. She is also a devoted mom to Whitney and loves being with her own family who lives nearby.

Jodi is a cowgirl at heart and by profession, but she also works in the Park helping with group sales and our mailing lists. She rode the Park's Shetland ponies before she could walk. Along the way, she taught herself to Roman-ride the Shetland ponies, performed with Sandy her trick horse, and took English riding and jumping lessons. She has ridden and won in cutting horse competitions and break-away calf roping on state and national levels. She fell in love with barrel racing in junior high school and won a truckload of belt buckles and trophy saddles. In 1990, she won the National Champion Barrel Racer title at the National High School Rodeo Association Finals in Shawnee,

Oklahoma. In 1998, she won the barrel-racing event at the Ft. Worth Livestock Show and Rodeo, and placed at or near the top of professional rodeos since. She now lives at the Park where she trains and sells barrel racing horses. Jodi has three hobbies: horses, horses, and more horses. She is also a wonderful mother to Taylor.

Jodi is married to Frank Cuccurullo. Even before Franko was part of the family, he was Jodi's high school rodeo friend and a pretty good team roper and baseball pitcher. He has a successful career selling heavy construction equipment around North Texas. His hobbies are tournament bass fishing, an occasional game of golf, hunting, and cleaning horse stalls.

By coincidence, Jodi and Annesa each won national championship titles in barrel racing during 1990, and kept their horses in the same barn here at the Park (Jodi on the high school level and Annesa on the college level).

The youngest generation was started with the birth of TJ. Tom F and Annesa keep him busy in sports and school activities. He is a redheaded bundle of action. His broad smile and friendly personality are reflections of Tom F and Annesa.

Whitney Anne is the first great granddaughter for Mom and Dad. David and Tori read books to Whitney from her birth, and it has been to her advantage. At an early age, she could sit at the dinner table and carry on a mature conversation. She works on a computer, and, best of all, she inherited the family sense of humor. Vickie and I think she got her funny bone from us, Mimi and Dandy. She also helps me with my computer when I get stuck.

The youngest member of the tribe to date is Taylor Ann. She favors both Jodi and Franko in looks and personality. Due in part to all four of her grandparents, she is very smart. She has a big smile, and early signs of athletic ability. Franko seems intent on teaching her to fish and play softball. I suspect that she may be interested if it can be done from horseback.

Track Section #II
(The late 1800s-1957)

C.P. Huntington - at the crest of a grade   stephen p. singleton '63

26. Turning Back the Clock

Granddad Rush passed away before I was born, but the things I have learned about his life help me have a bond which establishes him permanently on my list of heroes. He and my grandmother May Seymour (Mamo) grew to adults literally and figuratively in the heart of the Old West. Obviously, they never thought they would be founders of an amusement park or have descendents who would pursue that occupation into the twenty-first century. They traveled a long hard trail before their future unfolded.

Their childhood takes us back to the late 1800s. To put that era into perspective, one bit of Mamo's family history can be recalled and documented. Mamo's family lived in Spokane, Washington, where she was born in 1878. Her father, Edwin Seymour, and his brother worked on the railroad. Both were married and each fathered one child. Mamo and her female cousin were the about the same age, and by chance both of their mothers passed away while they were infants, leaving the two fathers with the two little girls, each three years of age.

Edwin and his brother decided to move back to Coffeeville, Kansas, where they had kinfolks who could look after the little girls. In July of 1880, they traveled east when most people were moving west, and they traveled in a covered wagon. They left Palouse, Washington, on July 27, 1880; the journal that the brothers kept relates the peril and difficulty of the journey. Imagine two little girls and two men alone in one covered wagon moving across the hot, dusty prairie, through rocky canyons and crossing rivers with no bridges. One note in the journal tells how they came to a campsite late in the day, only to discover that marauding Indians had vacated it only a few hours before. "The coals of their campfires where still warm to the touch," they wrote.

Another passage in the journal, dated August 8, 1880, addresses the plight of Mamo whose mother had passed from her life only a few weeks before. Edwin wrote, "May says she don't want to ride in old wagon to see grand ma. She has not mentioned your name (her mother) but one or twice until last night after we went to bed. She took to crying for Mama. I thought her little heart would break. She did not like Papa one bit but after a while she rolled over towards me and put her little arm around my neck and went to sleep."

Granddad Rush was raised in Coffeeville and met his future wife, May, while growing up there. He made the land run into Oklahoma Territory on April 22, 1889, when he was twenty-three years old. At noon that day, people lined up to make a mad rush into the area to stake a claim on free land. An individual could make a claim for land, but had to farm and build a house in order to "prove up the claim." Granddad waited for the flag to drop and a cannon's loud boom to signal the land opening. If you sneaked into the area and hid out prior to the designated time, attempting to guarantee yourself a prime piece of land, you were a "Sooner."

Dad tells how Granddad recalled when he was riding into "The Territory" in search of his own claim, he came across a secluded valley with a lean-to hut and new garden. The Sooners, who lived in the hut, said they had just arrived to stake the claim a few hours earlier. Granddad noted onions, boot-top high, in the garden and said to the man, "You better be careful when you plant corn. As fast as things grow in this valley, the seeds could sprout and hit you in the nose."

The early 1900s brought Granddad Rush and Mamo to Oklahoma from Coffeeville where they had married. Granddad eventually proved up his claim near Gotebo, Oklahoma, while he studied outdoors in the classroom of the Great Plains. He gained the ability to see how the land, along with the plants and animals that thrived there, could be managed and maintained.

He had also worked for Colonel Zack Miller, one of the owners of the legendary 101 Ranch, where his experience with livestock management grew into what would eventually give him the reputation as an expert in the field. The 101 Ranch was also in the process of organizing and producing the Miller Brothers 101 Ranch Wild West Show, but Granddad Rush was destined for a different avocation.

He became known as a naturalist. A naturalist was different and yet the same as what we know today as environmentalist. Back then, there

A pleasant day at the sod home of Frank S. (Granddad)
and May (Mamo) Rush near Gotebo, Oklahoma in 1901.

were a few people who realized the potential for settlement and growth
in the West, and, how at the same time, they could maintain the bounti-
ful natural resources. Granddad stood for the concept of preservation
co-existing with controlled development. Being proficient at ranch
work and handling livestock, he obtained the moniker of "Frank Rush,
the Cowboy Naturalist."

In 1907, Granddad Rush and Mamo had been married only a few
years. After working for himself and for the Miller Brothers, fate found
him heading to southwest Oklahoma to work for the government. No
doubt a little "showmanship" had rubbed off on him along the way as
can be seen in his style of dress, and because he was a champion fiddle
player.

179

This interior photo of the Rush home shows Mamo at the upright piano and Granddad holding his fiddle and bow. One neighbor lady was playing her guitar and the other neighbors were enjoying the entertainment.

The land, known today as the Wichita Mountains Wildlife Refuge, had been set aside from Indian land in 1901 as a National Forest by President McKinley. In 1907, it became the Wichita Forest and Game Preserve through efforts of President Theodore Roosevelt. Roosevelt had been invited to the Red River Valley for a wolf hunt. While hunting and camping along the southern border of Oklahoma, he saw the Wichita Mountains in the distance to the north. Low and rolling along the horizon, he realized that there was a natural beauty that he had the power to preserve. He had also visited Yosemite in California and introduced a bill that would start the wildlife refuge park system that we know today. Yosemite and the Wichita Mountains were part of this project.

Frank S. Rush in a beautiful Indian beadwork and buckskin
shirt and his trademark cowboy hat. c. 1927.

Mamo Rush holding an authentic war bonnet
in the office of old Craterville Park. c. 1950.

Granddad was recommended to President Roosevelt as having all the qualities to be the Supervisor of the Wichitas. In 1907, he accepted the position, moved to the area, and established his headquarters near the western border of the refuge. President Roosevelt's staff introduced Granddad to William Hornaday, chief taxidermist at the United States National Museum (later the Smithsonian). Hornaday had been sent to Montana during the late 1800s to collect and save a few of the last living American Buffalo. With the help of the American Bison Society, the buffalo were held in the New York Zoological Park. By 1907, the herd had grown large enough for some of the animals to be moved and established in a more natural setting. Granddad, Hornaday, the Wichitas, and opportunity came together to change the course of history for the buffalo.

President Theodore Roosevelt on the white horse
visits with Granddad Rush on the dark horse on his
visit to the Wichita Forest and Game Preserve.

An early day scene of the south gate entry
to the Wichita Forest and Game Preserve.

What a challenge and wonderful calling it must have been for Granddad to put together a refuge which would be a permanent home for wildlife and also be available for the public to visit and enjoy. Time would prove he was up to the task, and on August 8, 1907, he began the job.

The buffalo had disappeared from their native home in Oklahoma a few decades earlier. Longhorn cattle, which the Texas ranchers had grazed in the area on their way to market, were no longer to be found in managed herds. Wild horses were still ranging in the Wichitas. Deer and other species thrived there. The native grama grass, buffalo grass, and mesquite grass provided rich nutrients for the wildlife. Spring-fed supplies of pure water collected in the granite-lined pools along the creeks. Cattlemen of the area free-ranged or leased grazing contracts from the government to run their domesticated herds in the mountains.

The headquarters buildings were frame-and-log structures at first, but more durable cobblestones structures were built. Some of those buildings still stand and are unusual in their appearance. The round granite stones used in construction of the buildings are plentiful in the area. Most can be described as grapefruit-sized and have the typical brownish-red hues of the mountains.

The Wichitas are among the oldest mountain ranges in the nation. They lay at the western end of mountain ranges that stretch to the east and span several states. You can identify photos of the area by the rounded boulders that adorn the mountains. Only millions of years of wind and rain erosion could grind away the sharp corners of the majestic rocks to a nearly smooth surface while leaving them in place atop the sub-structure. The resulting sand, gravel, and stones washed down into the creek beds and valleys and made a wonderful and handy resource for endemic construction material. One only had to take a strong team of horses and a sturdy wagon and drive about the area to select the produce of Father Time's productive crop of cobblestones.

The headquarters building with typical cobblestone construction and a water fountain in the front yard.

Granddad Rush inspecting a section of the early day game fence
erected around the borders of the preserve under his supervision.

A road building crew under the direction of Granddad Rush
shortly after he became Forest Supervisor. c. 1909.

The roads were laid atop broad ridges or hogbacks between the
valleys and creeks. Granddad designed the natural curve of the roads
to take advantage of the scenic vistas as they wound through the area.
Bridges were built at accommodating narrow creek crossings along the
way, and turnouts for scenic views are great places to observe the animals, foliage, and the historic hills.

As projects were being constructed and planned, Granddad began
preparation for the buffalo. He was aware that yellow fever could kill
the buffalo when they arrived. Yellow fever is carried and transmitted
by ticks. Granddad successfully eliminated the pests from the corral area by repeatedly burning off the grass in the area. He also used
creosote oil with which to soak the ground and the animals after their
arrival. These precautions were successful in controlling the ticks and
the disease.

When the sturdy corrals were built and sufficient pasture had been properly fenced, he asked for the necessary funds and clearance to bring the buffalo home. The infrastructure preparation took place over a period of months, but the actual climax of the event took place over a period of a few days.

After much preparation, Granddad boarded the train in Lawton and traveled to Grand Central Station in New York City. Dad recalled his father's first-hand recollections of the trip. Granddad's personal ledger and expense records, in his handwriting, are compelling to read. A number of books, including *Buffalo Train Ride*, have been written about the events surrounding his trip, and I would recommend those books.

While in New York, Granddad oversaw the building of crates that could hold an individual animal with room enough for bedding, feed,

Granddad Rush standing on the front of the wagon with a buffalo ready for transportation at the New York Zoological park in 1907.

and water but portable enough to be loaded onto railroad cars. He wisely planned for the animals to have no way of escape in transport and was aware that the less they were jostled about, the better for their health and safety. He recalled how odd it was to realize the animals, which he would soon return to their native homeland, were passing through Fordham Station and the subterranean tunnels of New York City.

The trip back to Oklahoma was filled with scheduling and mechanical problems. The weather was typical of winter in the northeast. Granddad not only saw to it that the animals were cared for properly, he had to coax the railroad agents into special clearances so the railcars would continue to move. Great crowds gathered at train stations in cities along the way, and newspapers reported the progress of the animals.

The two train cars that transported the buffalo
displayed signs announcing the unusual cargo.

At last, the train pulled onto a siding at the station in Cache, Oklahoma. Indian chiefs, tribesmen, cowboys, town folk, farmers, ranchers, and politicians had gathered for the event days in advance. The Indians had bittersweet satisfaction when the crates containing their beloved buffalo were off-loaded onto horse drawn wagons for the final leg of their journey home. Among the Indians, celebration and ceremony were at a peak. Orations and kudos were on the agenda, but Granddad was eager to bring the buffaloes' journey to an end.

After their return to the West, the herd grew and prospered under Granddad's supervision and husbandry. Calves born in the spring the following year grew fat on the native grass and never realized that their sires and dams had been to The Big Apple. The buffalo were home.

The long journey home ended at Cache, Oklahoma where the crowd of onlookers gathered for a glimpse of the buffalo.

A mule and horse drawn wagon train traveled the last few miles across the prairies on the way to the holding pens in the exhibition pasture.

"Black Dog" was billed as the "largest buffalo in the world" with a weight of 2800 pounds and the monarch of herd.

In 1910, while living at the headquarters of the refuge, Mamo was largely responsible for reestablishing wild turkeys once native to the area. The turkey population had been depleted. Only a single turkey was reported inside the refuge. Mamo raised chickens for eggs and meat; and when I was a boy, she told me the following story: She asked Granddad to locate some breeding turkeys. He acquired a mating pair of Rio Grande turkeys from Texas, and one hen turkey from Missouri. She made use of the chicken pens behind her cobblestone house at forest headquarters, and the turkeys produced twenty-three eggs that season. She raised and released twenty-two young turkeys, plus the imported birds in the fall. From that brood, came the turkeys that populate the Wichitas and a great deal of Southwest Oklahoma today. Her contribution is scarcely mentioned in the shadow of Granddad's efforts to repopulate the buffalo, Longhorns, and elk to the area. She was not paid or praised for her accomplishment; however, this was a significant and historical deed.

Also in the shadow of Granddad's endeavors with the buffalo is the important accomplishment of reintroducing elk to the refuge. The native elk had been hunted to extinction in the area during the 1880s, and in 1911, Granddad was responsible for establishing the Wichita elk herd from the National Elk Refuge in Jackson, Wyoming.

Prior to his retirement in 1923, Granddad began selecting prime specimens of Texas Longhorn cattle to become the foundation herd of the Wichitas. He had unintentionally started the Longhorn herd a few years earlier with a single specimen named Old Whitey. He purchased the animal because of his great horn length and striking appearance and kept him as a pet for a few years prior to looking for breeding stock in earnest. Once it was officially decided to establish the Longhorns in the Wichitas, Granddad traveled to South Texas to inspect and purchase the foundation stock. Each Longhorn was chosen for color, horn shape, and size and conformation. Granddad looked for lean and lanky animals, characteristic of the breed, and specimens with gentle dispositions. The creation of the Wichita's Longhorn herd was just getting underway when Granddad retired, and even though he was instrumental in that endeavor, much of the process took place after he departed under the direction of Forest Ranger Earl Drummond.

Two typical Texas longhorns pose at the foot of Mt. Scott in the Wichitas.

Eventually the herds of buffalo, elk, and Longhorn cattle grew to such large numbers that they had to be thinned out. At first, they were culled and sold off for their meat. Later, they were sold for breeding stock. The buffalo and Longhorn auctions held at the refuge are annual events, which today are as much a social occasion as they are a necessity. The herds of nearly all of the privately-owned buffalo and most of the animals registered in the Texas Longhorn Breeders Association of America can be traced back to the foundation herds Granddad established in the Wichita Mountains.

In early days, only old cows and bulls were culled for sale. The animals were slaughtered for human consumption; and many school districts, including Cache, bought the meat at low prices and served it in the school cafeteria. At this point, I will remind you how delicious the tasty corn-fed buffalo meat was from Don Hight's ranch in South Dakota. At this point, I will also tell you about eating lunch at school in Cache and being served buffalo burgers, buffalo meat loaf, buffalo patties, and buffalo sausage. You will notice that each entrée contained only ground meat. In each case, no amount of A-1 sauce, catsup, Worcestershire, or any other flavor enhancer or innovative recipe by the cooks could disguise the taste. We were served the oldest, toughest, and rankest buffalo that were annually culled from the herd.

Granddad knew lakes were needed to provide a reliable water supply. Small dams were constructed, and plans for other larger lakes were incorporated into the long-term program. During the 1930s, the Civilian Conservation Corps, CCC, and the Workers Progress Administration, WPA, put people back to work during the depression. Most of the larger dams constructed by the CCC and WPA were planned by Granddad. Lake names like Jed Johnson, Quanah Parker, French, and Elmer Thomas were chosen in honor of worthy individuals. One particularly beautiful lake is named Rush Lake in Granddad's honor.

Granddad and Mamo wanted to reforest native cedar trees in the area. Early settlers to the area had taken their toll on the old-growth trees by harvesting them for log houses. Granddad and Mamo planned a nursery where they could start seedlings that could be transplanted

Granddad Rush, kneeling second from right, oversees the crew
at the cedar planting site with Mt. Sheridan in the background.

after a few years growth. A site near the north gate of the refuge was chosen. It was a field with rich soil, and an ample water supply was nearby. Several acres were planted with thousands of young cedar trees in evenly-spaced rows. Many small trees were transplanted by taking out every other tree, thus leaving room so the ever-growing forest could spread out into the newly-vacated space. Those trees that were never transplanted can be seen today growing in surreal alignments that stretch out in straight rows to every point of the compass. The trees have been threatened by forest fire numerous times. For some reason, perhaps in tribute to Granddad and Mamo, they have never burned.

The Holy City of the Wichitas was and is a landmark in the heart of the refuge. Buildings of native stone are reminiscent of buildings in the Bible. There is also a beautiful chapel where many weddings and church services have been held. In 1961, Big Tom and Suzy were married in the chapel.

The plan was to develop the Holy City for an Easter Pageant that would be held each Easter at sunrise, depicting the life story of Jesus Christ. There is a large, sloping hill facing the buildings where tens of

The chapel at the Holy City of the Wichitas
is a place of beauty and peace.

thousands of worshipers watch a volunteer cast of hundreds, in authentic costumes, reenact the story. The Easter Pageant gained national recognition and a great deal of history and tradition.

Mt. Scott is the most famous landmark of the Wichita Mountains. At two thousand, four hundred, sixty-four feet in elevation, the view from the top is awesome. Granddad was involved with the ambitious and bold idea of building a road to the summit. The road was conceived as a tourist attraction, which would become the crowning jewel for Southwestern Oklahoma. Granddad knew of the road up Pike's Peak in Colorado (completed in 1916) and realized that a gentle grade spiraling up the precipice might be possible. Armed with nothing more than determination, a hand-held surveyor's scope, and some geologic survey maps, he marked the path on which the road would be built. The result is a narrow two-lane highway that turns two complete spirals around and up to a parking lot and viewing area.

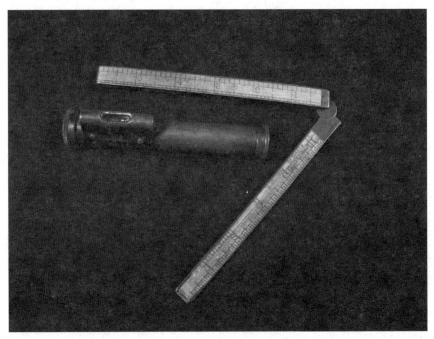

Shown here is the leveling eye glass and folding rule used by Frank S. Rush in the planning of the roads throughout the Wichitas.

The planners and construction workers who completed the job must have realized the road would be enjoyed by many tourists. They may not have fully contemplated how romantic, inspiring, and productive a moonlight drive to the top of Mt. Scott with your favorite girl might be.

When Granddad retired from the Forest Service, he moved to a location one mile south of the south gate of the refuge. The area was almost completely surrounded by mountains and looked something like a crater, thus the name Craterville.

27. Remembering Old Craterville Park

A township had been developed earlier where people could purchase lots for cottages in the foothills of the mountains. In addition to the principal acreage, Granddad Rush and Dad bought up the lots from the scattered owners over the years. Some people had already built a few cobblestone or wood frame cottages and were content with their ownership, but eventually almost every lot was added to the overall property.

While Craterville Park and Dude Ranch occupied the ground from 1923 through 1957, camping out on summer vacations was in vogue. There were few hotel or motel chains. Storytelling, sing-a-longs, hand fans, kerosene lanterns, tents, and camp fires were utilized, rather than televisions, refrigerated air conditioning, portable generators, RVs, and gas-fired barbecue grills. The simple pleasure of being in the out-of-doors, and away from home and work held the same appeal for many families then as now.

Granddad recognized people would not only come to camp, but if recreation were available, an enterprise would blossom in the granite hills. The pristine beauty of the Park and the location of the amusements as they developed over the years, combined to make Craterville a special place. A description and some old photos fall short of the experience that was Craterville, but let's journey to that magical place as best we can.

When you turned east off of the highway three miles north of Cache, the road rolled over a couple of low hills, through the oak trees, and opened into a meadow that was the heart of the Park. After crossing a bridge over a creek filled with persimmon and pecan trees, an icehouse, and grocery store were the first stops. The icehouse was considered a luxury for campers. Not only did bags of chipped ice cool beverages, block ice kept perishable foods fresh, and the ice was close at hand, not miles away. The grocery store on the opposite side of the main road sold fresh meats and fruit, eggs, milk, vegetables, and canned goods along with a supply of camping gear, swim suits, cooking utensils, and first-aid needs. There was a post office where mail could be cancel-stamped, "Craterville Park, Oklahoma." There was a large shelf filled with comic books for kids, as well as reading material for more mature readers. Candy jars, glass bottled soft drinks, and an ice cream box filled with five-gallon containers of Fairmont Ice Cream from Lawton were unexpected delights.

A view of a crowded day from the one of the mountains that surround old Craterville Park.

Next door, the main building contained the Park office; a fun house complete with a dark, walk-through maze; a glass house; and in later years, an electric Pretzel ride was added. Behind the main building were campgrounds with fire pits and tables, and an eighteen-hole miniature golf course built of cobblestones and cement. A refreshment stand served soft drinks, hot dogs, and hand-cut ice cream sandwiches with a sugar-wafer crust. Cotton candy, Sno-Cones, and giant dill pickles from a jar were popular treats as well. For the more daring customers, root beer was served from a wooden keg.

Next was the skating rink. The huge frame structure had a wooden skate floor and large screened openings that could be opened in summer and closed in winter. Clamp on skates with leather buckles were attached to your shoes, and off you went for a one-hour skating session. "A million dollars worth of fun, for only 25¢," was painted on a posted sign. Music played on the nickel jukebox, and the first thirty minutes were for clockwise skating only. A fifteen-minute session of reverse skating (counter clockwise) let everyone unwind and kept all the "lefties" from complaining. You got to skate clockwise again for ten minutes, then the last five minutes were for fast skating only. You were warned to get off of the floor if you didn't feel brave. If you wanted to skate another hour you had to buy another ticket, or "Shorty" Rowe, the rink supervisor, would call your name and send you to Mamo at the ticket booth.

Horseback riders stroll the midway at old Craterville.

The electric bumper car building joined the skating rink, and there was a nickel arcade where you could try a pin ball game, get your fortune told by a Genie in a glass box or mash a penny into a necklace with the Lord's Prayer embossed onto the metal on one side of the copper.

Mamo sold tickets in a glass-framed, elevated booth, and woe be the poor soul who misbehaved under her watchful eye. Once in a while, she would collect a silver dollar, which made a perfect gift for Suzy or me for making good grades or doing a chore for her. I have about one hundred of the big coins Mamo gave me, and have never been tempted to liquidate the treasure of silver eagles and golden memories.

Continuing around the perimeter of the Park to The Rush Inn, a seasonal restaurant welcomed guests, employees, and families in residence to hot meals prepared by the cook, Jimmy Stone. Alma Kirk ran the food line and made sure every child who passed along the cafeteria line in front of her had washed "both hands" before eating. Fresh homemade ice cream was in store for all who finished the meal. Upstairs over the restaurant was the employees' dormitory. Only single men were allowed to room there.

On the east side of the complex was Mamo's house. Mom, Dad, Suzy, and I lived next door. Dad built a home nearby for Bob and Alma Kirk and their daughter Nancy when they came to work for him. Continuing around the Park was the monkey zoo, the dude horse rental stable, Shetland pony stable, and the main horse barn.

Completing the live animal area was a "Real Live Rattlesnake Pit" and a display building for "Jimbo," the world's largest bovine. The rattlesnake pit was a popular attraction where for a small fee you could look down into a desert setting with two or three dozen live diamond back rattlers. Girls always screamed when the snake keeper tickled their ankles with a string on a stick, and every viewer was glad the snakes were in confinement rather than roaming the hills around the Park from where they had been captured.

As many as one hundred saddle horses were available for rent at the stable area. Pony rides for the little dudes were available at the building to the left of this scene.

Trail rides into the foothills of the Wichitas were a favorite attraction at the park.

Whistle Stop for Jimbo

Dad always liked giant cattle, and the steer Jimbo was his pride and joy. Dad had been acquainted with R. L. Davis of Scottsdale, Arizona, who owned a huge mixed-breed steer, Cimarron that was displayed at state fairs around the nation. The animal resembled a water buffalo but was billed as being the only animal alive which was a buffalo/Brahman cross. Cimarron's advertised weight was three thousand, one hundred and forty pounds. Dad had tried to buy Cimarron, but R. L. wouldn't sell the animal. Dad also kept a picture of three big Holstein steers that were owned by Joe Grimes of Kingfisher, Oklahoma. It is obvious that the photo had been doctored, but the weight of the animals, Tom, Dick and Harry, was three thousand, seven hundred and fifteen; three thousand, four hundred and ten; and three thousand, one hundred pounds respectively, according to the old photograph. The early-day picture of the Holsteins and Dad's acquaintance with Cimarron gave Dad the idea of searching for the world's largest bovine.

In 1954, the owner of the stockyards in Lawton called Dad and told him to hurry down because he had something to show him. Dad picked me up after school in Cache, and when we pulled up to the sale barn there was a giant brindle steer of mixed breeding looking over the top rail of a six-foot fence. The animal had been the family pet of a farmer down by Geronimo, Oklahoma. We were told that the farmer's children bottle-fed the orphaned calf, and he was so gentle that they just kept feeding him and letting him grow into a giant until he was too big to handle. Dad didn't want to seem too excited, but he knew the animal was bigger than anything he had seen and would make a great attraction for Craterville.

Jimbo was not only big for a three year old, but he continued to grow after Dad purchased him. We kept him on display for many years at Craterville and later at the Indian Curio store at Cache. At twenty-five cents a look, the animal paid for himself many times over. In 1964, Jimbo became ill and started to lose weight. We loaded

A photo of Bob-Cat Twister is part of the Frank Rush
collection of pictures of large bovines.

This picture from the collection has obviously been altered to make the
steers look much larger than a man but they are still impressive.

Mr. Davis' photo of Cimarron was a present to Dad
shortly after they became acquainted.

*him in a trailer and drove to the Paul Jones Lumber Yard scales in
Cache where we weighed the truck and trailer with Jimbo inside. We
then took Jimbo to the Kelsey Veterinary Clinic near Richard's Spur,
Oklahoma, where Doctor Charles Kelsey decided intestinal surgery
was the only chance the animal had for recovery. He also told Dad
that the surgery would probably be fatal. It was a tough decision, but
Dad gave the okay. Jimbo did not survive, but Doctor Kelsey found
the cause of his demise. When bovine animals ingest metal in their
feed, the material becomes imbedded in the lining of the stomach and
intestine. The result is known as Hardware Disease. Most animals are
slaughtered long before this becomes a life-threatening problem, but
Jimbo had succumbed to a handful of small pieces of wire, nails, and
various other metal items he had consumed in his hay and feed over
the years.*

*Only after Jimbo had gone on to greener pastures did we fully
realize how big he was. Big Tom and I went back by Mister Jones'
lumberyard that afternoon and weighed the truck and trailer minus*

205

Jimbo. The net difference in weight was three thousand, four hundred and twenty-five pounds. We estimated, conservatively, that Jimbo had lost another five hundred pounds during his three-month illness, so his total weight was at least three thousand, eight hundred pounds.

Dad called Mister Davis in Arizona and told him we had lost Jimbo, and we knew for sure that Jimbo weighed over three thousand, eight hundred before he died. Mister Davis revealed that Cimarron was never heavier than three thousand, two hundred pounds, but to maintain some bragging rights, he reminded Dad that Jimbo was a muley (no horns) and that Cimarron had large horns.

Frank Rush admires his pride and joy, Jimbo.
This picture is the "real deal." Jimbo really was this big.

28. Indian Stories

The most historic attraction at old Craterville was the Indian Curio Store and Museum. The Indian Curio Store completed the circle of attractions on the outer edge of the Park. It was a frame structure that sold all sorts of handmade Indian wares. Beautiful beadwork from the local Comanche, Kiowa, and Apache tribes were on display, as well as Minnetonka moccasins from Minnesota. Traders from Arizona and New Mexico delivered authentic handmade clay pottery, woven baskets, and turquoise jewelry. Collector-quality Indian blankets were popular, along with hundreds of other collectibles and trinkets.

A section of the store housed a museum. Granddad Rush had collected a great many artifacts and gifts from his friendship with local Indians, his tenure as manager at the wildlife refuge, and his years working with the Indian tribes at Craterville. Dad was also no stranger to collecting Indian artwork, crafts, and historic pictures, so the collection continued to grow.

The building also housed the original buckskin copy of the *Craterville Park Covenant* establishing an agricultural Indian fair. Also displayed was the certificate appointing Granddad as the supervisor and warden for the Wichita Forest and Game Preserve and memorabilia recounting his accomplishments.

Before he passed away, Granddad Rush received many gifts from his Indian friends. He was considered a trusted ally and was held in high regard by the Plains Indian tribes. He had lobbied for Indian rights and welfare with his many contacts in the state and federal government; in return, the tribal leaders took any opportunity to bestow the finest objects of Indian artistry.

Indians had frequented the area for centuries according to Indian lore and historical fact. As proof, a lucky individual or an archeologist would occasionally find an old arrow point or spear tip in the gravel washes. When the Park opened, Indians would return and camp for weeks during the summer. Powwows were organized for their enjoyment, and soon, other Park visitors started gathering to watch. Granddad began to hold scheduled powwows with dancing contests, a tradition that continued to grow when Dad inherited the reins as owner and manager. The dances had names such as the fast war dance, slow war dance, snake dance, and round dance; prizes were awarded to the winners. The drummers and singers were paid in cash, and the Indian families were given "camp meat" as a gift from the Park. Dad would order the best quality of meat from the dealers in Lawton, and as he moved through the camp passing out a proportionate share to each campsite, a great deal of ceremony took place. The Indians not only accepted the gift of fresh meat, they exchanged gifts and large quantities of verbal appreciation in return. Many times at old Craterville, we would awaken as the sun was rising and hear the drums and haunting chants of the singers as they ended a night of social dancing. What started as a social event for the Indians grew into a real tourist attraction.

A group of tribal leaders, including Horse, Buffalo, Sauppetty, George Cable, and others, called on Granddad Rush to join them in organizing an "agricultural Indian Fair" to give continuity and credence to the event. On May 25, 1924, *The Craterville Park Covenant* was signed by thumbprint of the tribal leaders and also Granddad's signature. For several years the event was held at Craterville. Horse races, traditional Indian sports, Indian dance contests, and many other contests were held as part of the event with Indian judges elected by tribesmen. Eventually, the official event was moved to Anadarko, Oklahoma, where it found a permanent home and was renamed the American Indian Exposition. Dad continued to hold powwows at old Craterville each year until the Park was displaced in the "land grab" in 1957. Other powwows could be found around the region, but the old Craterville gatherings were favored by many of the participants because of the relationship with Dad and the picturesque setting of old Craterville.

Granddad Rush standing in front of
the original Craterville Park Covenant.

The signers of the Craterville Park Covenant proudly stand for a photo on signing day. Not unusual is the fact that Indians are seldom seen smiling in a picture.

The Craterville Park Covenant. This covenant made and entered into by Frank Rush of Craterville Park, Comanche County Oklahoma, Party of the first part, and the Indians whose names are subscribed, party of the second part. Witnessth: it has become necessary for the American Indians to take steps for the advancement and uplift of their people and especially to teach their children the value of building character and becoming self supporting, this covenant is entered into as a means towards that end. Therefore, the parties hereto covenant and agree among themselves as follows, There shall be held annually at Craterville Park an agricultural Indian Fair. The object of this fair will be to create self evidence and to encourage leadership by the Indian for his people, a belief in the capacity of the Indian to better his position and to take his place on terms of equality with other races in the competitive pursuits of every day life, and a desire to accomplish the most possible for himself and his people. All Officers, Directors, Judges and Exhibitors at the aforesaid fair must be Indians, all said Officers, Directors and Judges must be elected by the Indians themselves. In Testimony, whereof we have hereunto set our hands this 25th day of May, 1924.
Horse, Buffalo, Sauppetty, Geo. Cable, Frank Rush
Written By, Freddie Dee

The text of the Craterville Park Covenant.

A photo of Frank Rush and Frank Rush III in front
of the Craterville Park Covenant inside the Curio
Store Museum shortly before it burned in 1955.

If you have ever heard the term "Indian giver," it refers to a custom long held by many tribes. If a gift was given to you, it was yours as long as you were alive. When you went on to the spirit world, the custodianship of the article was no longer your responsibility, and the gift giver could retrieve the gift. The custom was widely accepted as proper etiquette among Indians, but in later times, the term itself became a slur to describe a greedy or stingy person.

211

When Granddad died in 1933, many Indians came to Mamo and Dad to reclaim gifts given to Granddad. The issue quickly got out of hand because several individuals would see an article in the collection, and each would claim ownership. Indian friends of Mamo and Dad advised them to refuse all requests because hard feelings and disputes would cause more harm than good. Dad recalled how he and Mamo would tell inquiring Indians that the items were also given to her and she was still alive, and besides most of the items were on display in the museum. To their credit, the Indians understood and few, if any, held a grudge.

Fortunately, the museum displays had overflowed, and many items were stored in another building.

Mom and Dad were visiting friends in Ft. Worth in the late winter of 1955. Annie Duggins was the store manager and had left the building one evening after receiving a large shipment of goods for the upcoming season. An electrical fire started around 5 a.m. and spread quickly throughout the building. By the time Bob Kirk, the Park foreman, was made aware of the blaze, there was no time to save the building or the contents. Bob lamented later that if he had just had the presence of mind to back a truck into the sidewall of the building and collapse the section that housed Granddad's collection, he might have saved some of the keepsakes. Dad and Mom returned home and I recall how completely shaken Dad was. He seldom cried, but I know his heart was broken. To his credit, he hugged Annie and Bob and said he was thankful that no one was injured, and no blame was to be placed for the accident.

Dad made a call to Jesse and Red Robertson on the same day. You will recall Jesse was the man who built the Santa's sleighs, and Red later helped us open Sandy Lake Park. Every person who worked for the Park pitched in along with other volunteers from the community and started removing the rubble while searching any artifact that might not have burned. The Park was scheduled to open for the season in sixteen days. Bob Kirk was an excellent carpenter and between him, Jesse, Red, and forty or more workers, reconstruction quickly began. Annie, Dad, and Mom started ordering more inventory from traders in New Mexico and Arizona and also Brice Privette, who owned Pawnee Bill's Indian Trading Post in Pawnee, Oklahoma.

The *Lawton Constitution* reported that construction progress was moving along almost as fast as the building had been razed by fire. Electricians, painters, and decorators completed their work before the building itself was finished. Workers began unpacking Granddad's remaining stored treasures. The day of the Park's opening, only sixteen days later, a larger and more beautiful Indian Curio Store opened, fully stocked and ready for business. A big grand opening for the Indian Curio Store and Museum was staged, and the newspapers covered the event with front-page stories. Dad made a production out of the disaster. People said that Frank Rush was the only man in Southwest Oklahoma who could accomplish the task so quickly and beautifully.

Interior of the Indian Curio Store.

29. More About Old Craterville Park

The center of the Park contained the amusement rides and performance stage. While rides were similar to those we now have at Sandy Lake Park, they were not as sophisticated and closely inspected as we are today. There were kiddie rides, including a Roto-Whip, Midge-O-Racer, and Bulgy Fish and larger rides including a Merry-Go-Round, Rock-O-Plane, train, and Fly-O-Plane. In the earlier days, the Park had a raceway ride that was a cross between bumper cars and go-carts, which was eventually sold to make way for new rides. Prior to buying the Rock-O-Plane ride, an old Ferris wheel served as the high ride, and it had a bad habit of getting a car jammed and breaking the drive cable. If the wheel was loaded out of balance when the cable broke, the whole contraption would rock back and forth, giving the riders an unexpected thrill.

The performance stage was the site of a great many special appearances by popular celebrities of the era, as well as circus or specialty acts. Craterville drew crowds with public appearances, unlike Sandy Lake Park, which thrives on group picnics and the band festival.

The midway at old Craterville included a merry-go-round and Ferris wheel with a shaded entry. The Rush Inn restaurant is shown in the background.

The raceway cars were popular, however, the ride was removed to make way for new attractions about 1946.

Beyond the Fly-o-Plane ride was the performance stage where large crowds would gather to see the kaleidoscope of stars and circus performers.

Ollie Couch drives the colorful train at old Craterville.
Notice the "Rocking R" brands on the front of the engine.

Roy Rogers made an appearance at the Park. Dad's cousin, Art Rush, was Roy's manager, and when he had an open weekend, the arrangements were made for Trigger and Roy to perform and sign autographs. Roy had just finished a show in Chicago, and he and Trigger were flying to New Orleans. One open day in the schedule allowed their plane to land in Lawton. Trigger flew in a specially built stall on the plane with Roy.

Roy Rogers mounted on Trigger and backed up by The Sons of the Pioneers thrill a record-setting crowd at old Craterville.

Trigger, Roy and Dale Evans inspect a baby deer at the Lawton airport shortly before departing. The fawn was a gift to Roy and Dale from Dad.

There was a problem of major proportions. Some souvenir hunter in Chicago had found Trigger unattended and cut his tail off. Not the whole tail, but the hair had been bobbed off. The appearance would have had to be canceled but for the quick thinking of Roy's manager and Dad's cousin, Art Rush. He called RKO studios in California and had a false tail flown in. The tress arrived in Lawton about the same time Roy and Trigger landed. It was braided into place, and the audience never knew the difference.

There were many famous circus acts, including a high diver who dived from a one-hundred-and-twenty-foot tower into a tank filled with six feet of water. There were trapeze artists, bicycle trick riders, and LaLage, a beautiful blonde who did an aerial act. LaLage's routine is difficult to describe, but the finale was a series of one-arm "spin flips" while suspended only by a wrist loop. Her body would flip down, around, and up as the audience kept count of the cycles. She always attained a record number of flips by adding just one more to her previous record. After about one hundred arm-wrenching turns, the audience would gasp as she completed one hundred and one.

The family of performers who brought their bicycle act to the Park could ride anything on wheels. They had the world's tallest unicycle at twenty feet, the bicycle built for ten upon which all members of the family rode, and a tiny bike that was only eight inches tall. The entire family was very talented, especially the four voluptuous female members of the troop whose main contribution was to pose along the edge of the stage encouraging the audience to clap. The ladies were dressed in costumes, but "Wowee" what costumes! They left "almost nothing" to the imagination. While the men in the crowd were concentrating on "almost nothing," the cyclists performed their variety of tricks. I was a young lad at the time, but I still think that was the most memorable act that ever came to old Craterville.

There were trained dogs and monkeys, a lion tamer, and a bear trainer. The bear trainer appeared several seasons at the Park, but shortly after his final visit, he met an untimely end in Kansas City. We learned that one of the bears had cornered and killed him in his truck-mounted steel cage.

Benny and Betty Fox billed themselves as the Sky Dancers. The couple performed every style of dancing from ballroom, to waltz, to boogie-woogie and everything in between on a fourteen-inch diameter dance floor high atop an eighty-foot pole. Please note the platform was fourteen *inches*, not fourteen *feet*. The act had prerecorded music that bounced from one familiar song style to another as the Foxes changed dance steps and costumes in mid-air. Benny wore a white tuxedo, and Betty had a dress that could be quickly rearranged to match the dance style. It was a very novel act, not to mention the fact that there was eighty feet of thin air between the edge of the dance floor and solid ground.

The Sky Dancers played at both old Craterville and new Craterville. Dad thought of a publicity stunt for the duo in downtown Altus, the largest town near new Craterville. The tallest building in Altus was only six stories tall, but still an imposing height for the exciting plan. Mister Fox had another specially-designed dance platform, which could be suspended out eight feet beyond the edge of a rooftop. The dance floor disc and supporting steel structure, along with dozens of sandbags for counter balance, had to be lugged up six stories of the structure. A crew of Craterville Park employees labored for hours to put the prop in place on the roof. At noon on Friday, July second, the Fox team entertained surprised business people around the town square with a sample routine they called "Dancing On The Clouds." Publicity notices were scattered to the wind from atop the building. "Bring the family, friends and neighbors to Craterville Park July 3rd and 4th, and see the full show," announced the notices. The newspaper ran a picture, and the largest crowd ever to attend new Craterville was on hand that Saturday and Sunday.

The most beautiful act and the most dangerous were the Sky Kings. There were four one-hundred-foot poles set up in a square pattern about forty feet apart with brace wires running to the ground. Atop the braced portion of the poles were thirty-foot flexible mast poles on which four men performed acrobatic moves as the poles swayed back and forth under their weight. The song "Cherry Pink and Apple Blossom White" was the perfect match for the tempo of the swaying poles. For a finale, the Sky Kings would swap poles in mid-air. The fearless move was met by gasps and roaring applause from the crowd. The act visited both parks several times, and on one occasion during the pole change at new Craterville, two of the four performers accidentally wound up on the same pole. The combined weight of both men could have snapped the spring steel pole had they not quickly descended to the relative safety of the braced section. No one was harmed, but the crowd cheered even louder, thinking it was part of the act.

Hugo, the Human Cannon Ball, was fired, body and soul, from a truck-sized cannon into a suspended catch net some three hundred feet away. He never missed the net, but his life insurance policy had a special disclaimer attached. Hugo's wife was responsible for the control buttons inside the truck, and on at least one occasion she pulled the trigger slightly before Hugo was ready. Hugo wasn't happy even though he was not injured. Mrs. Hugo just laughed and said it gave a whole new meaning to the term "ready or not."

Hugo the Human Cannon Ball flies over the crowd at old Craterville.

Emmitt Kelly, one of the best known clowns of all time, made at least two appearances at old Craterville. He had a very small, battery-operated car, in which he could cram his large body and baggy clothes. The best part of the act was his arrival on stage. No one could believe that anyone could fit into such cramped quarters, inside the little car. When he emerged, he towered over the little coupe. His antics thrilled kids and adults alike.

Other famous stars from television and the *Grand Ole Opry* made special guest appearances each weekend all summer. Singers included Lester Flatt and Earl Scruggs, Roy Acuff, Homer and Jethro, Grandpaw Jones, Little Jimmie Dickens, and Brenda Lee. Western movie stars including Tex Ritter, Montie Montana, and Rex Allen drew large crowds at old Craterville. The Cisco Kid, Duncan Renaldo, performed several times and became a close friend of Dad's. Duncan fell in love

221

with the Park and told Dad, in all sincerity, he wanted to retire there, but it never came to pass. He sent Dad a Christmas card and letter every year until he passed away. Minnie Pearl came to both parks as well. Her "Howdee" opening line and price tag hat were her performance trademarks. Everyone, including our family, who met Minnie understood her loving personality and friendliness were even more impressive than her humor. During her first visit to old Craterville, she acted so at home at the Park, I thought she was related to us. Later, when she returned for a show at new Craterville, it was like old home week to be with her.

Dad's old receipt book shows where the fee charged for most personal appearances was "Paid in Cash" in the amount of $250. More popular stars commanded $750, an amount that wouldn't begin to interest any top artist today.

Rex Allen was billed as part of the 33rd annual Independence Day Celebration in 1954. It should be noted that all of the shows at old Craterville were free. The rides and attractions paid the bills.

Old Craterville had many other amenities as well, including a big spring-fed swimming pool about a half-mile north of the center of the Park. Back then, there were fewer requirements for safety. Lifeguards patrolled the pool and a sign stated, "Not responsible for accidents," but problems seldom occurred. The pool was a few hundred feet in length and lay behind a concrete dam that had been built in the early 1930s. You could dive or jump into the water from granite boulders up to thirty feet above water level. The water was held in the pool by a small gate in a children's pool, which also acted as a part of the dam. When the pool needed cleaning the gate was opened, and fresh water would gush through and cleanse the pool. There were fish, turtles, snakes and frogs in the water. People thought little of it because it was a natural pool and a wonderful place to spend a summer day.

This 1930s photo of the upper dam and the swimming
pool features the slide and a standing-room-only crowd.

223

Big Tom's mother and father, Dorothy and Dick Self, and his grandparents, Aunt Omah and Uncle Tom Howenstine, worked part-time at the swimming pool. There were dressing rooms and bathing suit rentals along with a small snack stand near the pool. Many Park customers enjoyed swimming in the pristine mountain pool. The pool was widely known as a landmark and was one of the main attractions for old Craterville.

By the 1950s when this pool picture was taken,
swimming attire had made some noticable changes.

Located between the pool and the Park were a number of rent cabins, which were former residences of previous owners. Employees or short-term renters stayed in the numbered cabins. Dad would hire people and give them a free place to live, which was an important benefit. The employees enjoyed living at the Park, and Dad knew they would always be near at hand when he needed them.

Bob and Alma Kirk lived in a house just behind the skating rink when they first moved to the Park. An Indian couple, Rusty and Maxine Wahkinney, helped run the Park and also lived in one of the cabins. Rusty and Bob would repair and maintain the Park and Alma and Maxine could do about anything else needed in the Park's operation.

There was a sense of family at old Craterville. Many teenagers from Cache worked at the Park at some point. There were a great many other adults who worked at the Park, raised their children on site, and considered the Park home. Mamo was the matriarch of the family. Even though she was a strong-willed businessperson, she always found time to visit with employees and customers in a friendly and pleasant manner. Dad and Mom were cordial hosts as well, an employee/employer relationship, which added to the success of the Park.

Dad was the hero and idol of every young child. They followed him as if he were a pied piper. He always let kids do a small chore, which made them feel important and useful.

A young Indian boy, Milton Peabshy, came to the Park and hung around Dad like a fly on a cotton candy cone. Milton's nickname was Beans, and the title stuck with him for life. Beans was a chubby kid who had a bad home life in Cache. His father didn't mistreat him, but his father also had a bad reputation, which often led to trouble in his family. Beans simply adopted Dad and moved in. Dad would send him home at the close of the day, and by daylight the next morning, Beans was back at the front door. Dad couldn't figure out how he got to the Park so early each day until he discovered that Beans had moved himself into a small storage room under the stairs behind the grocery store. Dad gave in and furnished the room with a cot and some essentials. Beans began working at the Park while he was in grade school, and as he grew older, became more and more involved. He never left the Park again, except to join the Army. He had an unwavering loyalty to Dad, and never failed to do any task asked of him.

When Beans finished school and joined the Army's 45th Division, he served his tour of duty, receiving honors and medals for his service. He loved to hunt and found military machine guns as easy to fire accurately as the old .30-30 rifle that Dad had given him for his sixteenth birthday. He started shooting competitively in contests held by the Army. He

225

won several championship machine gun competitions. He was proud of his Army service and would come home on leave clad in his finest army dress uniform, much to the delight and satisfaction of Dad.

I learned a lot of life lessons from Beans, at least one of which reflected Beans' upbringing by Dad. I have recalled the event hundreds of times since. Beans bought a new red and white 1954 Ford automobile. It was neat-o, to say the least, and he cherished the car. One day at the ranch, and long before I had a driver's license, I backed a farm truck into the driver's side door of Beans' new car and did a good deal of damage. I cried and confessed to Dad right away. I asked Dad to tell Beans because I was afraid to face him with the bad news. Dad didn't go for that. He told me I had done the damage and would have to stand up to the consequences. When I told Beans about my accident, his very first words were, "Are you hurt?" I tearfully said, "No," and the next thing I knew Beans was laughing and hugging me. I was startled by his reaction until he said, "Then don't worry, Frankie, I can get the car fixed." I never forgot his generosity in letting me off the hook, and I count the experience as my guide in similar circumstances with children.

After his Army days, Beans worked for Dad until we moved to Texas, but he didn't want to leave Oklahoma. He soon found a job with Dosey Davis at the Army Surplus Store in Lawton and later worked for the Gibson's store on Cache Road. I would go by Gibson's and visit with Beans every time we visited Vickie's mother in Lawton. The last time I saw Beans, he was suffering health problems, but it was not his nature to complain. He pulled an "Old Timer" pocketknife from his pocket and said, "This is a gift for you. Mister Rush gave me this knife when I first came to Craterville, and I have carried it everyday since." The blade had worn thin from sharpening, and like Beans, the knife showed the wear of many years of work. I told Beans that I could not accept such a valued possession, but he insisted. The next spring Beans passed away, and only when I learned the sad news did I realize why Beans wanted me to have the knife. It was a cherished gift to me as a life-long friend, and it gave me a whole new meaning to the term "Indian giver."

Other young people who were drawn to Dad include Big Tom and Walter Chris. Big Tom was a teenager living at the Park with his parents and grandparents while they worked there. Walter lived in Cache and worked at the Park as well. Big Tom and Walter ran rides on the weekends, but I believed they just had a lot of free time to hang out with me on weekdays. At least I thought it was free time. I didn't realize Dad and Mom had put Walter or Big Tom in charge of me as part of their job. We had the run of the place, and we were always fishing, riding, hunting, or just about any other activity young boys could think of. I realized later, when I had my children and grandchildren, my parents were concerned about general safety and thought an older companion would watch out for me.

The best result of their concern is the enduring friendship and fond memories I have with Big Tom and Walter. We had a lot of fun, and Walter, Big Tom, and I never did get into anything permanently damaging. Big Tom and I had one thing in common: we never did like school very much. Big Tom was like my brother before he became my brother-in-law. Walter moved to Texas and lives near Sandy Lake Park. He still helps out at the Park when we get in a bind, but also travels the world with the Texas Baptist Men helping with disaster relief. Walter says he owes much of his ability to work and organize relief efforts to his experience of working for Dad at old Craterville.

Suzy and I had chores at the Park when we weren't in school at Cache. Big Tom's mother, Dorothy, was a teacher at Cache, so Suzy, Big Tom, and I were always under her watchful eye at school. Big Tom and Suzy were no doubt better academically than I; however, I seem to recall Big Tom having more difficulty in the area of discipline.

I occasionally struggled with my grades. One time I came home with a report card that informed my parents that I had made four D's and one C. Mother was just about in hysterics about my grades. I thought sure my Dad would come unwound and do something bad to me. He studied my report card and said, "Son, this isn't good. Looks like you've been spending way too much time on one subject." Mom and I failed to see the humor in his observance, but Dad got his point across.

Suzy was busy skating and doing girl things with her friends, Nancy Kirk and Louise Rowe, but one time Dad wanted us to learn something about the family business. The process involved a modest amount of work. Dad took Suzy and me to the bank at Roosevelt and asked his banker, Carl Smelser, to loan us $60 each so we could buy some gumball and peanut machines to operate in the Park. We signed a note at the bank and formed a partnership. Dad said we could keep the profit from the machines after we paid for the necessary supplies and paid banker Smelser the $120 we borrowed. The first week we made $2.35 total, and Suzy decided she wanted out of our agreement. I told Dad that I would buy her half, but I still wanted the same no-sales-commission deal he promised both of us. I knew Dad had made arrangements for a man to display a young elephant in the Park during the summer and the peanut machine looked like a sure thing. Dad agreed, and by year's end, I was debt free and had a handsome profit of $42 to show for my effort. Suzy wanted back in the partnership, but Dad and Mom told her a deal is a deal.

Unlike Sandy Lake Park, old Craterville stayed open late each evening. Campers and day customers came and went at all hours and people respected each other's property and the Park property as well. There wasn't much trouble, but a good many pranks were played on anybody by anybody.

A constable by the name of Ray Powell would drive his old patrol car to the Park for conversation and free food. The boys were always making sport of Ray. One evening, a car pulled into the Park, cut a couple of donuts on the gravel and sped away down the road and out of the Park. "Did anybody get his tag number," hollered Ray. "Yeah, I did," replied one of the young employees. Ray wrote the number down and said, "By gum, I'll get that smart-aleck." Ray came back furious the next morning, looking for the boy who had given him the tag number to his own patrol car.

Old Craterville Park wasn't just an island in the vast prairies of southwest Oklahoma. It was southwest Oklahoma. The people that came there were from surrounding communities and towns and considered the Park their personal playground. Craterville was a familiar topic of conversation in a café in Hobart, a high school basketball game in Walters, a square dance at Faxon, or anywhere two or more people got together for a chat. It was the hub for family entertainment and a focal point for leisure activity. Without Dad and the people that surrounded him, the Park would have seemed less interesting, because they were the catalyst that gave it personality.

Whistle Stop for Papa Jack

One of those interesting people was Papa Jack Howenstine, a local legend, and perhaps a mentor to Dad and his insatiable appetite to make a horse trade whether a horse was involved or not.

Papa Jack lived on his Oasis Ranch just one mile south of the entrance to old Craterville. The ranch was a jumble of collectibles, tools, farm and ranch equipment, outbuildings, and assorted livestock. The inventory was kept in Papa Jack's head where he could recall each item and the amount of money he had paid or the trade deal he had made to acquire the object. He purchased cows by the pound and sold them by the head to insure a deal would be made in his favor. In other situations, he might reverse the procedure to gain the upper hand. In either case, he almost always got the best end of a trade. Papa Jack lived with a short cigar crunched between his teeth and had a sparkle in his eye that grew brighter when he was doing business.

Dad and Papa Jack were as close in their friendship as they were as neighbors. They would team up on a third party to make a trade, but it was great sport for the two of them to profit from a sale or swap between them.

One day, a couple of men showed up at the Oasis Ranch and approached Papa Jack about purchasing some yearling colts. Papa Jack knew Dad had some colts for which he was asking $350 a head. Papa Jack said he could provide the men with good colts for $400 each. Papa Jack figured Dad would be glad to pay him a $50 commission for providing the buyers. "Well, we were looking to buy some horses which cost a good deal more," one said smugly. Papa Jack quickly solved the issue. He said, "My neighbor, Frank Rush, down the road at Craterville Park has some good colts, and he'll take $800 rock bottom for 'em, if he likes the looks of ya." Off went the men, on their way to Craterville. Papa Jack quickly called the Park and told Dad the men were on the way, and to not price the colts for a dime less than $800 each. Dad had the boys gather the colts into the horse barn while he was getting acquainted with the gents. The men looked over *the selection, unaware they were the exact same colts Papa Jack had priced for $400 a short time earlier. They paid cash on the barrelhead for five of the animals, at the inflated price, and happily went on their way.*

Papa Jack and Dad split the profit and had satisfied the customers' wishes to boot. Papa Jack's eyes twinkled as he crunched a brand new stogie between his teeth.

This Papa Jack Howenstine drawing from Paul McClung's biography, *Papa Jack, Cowman from the Wichita* captures the old cowman in a typical expression and a perpetual cigar.

Paul McClung, a newspaper writer and close family friend from Lawton, Oklahoma, authored a book, Papa Jack, *and I would certainly recommend it. Paul's book and my acquaintance with him and his wife Jerry were part of my inspiration to write this book about Dad. Papa Jack was also Big Tom's great uncle, so the ties between the families are very close.*

30. Let's Rodeo

The rodeo grounds were located a short distance to the east of the main complex of old Craterville. Granddad Rush started producing rodeos on Fourth of July weekends in 1924, and grandstands that would hold a few thousand people were erected and enlarged over the years. Granddad passed away in 1933, but Dad continued the shows.

At first, the rodeo contestants were local cowboys, and there wasn't an arena fence. People just pulled their cars up in a big circle and the action took place in the field in the center. There was wild cow riding rather than bull riding, and when saddle broncs were ridden, the cowboys mounted in the middle of the arena without the aid of bucking chutes. Two hazing horses crowded the bronc between them, and a hazer placed a flour sack over the bronc's eyes to quiet the animal. The contestant climbed over the back of a hazing horse and down onto the saddle. When things were ready, the hazer pulled the sack from the horse's eyes, and the cowboy rode the horse until it quit bucking. To attract the attention of the judges, a bronc rider might flog his mount with his hat, an act of bravado that would draw a stiff fine in a rodeo today. But even then, cowboys had respect for the animals. Once a cowboy was safely on the ground, and after an especially good effort on the part of his mount, a cowboy might tip his hat in salute to the animal.

As the sport progressed, calf roping and steer roping events were added, along with roping and bucking chutes similar in many respects to modern rodeo arenas. Old films reveal how big and tough the animals were and how the sport closely resembled every-day ranch work. There were no bucking bulls, trophy buckles, or ceremonies at first, but times were changing. New contest rules and innovations were being introduced to the show, and the popularity of the sport was catching on.

231

There was almost too much action for one page of advertisement at the 16th annual rodeo in 1940.

Dad hired a famous rodeo announcer and producer named Foghorn Clancy to help add color and structure to the rodeo. Foghorn used a megaphone to announce the events, and his booming voice carried to the far corners of the grandstands. Cowboys such as Windy Ryon, Todd Whatley, Freckles Brown, and Buck Rutherford were coming from Texas and Oklahoma to show their talents and win the jackpots. Grand entry flags, a rodeo band, and specialty acts were added, and the crowds grew each year.

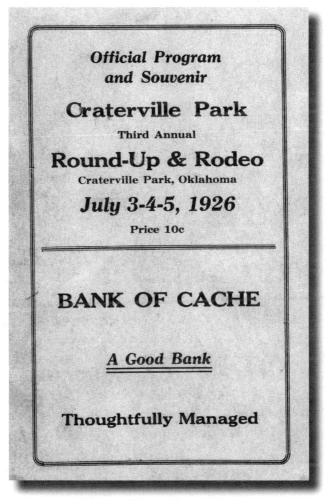

The 1926 program for the third annual Craterville Park Round-Up and Rodeo.

SATURDAY, JULY 3

Calf Roping.
Half Mile Dash (Indian).
Wild Cow Milking.
Bell Calf Roping.
Three Quarter Mile Race (Indian).
Three Eighths Mile Race (White).
Half Mile Dash (White).

EXHIBITIONS

Bronc riding. Riders, Tye Jones, O. K. Jones, "Goober" Roach. Riders will draw from following horses: Rosebud, Vinagaroon, White Angel, Fort Worth Anna, Skyrocket, Saxaphone.

BULL DOGGING, TYE JONES
Saturday Night

Indians will give war dances. Natives, painted, crouching, and chanting to the weird music of beating toom-toms, dance the wild and picturesque war dance.

NOTE—The management could not secure the names of all the entries in the contests as the drawing for places and so forth did not take place until a few minutes before the contest, hence they were omitted to avoid mistakes. For the benefit of the spectators the announcer will give all such information as each event is given.

SUNDAY, JULY 4

Unveiling of Liberty Bell—11 A. M. An actual full size reproduction of the original Liberty Bell.
Patriotic Speech, by O. O. Kirkham of Lawton.
2 P. M.—Baseball Game. Craterville vs. Chattanooga.
Calf Roping.
Exhibition Riding—Tye Jones, Goober Roach.
Exhibition Bull Dogging—Tye Jones.
Wild Cow Milking.
Exhibition Steer Riding.
Bell Calf Roping.

MONDAY, JULY 5

Calf Roping.
Half Mile Dash (Indian).
Wild Cow Milking.
Three Eighth Mile Dash (White).
Exhibition Bronco Riding.
Cowboy Barrel Race.
Exhibition Bull Dogging.
Three Eighths Mile Dash (White).
Steer Riding Exhibition.
Three Fourths Mile Race (Indian).
Bell Calf Roping.

MONDAY NIGHT

Indian War Dances.
Dazzling Fireworks Display.

RECORDS OF ROPING

The world's fastest records in steer roping and tieing are: 17 seconds, made by J. Ellison Carrol in 1906, and Clay McGonigal in 1908. The world's fastest records in calf roping are 18 seconds made by Jack Degraftenreld in 1921, 17 1-2 seconds made by Henry Saddler, February, 1923, and 16 4-5 seconds made by Lee Robinson March, 1923.

The world's fastest records in bull dogging are: Mike Hastings, 1916, 12 seconds; Slim Caskey, 1920, 11 4-5 seconds; Shorty Kelso, Watonga, Okla., 9 3-5 seconds; Frank McCarrol, 1921, 7 3-5 seconds; Mike Hastings, 1922, 7 seconds; May, 1924, Rube Roberts, 6 2-5 seconds; June, 1924, Johnnie Roberts, 5 4-5 seconds.

The program details are complete with sponsor's ads from 1926.

Fagon Miller, a young boy from Odell, Texas, had come to the Park on a family vacation and got to hanging around Dad. Fagon was a ranch-raised cowboy and could handle any chore with horses or cattle. Dad put him to work in the Park, and in the winter, he started milking cows at the barn to earn extra money. Fagon also worked with the saddle horses in the dude string. He and Dad bought a pair of paint horses and decided they wanted to learn to trick ride. There was a lady named Teddy Jacobs who came from Wells Point, Texas, with her sister to ride in the women's bronc riding, and also perform their trick-riding act. Dad saw no reason to hire an outside act when he and Fagon could do the job. They purchased some trick riding saddles in Vernon, Texas, and taught themselves to do all of the tricks the rodeo professionals could do. Anytime I tell people Dad was a trick rider, they look at me with amazement, but Dad and Fagon got very skilled as they practiced. Besides, "Trick riding is a lot more glamorous than milking cows," according to Fagon.

One old movie of Dad trick riding at old Craterville shows him doing a tail stand on Tony, his trick riding horse, as they sped around the arena. A trick not all trick riders would attempt, a tail stand required him to hold on to the cruppers or handles at the rear of the saddle and do a headstand with his head down by the horse's tail and his body vertical above. Mother swears to this day, the reason Dad complained about a sore neck is because he would occasionally fall off of Tony on his head. Mom recalled, "He bounced three or four times on his head, just like a pogo stick with arms."

Frank Rush performing a shoulder stand on his speeding horse Tony in front of the crowd and the giant loud speaker horns at a Craterville rodeo.

235

Whistle Stop for Ridin' and Shootin' with Mom

Mom tries to keep peace in the family as neatly as she keeps her home. She is a classy lady, and beautiful, even at an advanced age (which a lady never reveals). People always recognize those good qualities and many more in Mom. But there are a couple of things about Mom most people don't know. She could ride horses and shoot a shotgun with the best of 'em.

Mother had purchased a gorgeous black high school (trick) horse, Ace of Spades. He was jet black and stood sixteen hands tall. Ace was a cross between a Standard Bred and Tennessee Walker, and he was an eyeful. Mom recalls how everything about Ace said, "Look at me." He was trained for dressage work as well as circus stunts, and Mom soon had her own specialty act for the rodeo. People didn't get much of a chance back then to see show horses of that quality. Even though there were cowponies and draft horses that were still being used on the job, it was entertaining to see such an unusual animal as Ace being put though his paces in a rodeo arena.

Mom's experience with Ace of Spades and other horses around old Craterville cultivated a God-given skill that was apparent when you saw her ride. Mom had a natural seat in the saddle or as horsemen say "she could sit a horse." She was a good instructor as well. She taught Suzy and me to ride. She could walk up to you while you were mounted and move your leg or touch your hand and say, "See how that feels?" or "Think what the horse feels when you do this." She would watch you ride and would encourage your good qualities and correct your bad habits in a way that made riding feel right and look good at the same time. Mom taught us that if you ride correctly, it is comfortable and fun, and the animal will respond.

At old Craterville, Dad and Mom built a trap-and-skeet range for shotgun practice. The officers with the Oklahoma Highway Patrol and agents with the FBI would come to the Park and visit. Sometimes they just stopped by in their squad cars, and often they would move into one of the cabins and spend a few days relaxing. Dan Combs with the

236

OHP and Spot Gentry and Jelly Brice with the FBI were among Dad's guests. Dad and Mom spent a good bit of time at target practice with their officer friends.

Mother had a little 20-gauge Remington shotgun with a custom fitted stock and a modified barrel choke. A round of shooting consisted of firing twenty-five shells at clay pigeons at various distances. Mother could typically hit twenty-three or twenty-four targets on skeet and

Genelle Rush and Ace of Spades saluting the crowd at old Craterville.

237

twenty or more on the trap range. For a police officer or a skilled hunter, those scores would be considered excellent. For a little lady who had no formal training, the scores were outstanding.

The original hand-written score of "Thoughts of Love"
composed by Genelle Rush.

Mom adapted to Dad's interest of hunting and riding, but she also possesses the only musical talent in the family. She sang and played the piano on the radio in Elk City and Altus as a teenager, and she accompanied the choir at the First Methodist Church in Cache until we moved to Texas. She also composed a beautiful love song for Dad titled "Thoughts of Love." Mom always filled the request to play and sing the song at family gatherings. At every family wedding, birthday, and anniversary, our friend Allison Snyder has performed the song. In the tradition of the ballads of the '40s and '50s, the tune always brings joy to sentimental hearts.

31. The Rodeo Showdown with the Turtles

In 1936, a group of cowboys threatened to walk out, or strike, during a rodeo in the Boston Gardens in Massachusetts if their entry fee was not added back into the prize money. The group became a labor union of sorts, with a goal to improve the money paid and other conditions such as rodeo livestock selection. The group called themselves the Cowboys' Turtle Association. Rodeo history tells us the rodeo cowboys used the word turtle in their title because officials had been "slow as turtles" to act on their demands. Dad joined and paid his dues for a number of years as member number 1410. A few years passed and things were getting better not only at Craterville, but at rodeos around the country.

Frank Rush's Cowboy's Turtle Association card.

240

In 1943, just before the rodeo grand entry at Old Craterville was to start and with the grandstands full of people, the cowboy contestants threatened to strike at Dad's rodeo. They told Dad that they wanted even more money added to the advertised prize money or they would not ride. Dad got hopping mad and told them they had made a deal, and they should stick to it. After all, he was also a CTA member. He had supported them with the issue about the entry fees being added into the prize money, but he didn't like the idea that they were threatening a strike if they didn't get more money than advertised. There was a confrontation, and the cowboys not only threatened to leave but do a little damage to Dad and the rodeo arena on the way out.

Dad had hired the Cowboy Band from the Oklahoma State Reformatory in Granite under the direction of Major Fred W. Pike to perform and provide music for the show. The band members were prisoners on trustee status, and between them and four armed guards, they were a formidable group. The head guard could see that the cowboys had Dad up a tree and motioned to Dad to come over to the bandstand. Dad said the guard told him to stay next to the band, and they would see that no harm came to him. Cowboys have a reputation, occasionally deserved, for enjoying a good fight. This bunch would have no doubt upheld the tradition had it not been for the prison band.

Dad had to agree to pay the extra prize money to avoid a strike. The show went on as scheduled, but he never again held a professional rodeo at Craterville. The old Cowboys' Turtle Association became the Rodeo Cowboys Association (RCA) in 1945 and in 1975 was renamed the Professional Rodeo Cowboys Association (PRCA). Dad had hard feelings against some of the early-day cowboys, but many of them remained his lifelong friends. He never outgrew his love for the sport.

THE LAWTON CONSTITUTION

TUESDAY EVENING, JULY 1, 1941.

FAMOUS COWBOYS TO COMPETE FOR $1,500 IN PRIZES

100 Professionals Expected To Take Part In Contests At Craterville

CRATERVILLE PARK, July 1. —Fans who watch the four rodeo performances here Thursday and Friday will see the best rodeo professionals in the business as they contest for purses in the respective events.

Frank Rush, jr., who with his mother, Mrs. Frank Rush, sr., is managing the celebration, explained that the winners of the world's greatest rodeo shows are residing in Oklahoma and north Texas.

100 Professionals to Enter

He predicted that at least 100 professional cowboys would enter the show. More than $1,500 in prizes will be warded.

He mentioned such well known rodeo names as D. Burk, calf roper from Comanche. Burk is said to be faster than his brother, Clyde Burk, world famous roper.

Also coming are George Wilderspin, Fort Worth, Tex., calf roper and bulldoger, and Houston Burns, Ryan.

Dick Shultz To Ride

One of the outstanding rodeo performers will be a former Law-

COLORFUL BAND DIRECTOR

Maj. Fred W. Pike, veteran band director, is shown above in the colorful cowboy regalia he will wear at the annual Craterville Park rodeo, July 3-4, as he directs the Cowboy Band of Oklahoma State Reformatory, Granite, one of the nation's outstanding rodeo bands.

ton man, Dick Shultz, Wichita Falls, Tex. He is now the championship bronco rider of the Southwest Rodeo association, which includes 40 shows.

Many of these cowboys make a living contesting in rodeos, Mr. Rush said. Some of them have become independently wealthy from the sport.

The rodeo here is a member of the Cowboy Turtle association,

which means it is recognized nationally.

Most Hazardous Sport

The rodeo business, which is termed by cowboys as "the greatest American sport," is said to be the most hazardous sport in the nation.

"If anyone doubts this, let him come to the rodeo and watch some of the breath-taking acts, Mr. Rush said.

The ropers have the best horses that money and careful selection can provide. Mr. Rush said he doubted if very many of the roping horses could be purchased at any price. They have been trained for years.

Red Cross To Have Stations

All during the celebration, there will be field stations of the Comanche county chapter of the American Red Cross stationed throughout the park. They will be ready for any emergency from injury to rodeo performers or minor injuries to the fans.

In addition to the rodeo there will be free swimming in the Craterville pool. The entire park will be supervised, Mr. Rush said.

Among the 20 events at each of the two-hour performances are acts by Mrs. Genelle Rush on her educated horse, "Black Beauty."

Other Rodeo Acts

Other acts are calf roping, bulldoging, trick riding, trick roping, bronco riding, steer riding, implement throwing by Steve Clemento, a bullwhip act by a blacksnake expert and others.

Dr. E. B. Dunlap, jr., son of Dr. and Mrs. E. B. Dunlap, sr., will sing a patriotic musical selection at the beginning of each performance. The opening of each rodeo, at 2 p. m. and 8 p. m., will be heralded by a patriotic observance.

Warren Wolverton, Lawton, will announce the rodeo from the arena. Each afternoon the show will be broadcast over KSWO.

Every minute, 19 persons are accidentally injured in the United States.

Major Fred W. Pike, director of Oklahoma State Reformatory Cowboy Band.

32. Around the World in 80 Days and National Geographic

Dad's friend, Bill Wilkerson, who owned the Indian Store at Disneyland was also an actor, mostly in roles that required an authentic-looking Indian chief. Bill had a lot of contacts in Hollywood, including a filmmaker/director named Lou Borzage. In 1954, Lou was looking for locations for the buffalo stampede, Indian camp, and train ride scenes for Jules Verne's *Around The World In 80 Days*. Mike Todd of Todd-AO was to direct the movie. Bill put Lou in touch with Dad, and the location was scouted. The old fair grounds/rodeo grounds at Old Craterville was perfect for the Indian camp scene and a scene where the train was delayed by a herd of buffalo crossing the track.

A few days prior to the actual filming, big equipment trucks started rolling in. Dad had arranged for several hundred Indians to be dressed in costumes and act as seconds. Tepees were set in place as background for the scene. The beautiful granite hills, oak trees, and all the Indian camp trappings made an outstanding setting. The Indian camp was reminiscent of bygone days, but the behind-the-scenes action made for a great deal of excitement among the locals.

The wardrobe crew passed out fake but authentic-looking bows, arrows, war clubs, shields, and all manner of Indian gear. The Indians had their own costumes, but some of them wore eyeglasses and had modern haircuts. The eyeglasses had to go, and the wardrobe department issued long, black wigs to the Indians who needed them.

The days of preparation were long, and everyone was standing around waiting of the film crew to get set. No one complained because everyone was on the payroll at the actors' scale rate of pay, which was more money than most were use to making. Mike Todd showed up with his entourage on the day of the actual filming. He barked orders and made a few changes, but when he finished filming he told Dad it was exactly what he had in mind for the film. Everyone involved had cooperated and done a first class job. Bill Crawford's account in the *Lawton Constitution* recalls the filming took place at Old Craterville in early October 1955.

LAWTON CONSTITUTION and MORNING PRESS, Sunday, October 9, 1955

MOVIE JOKE. Mike Todd impresses these Indian youths with some wild Hollywood tales before giving them hints on the technical phase of the motion picture industry. Spectators jammed the Craterville Park area Saturday afternoon to watch the movie crew and Indians in action. Many Lawtonians and Fort Sill personnel lugged their own cameras to the location. See story, page 1.   (Staff Photo)

Mike Todd visiting with Indians during the filming of scenes for *Around The World In Eighty Days* at Craterville Park.

This photo appeared in *National Geographic* in the May 1957 issue and shows the Indian encampment, dancers performing a round dance, and the film crew in the foreground. Photo copyright *National Geographic* magazine.

The Indians were asked to turn in their wigs and props to wardrobe, which turned out to be a small problem. The wardrobe manager started to take some of the personal items the Indians had brought, and the Indians claimed some of the wigs were actually their own real hair. One Indian yelled loudly when the wardrobe man tried to remove what he thought was a wig from the man's head. The other Indians started talking in their native tongue and making threatening gestures as they surrounded the paleface. Smiling and apologizing, the shaken wardrobe man decided to let all of the others turn in their wigs voluntarily. Some did and some didn't. For several years following, Indians would come over to Dad at powwows, pull up their fake wigs and ask jokingly, "When Mike Todd comin' back?"

This photo showing Bob and Alma Kirk, Genelle and Frank Rush mounted near the refuge gate also appeared in the *National Geographic* article in 1957. Photo copyright *National Geographic* magazine.

In 1956 and 1957, Mister Woodbridge Williams, a photographer for the *National Geographic* magazine, came to the Wichitas and Craterville to take photographs for a story. In the May, 1957, edition of the *National Geographic,* a wonderful article, "The Wichitas—Land of the Living Prairie," gave a thorough account of the splendor of the Wichitas. Pictures showed Mom, Dad, Bob, and Alma Kirk and the rest of the family on horseback and carrying out various other activities.

Mister Woodbridge resided at the Park for several weeks while writing and taking photographs for the story. He and Dad spent hours visiting about the lore and history of the area.

On a few occasions, Dad allowed me to tag along with Mister Woodbridge on his photographic journeys in the Wichitas. We would sit for hours in a concealed location or a portable blind with his camera at the ready, waiting for a bird or an animal to appear. At first, I was impatient. By the end of the experience, I learned to observe detail and color of everything in view. Unexpected joy could be found in the solitude. Mister Woodbridge possessed the patience and skill needed to take the exceptional and unusual photographs for which the magazine is known.

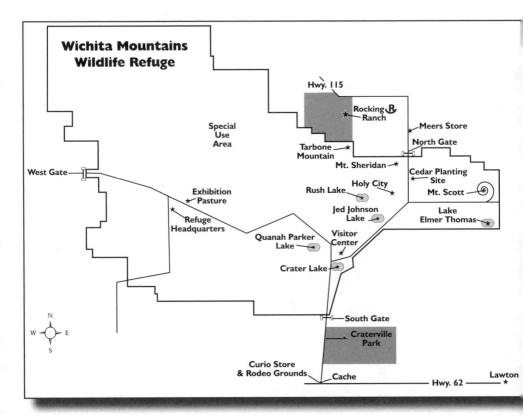

The Wichita Mountains area shows the location of landmarks
in the refuge and points of specific interest nearby.

33. The First Rocking R Ranch

Old Craterville had a public side, but it also was headquarters for Dad's more personal cattle and horse operations. The eastern portion of the property was a few hundred acres of land, ideal for the registered horned Hereford cattle and horse herds Dad so dearly loved. He and Ted Warkentin of Lawton purchased about one hundred head of Hazlett-bred cattle, a popular bloodline of the time. Ted owned Southwestern Stationery and Supply in Lawton but longed to be in the cattle business. I asked Dad how he and Ted got to be partners, and he told me, "Ted had the money, and I had the grass."

Horned Herefords were registered with the American Hereford Association and had their registration number branded on their horns. At the time, registered horned Hereford cattle were the most trendy of species. The cattle market was good, and there was plenty of little bluestem grass and other forage for the animals.

On January 4, 1945, Dad and Ted held a Warkentin & Rush Production Sale at Old Craterville. Twelve bulls and thirty-eight females were offered. Offspring of Hi Rupert, T Royal Rupert, and Hazford Rupert were on the sale docket. Honorary guests from the American Hereford Association, the *Hereford Journal* and Oklahoma A&M College were on hand. Representatives of the most popular journals and livestock publications covered the sale, including Frank Reeves of the *Ft. Worth Star Telegram*, Bobby Vincent of *The Ranchman*, O. R. Peterson of *The Cattleman,* and Jewett Fulkerson of the *Hereford Journal*. The sale was very successful, and brought much notoriety to the partnership. Dad and Ted were successful in their cattle venture. The business partnership eventually ended, but not their life-long friendship.

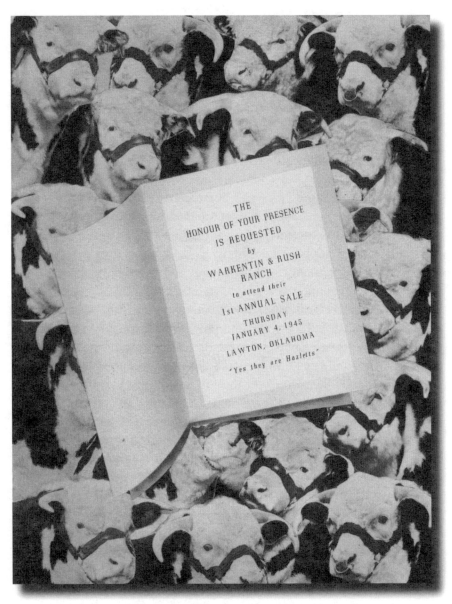

The cover page from
the Warkentin and Rush Hereford sale.

OFFERING

A HANDPICKED GROUP OF OUTSTANDING
HAZLETT YOUNG BULLS AND FEMALES

12 HERD BULL PROSPECTS

38 FEMALES

MOST OF THESE HEIFERS ARE BRED, THE BREEDING DATA
WILL BE ANNOUNCED BY ART THOMPSON AT THE SALE.

THURSDAY
JANUARY 4th, 1945

SALE STARTS PROMPTLY AT 1:00 P. M.

THIS SALE WILL BE AT CRATERVILLE PARK, RANCH HEADQUARTERS, 14 MILES WEST
OF LAWTON ON HIGHWAY 62, 3 MILES NORTH OF CACHE. ALL ROADS PAVED.
SEE MAP PAGE 17.

HONORARY GUESTS

R. J. Kinzer	American Hereford Association
B. B. Anderson	Sec. American Hereford Assn.
Roy J. Turner	Pres. American Hereford Assn.
Haves Walker, Jr.	Hereford Journal
Dean Blizzard	Oklahoma A & M College
A. L. Darlow	Oklahoma A & M College

WARKENTIN & RUSH RANCH

The introductory page from
the Warkentin and Rush Hereford sale.

The story of the cow in the well started rather unceremoniously when one of Dad's cows fell into a previously unknown and abandoned well. The well had been located by an old homestead on the east side of the ranchland at Old Craterville. Dad missed the cow one day when he made his daily herd check; while he was searching for her, he ran across the caved-in well opening only to discover her looking up at him from the mud some twenty feet down. Some ranchers might have put the cow out of her misery and filled her grave and the well at the same time. Dad, seeing an opportunity to save the cow and get a little publicity, called a wrecker and a photographer from the newspaper. As the photos show, the cow was successfully extracted and gave birth to a healthy calf a few weeks later. Newspapers ran the pictures and mentioned the cow belonged to the owner of Craterville Park. Curious

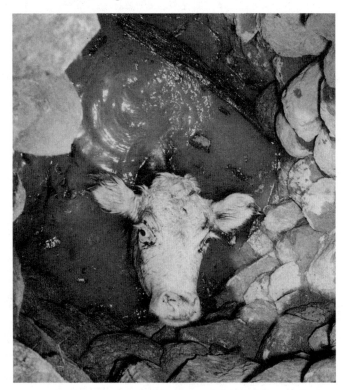

These unusual photos of the cow in the well were displayed in the Indian Curio Store Museum and were always a source of great interest to visitors.

people came to the Park for years and asked about the cow. Dad always had the cow (or a similar looking cow) standing around the corrals to satisfy the curious public, and if they spent a little money in the Park while they were there, so much the better.

The cow was successfully extracted and gave
birth to a healthy calf a few weeks later.

Dad also raised horses and began to purchase some registered Appaloosa mares. Dan Coates, Dad's friend from Ft. Worth whom he had known since the rodeo days, owned a registered Appaloosa stud, Son of Quanah. Quanah, as we called him, may have been one of the best Appaloosa horses of all time and certainly had one of the most popular bloodlines. He had the conformation of a quarter horse and the best qualities of his breed, including stamina and eye-popping color. He was black and gray with a snow-white blanket over his hips with typical Appaloosa spots over the blanket. Picture the most majestic painting by Russell or Remington with an Indian chief on a hill, mounted on his spotted war pony. The horse could have been Quanah. Dad and Dan made a deal for Quanah to stay on the ranch at Old Craterville and sire the colts for Dad's equally-beautiful herd of mares. It was a good partnership, and Dad and Dan sold lots of colts from the herd that went on to show and perform on a high level in the Appaloosa association.

While it was always a sight to see Quanah and his herd grazing in the red granite foothills of the Wichitas, the stallion did have one bad habit. If you rode horseback into his pasture, you'd be wise to take some precaution. He would see you coming and hide in the trees or behind a hill to ambush the horse and rider. It wasn't a game for Quanah. He was protecting his mares and would knock a rider from the saddle and attack his mount. The only defense was to dismount, find a big stick or a handful of rocks and make sure you stayed between Quanah and your horse. He had more respect for a man standing on the ground than he did a mounted rider, but more than once did one of us come walking home without our saddle horse. Usually the saddle horse had the good sense to hightail it away from the biting, pawing, and kicking defender and head for the barn.

Son of Quanah

In addition to being a great livestock range, there was plenty of good hunting and fishing on the ranch at old Craterville. Several lakes and farm ponds provided duck hunting and were brimming with game fish. White tailed deer were plentiful, and Dad invited friends to hunt and fish, sports that he relished as much as anyone. Big Tom and I took every opportunity to "wet a hook" or "bust a cap" as well.

Dad's love for hunting was always part of his life. He started hunting quail at Blair when he was dating Mom, and he began hunting pheasant in South Dakota in 1945. He kept some pointer bird dogs, which doubled as family pets when he wasn't using them on local hunts with his buddies.

Dick Self, Big Tom's father, lived in Cache and was always among Dad's quail-hunting pals. Between them and J. B. Long, Bill Red Elk, and Clinton Reeves, many days of quail season were spent harvesting birds from the plentiful Bobwhite population around Cache, Indiahoma, and Chattanooga.

Dad would hunt during the day, then pick me up after school. We would hunt together until sundown. I always wanted him to wait on me to hunt, but he said he was mostly looking for coveys of birds and exercising the dogs in the morning so we would be more successful in the evening. Yeah, right!

Dick Self had birddogs that were well trained to point, back, and retrieve; and we loved to watch his dogs work a field or creek bed. J. B. "Gabe" Long had two or three big rangy pointers, which he "kept thin so they didn't have to drag all that extra weight around." Bill Red Elk was a local Indian man who kept birddogs as well, but he didn't always need them. Bill could track birds, even in heavy grass, and tell you, "Get ready, we're getting close." You better have your gun loaded when he said that because you would soon flush the birds or the dogs would go on point. One might be skeptical about Bill's uncanny ability to track birds, but his Indian instinct was often successful. More than anything, I had unabashed fun hunting with Dad and his buddies, and in the process was taught how to be a safe hunter, a sportsman, and enjoy true friendships.

The first Rocking R Ranch helped fulfill Dad's dream of being a sportsman, cowboy, and rancher. Like the public part of Craterville, it was idyllic, but the days were numbered until it would no longer be in Dad's possession.

34. The Land Grab

After the Korean War, the military was cutting back the number of operational bases, just as they have done on a number of occasions. At the same time, long-range missiles with more firepower were advancing, and the Cold War had everyone scared. Fort Sill was an important training facility for artillery; however, the cutbacks were a major threat to the base. The Army was looking for a larger firing range, possibly in Arizona. There were already rows of empty houses in Lawton, and rumors about moving the base to Arizona caused concern to grow.

Fear grew the installation would be closed if steps weren't taken to bolster the importance and size of the facility. For a time, the base's title was changed to Artillery and Missile Center to enlarge its scope and mission. The proposed land expansion also played a key role in turning back the threat of closing.

Closing or reducing the facility would deal a blow to the local economy. Many business people in Lawton thought more troops would build their customer base if the facility were enlarged. They also thought the land to be condemned was of little value, and the loss of Craterville Park and Comanche Chief Quanah Parker's historical home and grave site was of no consequence, so they backed the idea.

Politicians were lobbied and community leaders pressed the idea that Fort Sill needed to be enlarged. Government officials and legislative committees were sold on the concept of enlargement of the existing facility. When the official news came that the firing range at Fort Sill would have to be expanded, it meant a lot of people to the west of the base would lose their land, Old Craterville included. There were public meetings, bitter disputes and hard feelings, but the government brass would not be swayed.

Politicians publicly showed support for the landowners and said there was no reason to take away the private land, but they also wanted to have more government money spent in their district. They did not want to have a possible economic disaster while they were in office, regardless of who was hurt. Fear was an ally for those who didn't have land involved in the deal. It was easy to argue that the land was needed for defense of the nation.

The Right of Eminent Domain made it easier for the government to take private land back then than it is today. The Army Corps of Engineers was the government department that dealt with landowners, and the Corps used any tactic to accomplish its goal. The first thing anyone knew, the Corps persuaded one or two land owners in the western end of the land in question to make a deal to sell out. Therein lay the strategy. First, the Corps said some land had already been purchased; therefore, the land in the middle must be condemned as well to connect new land to the base. Old Craterville was directly in the middle, and condemnation was unavoidable.

Next, the Corps said the land that they had already purchased, set the market price for the other land. While those few farmers who sold out early were pleased with their price, there was no comparison in actual land values. Also, the Corps did not want to pay extra for improvements, such as Old Craterville Park. Land was just land to them, and the fact that Dad's property would be expensive, if not impossible to replace at any price, did not concern them.

It wasn't just Old Craterville property in dispute. Lots of people were livid that their family homes and businesses were to be uprooted. The "land grab," as it was known, became a community-splitting upheaval of the first order.

Dad was served with papers that ordered him to allow appraisers to come in and place a value on the property. He flew to Washington, DC, with a group of other landowners to talk to congressmen, senators and committees about the issue. Victor Wickersham was the congressman from the sixth district and vowed to fight for his constituents. The process moved along. Some landowners settled and some were heading for court, but one thing was certain, Old Craterville was going away.

Heartbroken and angry, Dad and some other owners hired lawyers and brought suits in Federal Court to fight the action. Congressman Wickersham sold out and did not fight as he had said he would. He voted for the land expansion, and many other congressmen followed his lead since the land was in Wickersham's district, and he was the apparent authority. Dad's lawyer, Curtis Harris, took his fee, did a weak job of preparing a case and was defeated by the powerful federal lawyers during the trial in Tulsa. Dad recalled how Mister Harris turned to him and said, "Frank, you better take what they offer because that's more than your old Park is worth, and I can't help you anymore."

The Federal Judge made a finding in favor of the Corps' appraisers, and did not agree with Dad's appraisers. The judge did leave a little bit on the table, "to be mitigated later." The judge ruled that if expenses of relocating the Park exceeded the amount paid, Dad could bring suit on the government for an amount not to exceed two hundred thousand dollars. Though the expenses of moving greatly exceeded that amount, the government would later tell Dad that there were no funds available to pay such a claim, even if he were successful in court.

In the fall of 1956 and the winter of 1957, Old Craterville was stripped of improvements and abandoned as ordered, and the historic playground, the home and workplace for a community, faded into history.

Two things never came to pass. First, the government claimed the property would be a dangerous place after the shelling practice began. Also, the highway from Cache to the south gate of the refuge would have to close to public traffic because it would be too dangerous for cars to travel through military property. The Corps said that the land would be like a war zone. Unexploded shells, land mines, and live fire training for solders would make the land extremely hazardous to anyone who might trespass. The picture they painted in the communities mind was devised to persuade landowners their property was vital to the security of the country and would be used for that purpose only.

In the early fall of 1977, when Vickie and I were visiting friends in Cache one Sunday, we decided to take David and Jodi up through the Wichitas. About noon, we headed north along the old highway, and when we got to the Old Craterville entrance, I pointed out the army sign that read "Camp Eagle," where the old Craterville Park sign had once stood. Oddly enough, the gate was open and while there were signs warning against trespass on government property, there was also a paper sign taped to a post that announced "Officers Fall Picnic" with an arrow pointing down the old entrance road.

I turned in and figured the worst they could do was toss me in jail, take our car, and put the kids and Vickie in some kind of protective custody. Down the road we went, and to my surprise, there were about five hundred people in uniform and their families standing around tables with white tablecloths and a big catering truck. The setting was exactly where our homes once stood, and the Park property was neatly mowed. The old store building and the restaurant still stood in place. Signs on the doors directed military personnel to the offices used to direct recreational activities. To the east, families fished and camped at a lake with a big cement dam, which was on Dad's former ranch. I learned later Old Craterville was often used for army social events, and military hunters and fishermen who found those sports at their disposal.

We had a similar visit to the old Park in 1984. There were military families playing in the picnic grounds and climbing the mountain that bordered the Park on the south. No one asked who we were. The kids and I climbed the rocks and took pictures. No unexploded bombs or land mines were there, just the same trees, rocks and land where Old Craterville once stood.

I never had the courage to tell Dad or Mom about our visits to Old Craterville, now Camp Eagle. There was no need to break their hearts again.

Southwest Oklahoma lost what would probably remain today as the largest and most entertaining tourist destination in that part of the state. A family-run business, led by one of the most innovative men in the amusement business, might still be a part of the culture and diversity of the community. In addition, no one can prove the security of the United States of America would be any the worse if the land grab had been defeated.

Dad, and our family, never recovered from the pain of losing our home, but the Lord gave us the strength to move on. The direction of our lives changed, possibly for the better. Old Craterville was moved to New Craterville, and we moved to a wonderful ranch north of Meers. Dad and Mom lived a long and interesting life together. Big Tom and Suzy probably would have wound up married anyway, but Vickie and

I were not likely to have crossed paths. We would not have wound up with a successful business at Sandy Lake Park, otherwise. The prospect of not having Vickie in my life and having our children and grandchildren makes me believe it was our destiny.

Track Section #III
(1958-1971)

35. Moving on Down the Track to New Craterville and Beyond

Mom was born and raised in Blair, Oklahoma. Her parents, Dandy and Maudie, lived in Blair, and in the early '30s, they would come to old Craterville to camp every summer. Mom, her brother Royce, and her sister Jessie enjoyed the Park. Soon Dad discovered Genelle (Mom). He claims it was love at first sight. Mom was a beautiful young teenaged girl a with talent for singing and playing the piano. She fell in love with the Park and fell even more deeply in love with Dad.

Over the years, Dad and Mom continued to visit Blair, and Dad had noticed the area around nearby Quartz Mountain State Park was a place that resembled old Craterville in some respects. Years later, when he realized he was going to lose old Craterville, he began looking for a place to move the Park. Uncle Royce, Bob Kirk, and Dad road-sided the area and came up with the plan to build a new park on a piece of property which was near the entrance to the state park.

One event indicated that Dad was not single-minded about the Quartz Mountain location. One day, again about the time he realized losing old Craterville was inevitable, he took Mom, Suzy, and me to Turner Falls, a famous landmark a few miles north of Ardmore, Oklahoma. The swimming pool and campgrounds lay alongside the route of Highway 77 and the developing Interstate 35 between Dallas and Oklahoma City. The facility was for sale, and Dad had a pretty good idea that with the addition of amusement rides and other attractions, the place could become his new park. A large ranch called the Diamond T lay a few miles south. The Diamond T would be ideal for his cow and horse operation. Dad was very enthusiastic about the prospects, but Mom, Suzy, and I protested. For once, Dad changed his mind.

Mom took more interest in the Quartz Mountain location because her family lived nearby, and there were some other advantages as well.

Dad didn't want to give up the business, and he thought the new park would draw customers from the old park even though the two properties were about sixty miles apart. The Quartz Mountain location was very close to the mountains that made up the western end of the Wichita Mountains range. Next door was the beautiful Quartz Mountain State Park with hotel rooms, campgrounds, and boat docks that provided a readymade customer base. The land was not expensive, and the shape of the property was ideal for the placement of the various attractions to be installed. Water and electricity utilities were close at hand, and the property had frontage for good exposure on a newly-paved road.

There was one other advantage which clinched the location in Dad's mind. Altus Air Force Base was just sixteen miles down the road on the east side of the city of Altus. Dad had always cultivated the business that Fort Sill military personnel provided at old Craterville, and he realized the servicemen in the Air Force would make good customers just as the Army had provided.

As old Craterville was being dismantled, the decision was made to construct new Craterville near the entrance of Quartz Mountain State Park. Uncle Royce, dirt placement expert, took on the task of bulldozing the sand hills and shaping and paving the property in preparation for the upcoming move. Using these same skills, Uncle Royce would help us recover from the flood at Sandy Lake years later.

Bob Kirk and Rusty Wahkinney worked at old Craterville and moved to the new park to continue their jobs. Bob and Rusty, along with Jesse and Red Robertson, were in charge of building the various structures for the park and getting the infrastructure for the rides in place. Bob was a carpenter by trade, and he and Rusty knew what Dad was looking for because of their involvement with old Craterville. Laying out a park that appealed to the eye, allowed for good traffic flow, and fit the footprint of the property was a challenge. In the capable hands of Uncle Royce, Bob, and Rusty, and with Dad directing the operation, new Craterville was brought to life.

Meanwhile Dad was also directing the development of the Indian Curio Store and a new rodeo arena in Cache. The site was at the intersection of Highway 62 and the road that led to old Craterville, just three miles north.

Dad also found a location for the Rocking R Ranch, fifteen miles to the north, at Meers, Oklahoma. The three thousand, two hundred acre ranch property bordered the wildlife refuge on the north, just as old Craterville had bordered the refuge on the south. Dad's roots were buried deep in the granite mountains, and he didn't want to move away. He purchased the ranch property, and began moving his cattle and horse operation there.

Dad was spending money like there was no tomorrow. He always made a good profit at old Craterville and felt like the investment of his savings in the three new operations would return good profits as well. Dad didn't mind at all the thought of spending whatever it took to develop three first-class operations. At the time, he still believed the legal appeals filed disputing the value the government had placed and paid on old Craterville, would be ultimately successful in forcing the government to pay more money. He was also under the false assumption the $200,000 the judge had promised could be easily claimed once his moving expenses were shown to exceed the original settlement. He was betting on the come, but in the meantime, it was full steam ahead.

At new Craterville, the main building housed the office, a dark house walk-through maze, a glass house, the Pretzel ride, skating rink, and bumper car building. It was similar in design to the main building at the old Park, but the skating rink and bumper car ride were attached. All of the buildings had log-looking exteriors created by half-round two-by-six pine boards and with a sloping shingle-roof trim. The style gave the buildings a rustic yet modern appearance. This was the style Dad favored from the days when he rebuilt the Indian Curio Store building at old Craterville. We also used the same look at Sandy Lake Park years later.

The rides were clustered in the middle of the property at New Craterville, and the track for the miniature train was in a big loop toward the back of the property. Inside the loop created by the train track was the Park stage, similar to old Craterville. Houses were moved to the location from old Craterville as well. There was a monkey pen, a snake pit, and a big picnic pavilion constructed on the opposite side of the rides from the main building. There were horse stables for dude horses. A maintenance building stood near the rear of the property with a cook shack nearby, where employee's meals were prepared. In the middle of the rides was a combination Indian Curio Store, refreshment stand, and an awning to cover the kiddie rides. The same ride equipment was moved to the new location so the place looked similar, in some respects, to the old Park.

There was no swimming pool or miniature golf course at new Craterville, but Dad did add a couple of new attractions. He added a four-stall carnival game section, even though he never liked the idea of having the Park look too much like a carnival. Everyone kept pressing Dad, trying to convince him there was not a bad connotation associated with those games, and they would make money. The games did make a profit on good days, but because it took one operator for each game, the labor cost made for a losing deal on slow days. Dad did not like the idea of closing any attraction when the rest of the Park was open, so he grumbled about the games the entire time he owned new Craterville. He also never gave into the temptation of including carnival games at Sandy Lake Park.

The dude horse rental business was good at first but was getting difficult because gentle horses were getting more expensive. Also, insurance claims were starting to be a concern. There was a huge sand hill on the south edge of the property, which didn't have much use except as a dude horse riding area. Dad began to look for another attraction to put the area to better use.

Dad had a friend, Lanny Edwards, who was a racecar driver at the old Lawton Speedway. Another man, Clinton Herring, owned an automobile dealership in Lawton; and he and Dad had promoted some stunt car shows together. Lanny and Clinton convinced Dad a quarter-mile dirt track would be a sure thing for weekly races at the Park. Dad liked the idea, but there was a problem with the fact that any racecar driven over the sloped embankment of the track would run into the nearby amusement rides and other attractions.

Uncle Royce convinced Dad all that was needed to keep the cars from leaving the track was a solid retaining wall. Closely spaced telephone poles and rough cut four-by-twelve oak lumber could be used to do the job. He also told Dad that he could shape the sand hill and build concrete bleachers on the front side to seat four thousand people. In front of the bleachers, red clay for the track could be brought in to provide an ideal surface for the car races.

Lanny had traveled across the country with racecars, and he told Dad there were paved tracks with concrete walls where the Indy-type cars raced. He also noted that fences kept the cars from hitting the bleachers at every track, but he didn't know of a small dirt track with a wall completely around the outfield. Dad asked, "Well, will it work?" The reply was, "Well, yeah, I guess so." Dad asked if a rodeo arena could be placed in the center of the track so the facility would have dual use. Again, "Well, yeah, I guess so." Dad's reply to Uncle Royce was, "Royce, let's get started."

In addition to Bob and Alma Kirk and Rusty and Maxine Wahkinney, several of the former employees from old Craterville came to new Craterville. Wayne Young and Robert Barfield were both young men who had grown up working at old Craterville. They moved to the new park and hit the ground knowing what needed to be accomplished. Robert eventually met and married Judy Cypert, who lived in the area and also worked at the Park.

Local teenagers and adults applied for work, just as they had done at old Craterville. In many cases, there were several families with two or more family members working at new Craterville. Members of the Cypert, Chastain, and Foster families were among those who worked at the Park.

Joan and Lynn Foster lived in nearby Granite, Oklahoma, and came to work in the Indian Curio Store. Both of them were, and still are, really cute. I hung around them pretty much every time my family was at the Park working. Not that they had much choice about putting up with me, but they were sweet as sugar, and I kinda' had a crush on both of them. Little did I know they had a younger sister named Vickie who was equally pretty and sweet but too young to work. I also had no way of knowing Vickie and I would cross paths a little later in life and eventually go on to be married.

As for the special acts on the stage, Dad took the same strategy at new Craterville that he did at the former location. Television and radio were simpler then. Radio offered only a few stations, and there were just three television stations on the air. Thus, nearly everyone was familiar with almost every star. Each television or *Grand Ole Opry* personality was popular with a wider audience, making it easier to draw a crowd.

Personal appearances drew impressive crowds for Southwest Oklahoma or anywhere else. A few thousand people would show up, and there were lines at every attraction. It was exciting to actually meet Rex Allen, Minnie Pearl, Homer and Jethro, or any of the other popular personalities. The Sky Kings, The Sky Dancers, the lion act, and the high-diving mules were among the circus acts.

Several of the same stars that had been at old Craterville returned for engagements at the new park. Popular TV stars including Robert Horton of *Wagon Train*; Clint Walker of the series *Cheyenne*; Donna Douglas of *The Beverly Hillbillies*; Dan Blocker (Hoss Cartwright) and Michael Landon (Little Joe) of *Bonanza*; Dale Robertson, star of *Tales of Wells Fargo*; and Rip Masters and Rin Tin Tin were there.

Donna Douglas and Dale Robertson, and especially Minnie Pearl, were the nicest of the bunch. They were down-home folks who were easy and fun to talk to. Most of the artists were very friendly and glad to sign autographs.

Robert Horton was the handsome star of *Wagon Train*. When he came to the Park, there were lots of kids, but the main part of the crowd was young girls and women. He was so handsome, it was a little like an Elvis concert. The ladies screamed and tried to get close enough to touch him. The crowd nearly got out of hand, but the Park employees kept him secure enough to sign autographs without having his clothes torn off. There were always two or three state troopers in Oklahoma Highway Patrol cars at the Park to help direct traffic and keep things orderly. Dad asked one of the troopers to pull his car near the autograph platform where Horton was still signing everything offered to him. Finally, after it was long past time for Horton to leave, he was escorted into the back seat of the cruiser. With lights flashing and siren wailing, he left the Park for the airport. Boy, was Dad happy!

In 1959, another Horton, made an appearance. This time, it was Johnny Horton. He sang his hit recordings, "The Battle of New Orleans" and "North To Alaska." He was also known as the Singing Fisherman because he owned a fishing lure company. A few days after his appearance, I got a shoe-box-sized package addressed to me personally, filled with a variety of his company's fishing lures and a note that said, "Frankie, catch a big one for me. Johnny Horton." Boy, was I happy!

The Grand Ole Opry stars always drew big crowds. They usually accompanied themselves with a guitar, but sometimes they had a two or three-piece band. Little Jimmy Dickens and Brenda Lee sang for over an hour on stage in the hot sun, then autographed pictures until everyone had a copy.

In the later years at new Craterville, Dad started hiring professional wrestling stars. He had a wrestling ring built on the stage complete with a semi-flexible floor and rope side fences. Dan Coates, Dad's Appaloosa horse partner, was also a famous rodeo and wrestling announcer from Ft. Worth. He helped Dad get started booking the shows, and he also was hired to announce the matches. Danny "The Bull Dog" Fletchis was not only the popular bad guy, but he was also one of the main promoters for the other wrestlers. The announcer would caution the crowd not to "bark at The Bull Dog," which would always bring howls and yaps from the audience. Fletchis would hold his ears and run around the stage in perceived agony causing the crowd to bark louder.

The wrestlers traveled on a regular weekly circuit. They wrestled in Shreveport, Louisiana, on Friday night and the Sportatorium in Dallas on Saturday. On Sunday afternoon, they would stop by new Craterville for a match on their way to Amarillo for a Sunday evening show and then back to North Side Coliseum in Ft. Worth for the televised *Monday Night Wrestling Show.*

Usually, the wrestling shows were held at 3 p.m. on the open-air stage, and it was often sweltering, a condition which the wrestlers and fans paid little attention to. There were the usual bad-guy/good-guy matches, and even women wrestlers and midget wrestlers made special appearances. The audience would take sides and come back the next weekend to see a promised rematch or grudge match for their hero. The wrestling grew wilder and more popular each week.

One unusual thing, which few people realized, was the four wrestlers and the referee traveled together in the same car. This was a "show" or "wrestling demonstration" for the pros, but it was the real deal to the customers. When the five-man crew would arrive, Dad would hide them in one of the houses at the Park where they could get dressed and ready for the match. He would have one of his employees load two wrestlers in a hidden car and bring them to the stage from a different direction so people didn't realize they'd arrived together. When all four wrestlers got on the stage, the mayhem and chaos started in earnest. Pro wrestling is like a soap opera, gym meet, dinner with your in-laws, and a cockfight all rolled into one. If you asked a wrestler if it's all an act, they would likely invite you into the ring to find out first-hand. Most people should never accept that challenge.

On one occasion, Dan Coates had our friend J. W. Stoker, the trick roper, drive him up to new Craterville from Ft. Worth so Dan could announce the show on Sunday. Stoker always drove a new white Cadillac. The car fit Stoker's image, and he was very particular about keeping his image and the car intact. During the wresting match, things got out of hand, as planned. For a finale, the two good-guy wrestlers started chasing the other two bad-guy wrestlers around the Park while throwing pop bottles and rocks at them. The crowd went wild. Unfortunately, the place the bad guys chose to take shelter was behind Stoker's Caddy. Stoker about had a stroke as he watched pop bottles and rocks bounce off of his car. The crowd couldn't believe their eyes. Someone was overheard saying, "Frank Rush must have arranged for that white Cadillac to be destroyed. What a showman!"

Dad paid for the repair on Stoker's car and had a strict understanding with the wrestlers. He told them, "You might be bigger and stronger than me, but you're not half as mad, and I do keep a loaded shotgun in my office." I think they believed Dad would make good on his implied threat, and similar stunts were never attempted again at new Craterville.

The stock car races at new Craterville were a "good ol' boys" delight. Lanny Edwards or Clinton Herring were in charge of lining up the races, taking the entry fees, and classifying the cars into various groups. Anyone could get an old junk car, do a few modifications, hand paint a number on the side, and get in a race. The car owners usually didn't have more than a few hundred dollars invested, so they didn't mind tearing up the rig in an attempt to win a race. Cash prizes and trophies were offered and there were usually forty to sixty cars and drivers entering the races from nearby towns. This created an enthusiastic audience to cheer for their hometown favorite.

It was not uncommon for a race to be followed by a fistfight or a cuss fight in the pit area, which was in easy viewing distance from the grandstands. We didn't charge extra to view the disputes, and Lanny or Clinton and the security force would occasionally permit the groups involved to go at it for a while, which added to the excitement.

Car mufflers were not a requirement, and the wooden fence around the outer edge of the track helped amplify the car noise. It was ear-splitting. Dad was usually the announcer, but he let me take over the duty when he was busy elsewhere. I was announcing rodeos at Cache, but I thought announcing stock car races would be more difficult. Actually, it was the easiest job I had. All I had to do was introduce the car by driver's name, hometown and car entry number. As the cars warmed up, I would announce the number of laps and the title of the upcoming race.

When the race started when the green flag dropped, the announcer's job consisted of screaming into the microphone and sounding excited. No one could understand what you were saying because of the noise, but the blaring PA system added to the exhilaration. On the last lap of a close race, when the crowd was screaming and the noise was the loudest, I would occasionally scream something over the public address system that was completely unrelated like, "I ate two eggs, bacon, and toast for breakfast this morning!" The crowd, hearing any excited announcement, would cheer even louder.

Dad produced rodeos at the new Craterville Arena as well. The Altus Riding Club and the Duke Riding Club sponsored two of the rodeos, and they would sell tickets and get a percentage for their treasury. Those rodeos were usually among the wildest shows at the Park. Our rodeo stock was trucked in from Cache and Meers, and there were some good contestants entered in the various events. The action took on a more festive atmosphere when cowboys ignored the "No Beer Allowed" signs posted in the horse trailer parking lot. Not unlike the stock car races, the cowboys would occasionally settle their differences the old-fashioned way before the night was done.

36. Cowboys and Indians at Cache

When old Craterville was abandoned, Dad removed everything that wasn't tied down and a lot of things that were. The Corps of Engineers didn't pay for anything except the land, so the improvements belonged to Dad. The new Indian Curio Store that replaced the burned building only a couple of years earlier was too good to leave behind but too large to move. Jesse and Red Robertson and Bob Kirk came up with a plan to saw the building into two pieces so that each half could be hauled separately. The plan worked; and when the building was put back together at the new location in Cache, anyone would be hard pressed to find where it was cut.

To add to the attractions at Cache, a building to house Jimbo, the giant steer; and the Snake Pit were added, along with a refreshment stand. We also offered stagecoach rides on weekends. In 1961, Dad installed a train track around the property and purchased his first C. P. Huntington #8 miniature train from Chance Mfg. in Wichita, Kansas. The train had been little used, and the train from old Craterville needed replacing, so Dad moved the Huntington train to new Craterville in 1962.

Dandy and Maudie Walker, Mom's parents, moved to Cache to run the Indian Curio Store. Suzy had started another museum about Granddad Rush and old Craterville in the back room of the Indian Curio Store. The museum included pictures and artifacts that did not burn in the fire at old Craterville. There were still a good many original pictures and items for a nice display, but precautions were made to use more copies and duplicate items in case there was another fire. Unlikely, but true, there was yet another fire. The structure and many of the items were saved from the second fire, but considerable smoke and water damage took its toll. The store continued to be open after repairs were made, but it was too expensive to completely rebuild, so there were traces of charred wood along the edge of the ceiling.

37. Rocking R Ranch Rodeos

In 1958, Dad decided he wanted back in the rodeo business. He erected a new steel arena, bucking chutes, roping chutes, and bleachers at Cache near the rear of the Indian Curio Store property.

The Rocking R Ranch Rodeo Company began holding weekly rodeos at Cache. Dad hired Bill Yale from Texas to bring the bucking stock. We owned our own roping calves and dogging steers, and soon Dad decided to purchase his own bucking stock rather than lease. In 1960, Dad sent Clinton Reeves and me to Tommy Steiner's ranch north of Austin, Texas, to pick up a load of ten bucking bulls Mister Steiner sold to Dad. Mister Steiner was a top rodeo producer in the RCA and was well know for his high-quality bucking bulls. Clinton and I took a big Chevy stock truck and headed south. When we got close to Steiner's Ranch, just downstream of the dam of Lake Travis, we dropped over a steep hill into a deep valley along the Colorado River. Ahead, the river made a big horseshoe bend around the ranch headquarters. Clinton and I were both impressed with the ranch. It was cowboy heaven with plenty of rodeo equipment and Western atmosphere. Mister Steiner was waiting and let us select ten bulls from a heard of about fifteen animals. We loaded the bulls and got ready to head back to Oklahoma.

To top off our day, a speedboat came flying up the river with a girl water skiing. She waved and smiled as she went by, and Clinton and I realized all she was wearing were two water skis and a life belt. After we put our eyes back in their sockets and picked our jaws up out of the dirt, Clinton asked Mister Steiner's cowboys, "Does that happen often?" The cowboys said it happened every day but more on the weekends. On the trip home with the livestock, we agreed to volunteer to drive back down to Mister Steiner's if Dad needed more bulls.

Dad bought a few more bulls and most of Bill Yale's bucking horses, and the rodeo schedule started branching out. Every town within two hundred miles of Cache held a summer rodeo. When the rodeo committees noticed how good the rodeos were at Cache, they started asking Dad to produce the shows in their hometowns. For the next few years we would have about fifteen rodeos away from home on Thursday, Friday, and Saturday nights and then come home to Cache on Sunday afternoon for another show. The circuit included the towns of Apache, Chattanooga, Walters, Fairview, Rush Springs, Mountain View, Carnegie, Hollis, Walters, Waurika, Guthrie, and Anadarko; all in Oklahoma. The Altus and Duke rodeo committees sponsored events at new Craterville. Rocking R Ranch rodeos in Texas included Burkburnett and Bowie. On Labor Day, July Fourth, and Memorial Day we stayed home and had three-day rodeos in our own arena at Cache.

One year we went to Muskogee in eastern Oklahoma. They had a grandstand full of people for a four-night rodeo, and Dad made a lot of money on the deal. The rodeo was well attended and successful in every way expect one.

Dad was announcing and Big Tom was running the bucking chutes. We brought our own rodeo judges, one of whom was Gene Snider from Cyril. Jerry Duke, Jake Hickox, and a couple of other cowboys had come with us to work stock and help with the show. Louie Meyers and I were the pick-up men, and I ran the roping chute as well. There was a man, Jim Starr, who had a semi truck that hauled our bucking bulls and horses. The steers and roping calves were hauled in our red bobtail stock truck. The rodeo equipment had a trailer of its own and the pickup horses and flag-horses rode in another trailer. Mom operated the special recorded rodeo music on a tape player themed for the grand entry and each event. The music gave the rodeo a professional feel. Suzy was the rodeo secretary and took the entry fees, acted as timekeeper, and paid the cowboys their prize money. In all, it took about fourteen people to run the show, and each one had a job and did it well.

At the Muskogee rodeo, several of our regular contestants from "God's Country" in southwest Oklahoma traveled to Muskogee to compete. The one and only controversy arose on the final night of the rodeo, when there was a dispute over a judge's ruling in the calf roping. The contestant involved was from Muskogee, but, that fact aside, the judges ruling was correct and accepted by most, including every contestant from the southwest part of the state. We knew trouble was brewing when some of those hillbilly cowboys from Muskogee decided they were going to gang up and whip the judges and our crew before we left town.

In rodeos produced by other contractors, it was the usual custom for two or three hours to pass before a rodeo secretary could figure the books and have the payoff ready. Assuming that to be the case, those hillbilly cowboys figured they had time to make a beer run, let the crowd clear out after the rodeo, come back for their prize money; then beat the daylights out of rodeo judge Gene Snider and the rest of us to boot.

They would have had to whip the whole crew and also the contestants from southwest Oklahoma, but Dad had another plan. While the bull riding was finishing up as the last event, the bucking horses were loaded in the front of Jim Starr's big semi. The steers and calves, horses, and equipment were loaded in other trucks for the trip home. Suzy had already paid off the other event winners. When the last bull bucked, we herded him into the strip chute, removed his flank strap and loaded him behind the other bulls waiting in the truck. We jumped the pickup horses and flag horses in their trailer, saddles and all. Dad had already settled up with the rodeo committee. Suzy paid off the bull riders, and in ten minutes flat we passed the city limit sign of Muskogee, vowing to never return.

Don't get me wrong; we didn't run from a fight. All we would have to do was put Jerry Duke and Jake Hickox in the middle of the arena with as many of those hillbillies as wanted to show up, and the rest of us could have stayed busy stacking them up like hillbilly cordwood. Dad just figured if the Muskogee police and the Muskogee jail wouldn't be tough enough to deal with, a Muskogee judge might be.

The whole caravan pulled into a truck stop in Shawnee about 1 a.m. to eat a steak. We had a big laugh wondering if the drunken hillbilly cowboys took their anger out on someone else or each other.

Trouble still lay ahead. By the time we got close to home before daylight, it had rained several inches. The creeks were out of their banks and the gravel road to the ranch had eroded into a muddy mess. Jim's semi-truck couldn't make it up the last hill. He got stuck about a half a mile away from the ranch gate. We jumped the saddle horses out of the trailer and opened the tailgates on the semi and the stock trucks. The bulls, bareback horses, dogging steers, and roping calves jumped out of the trucks; and the short trail drive home was on. We herded them into the front pasture where they dropped their heads and began grazing as it began to get daylight. Later on that day, when we finally got the trucks and trailers out of the mud, I noticed the rodeo stock lying down in the pasture with their bellies filled with Rocking R Ranch grass. I know they were just as glad as we were to be home safely from Muskogee.

The rodeos on the road went remarkably smooth. The rodeo crew was made up of outstanding cowboys. The contestants respected our judges and understood they would get a good call and a fair score. Well, everywhere but Muskogee. The crew had satin rodeo shirts that matched. Along with the special recorded music, we also had a printing machine in the equipment trailer that custom-printed rodeo programs with the contestants name and their stock draw. Most rodeo producers didn't bother to put a polished production together like Dad.

Another real plus for Rocking R Ranch rodeos was the rodeo stock that Dad purchased. The bulls and horses from the Tommy Steiner ranch and Bill Yale herd were of the same quality you would see in today's top pro rodeos. One bull, Joe Louis, went unridden for three years. Other bulls such as Mighty Mouse, Pee Wee, Tiger, and the rest were topnotch performers as well. Dad always had herds of good even, bareback horses, calves, and steers so the draw was as consistent as anyone could expect when dealing with rodeo livestock.

Dad and sixteen-time World Champion Cowboy Jim Shoulders were good friends. Bull-riding legend Freckles Brown had been acquainted with Dad since the old Craterville rodeo days.

In early 1965, Dad came up with the idea of having a matched bull riding between the superstar bull riders at Cache. The event was probably the first matched bull riding involving top contestants ever promoted by anyone. Dad made a deal with Freckles and Jim to ride for a $300 winner-take-all purse. We advertised around Southwest Oklahoma; and come the day of the event, May 2, 1965, there were over five thousand people who bought tickets to the event in our arena built to hold three thousand, five hundred.

THE LAWTON CONSTITUTION, Thursday, November 4, 1965

This photo was part of a story on the bull Joe Lewis by Paul McClung which appeared in the *Lawton Constitution* in 1965. The picture also show shows Frank Rush III petting the bull. Joe Lewis was reasonably gentle while at home on the Rocking R Ranch but took on a different personality in the rodeo arena.

25c

No. 215

Souvenir Program

World Champion
Bullriders Contest

Freckles Brown

vs.

Jim Shoulders

May 2, 1965

ROCKING R RANCH

RODEO ARENA—CACHE, OKLAHOMA

Clowns and Bullfighters—Buck LaGrande and Tommy LaGrande
Morris, Oklahoma

Announcer—Frank Rush

Secretary—Suzy Self

The souvenir program from the first matched bull riding
at the Rocking R Ranch Rodeo Arena in 1965.

Jim Shoulders in his classic style at Cache.
Photo copyright 1965, The Oklahoma Publishing Company.

Dad used his bulls and Jim Shoulders supplied some bulls as well. In addition to the advertised match, a jackpot bull riding was held for other cowboys as a separate event. Big Tom recalls Jim Shoulders pointing out one of the contestants who was entered in the bull riding jackpot. According to Big Tom, Jim said to him, "That cowboy will be a world champion soon." The cowboy was none other than Larry Mahan, and the following year Jim's prediction came true.

Buck and Tommy LaGrand were contracted to be the clowns and bull fighters. The LaGrands were popular enough to attract their own crowd. The Lawton Rangers Rodeo Club Mounted Drill Team performed and added a lot of color to the show.

281

Freckles Brown riding a tough one as the crowd looks on from the grandstands. Photo copyright 1965, The Oklahoma Publishing Company.

The Daily Oklahoman newspaper wrote a feature article in the "Orbit" section of the paper. The reprint of the story shows some of the action. The event was successful, and all expectations were exceeded.

More matched bull rides were scheduled at Cache, including one between Freckles Brown and Bill Kornell on June 6, 1965. Bill Kornell had won the title of RCA World Champion Bull Rider in 1963. Gene and Bobby Clark, like the LeGrands, were famous bull fighters and clowns. They were hired for the second match, and people looked forward to seeing them perform. Another standing-room-only crowd was on hand. During the second match, Dad's little gray bull, Mighty Mouse, bucked off Bill Kornell; and as usual, the bull was looking for someone or something to hit before he left the arena. Louie Meyers and I were the pickup men, and we knew to give Mighty Mouse all

The Orbit section of the *Daily Oklahoman* newspaper featured the matched bull riding event in an article titled "Eight Second Fight." Frank Rush III holds the American flag and looks on as the grand entry serpentines through the arena during the opening ceremony. Photo copyright 1965, The Oklahoma Publishing Company.

the room the arena would allow. I told Bobby Clark, who was in the barrel, to watch out for the deceptive little bull. Bobby's barrel had been the target of the toughest bulls in pro rodeo, but he didn't seem to think little Mighty Mouse would be a problem. When Mighty Mouse saw the clown's barrel, he charged full speed; and when the bull and barrel collided, there was a resounding impact. The reinforced barrel was cracked, and Bobby was knocked unconscious. His head came out one end of the barrel and his feet the other. It took several seconds to distract the bull; and when Bobby finally woke up a few minutes later, he had a whole new respect for Mighty Mouse. The crowd got their money's worth, and another Frank Rush promotion became legend. As a footnote to history, Freckles won both events.

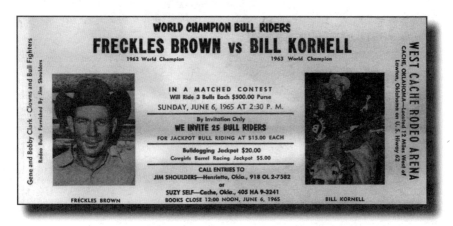

An advertising brochure for the
Freckles Brown/Bill Kornell match in 1965.

At the NFR in December of 2004, I asked Jim Shoulders if it was the first time he remembered a matched bull riding. He told me that there had been some rough stock buck-outs which included top professional saddle bronc, bare back, and bull riders, but as far as he could recall it was the first time an event had been billed as a one-on-one match. Dad helped rodeo contractor, Tommy Steiner, get the contract for a rodeo during the State Fair of Texas when Wayne Gallagher was president of the fair. I recall he told Dad, when he heard about the matched bull riding at Cache, that he thought it was a great new idea. I have also been told the idea of the matched bull riding events stayed in the minds of some other rodeo producers for years, and they no doubt had influence on similar promotions that developed into what we know today as Professional Bull Riders or Xtreme Bulls events. Dad was not responsible for the PBR or Xtreme Bulls, but he did have an innovative idea that had not been produced prior to that time.

The championship buckle presentation for the top annual money winners at Rocking R Ranch rodeos in 1965. The photo was taken by Frank Rush and includes from left: Frank Rush III, announcer and pickup man; Pepper Morgan, calf roping champion; Bill Abbott, bareback riding champion; Ken Williams, bull riding champion; Suzy Self, rodeo secretary; Gene Snider, rodeo judge; Nelda Patton, champion barrel racer; Donnie Bowles, champion bulldogger; Wild Willie Windsor, clown; and Tom Self, arena boss. The two cowboys looking on are unidentified.

Rodeos at Cache and new Craterville took place from 1959 through 1966. Early on, Dad hired Dan Coates from Ft. Worth, Texas, to announce the shows. In the minds of most people who ever heard him, Dan had the best microphone voice of any person who ever announced a rodeo, before or since. There was a timbre in his voice that was unforgettable; and his knowledge of the sport was used to convey to the audience a vivid and colorful oration, which added to the action in the arena. Dad was also an accomplished rodeo announcer. He was a natural conversationalist and loved to announce the action and keep the show moving. I learned everything I know about announcing from Dan and Dad, and I am sorry I don't have a recording of either of them at the microphone.

Eventually, Dan got too busy to come to every rodeo, and Dad and Mom were needed at new Craterville to run the Park. Suzy, Big Tom, and I were left to run the rodeos at Cache on Sundays. I started announcing, Suzy ran the books, and Big Tom ran the arena. Dad left us in charge, and we received a good education in responsibility as a result.

There were lots of great cowboys like Pepper Morgan, Alton Cox, and Junior Garrison along with others who made the shows enjoyable. Pepper was an Indian man who was fast on the ground in calf roping. Alton Cox was a cowboy from Lawton who had to rope in high-top tennis shoes to protect his bad ankles. They made fun of him at times, but he got his share of first-place money. Junior Garrison roped with us as well and went on to become the RCA World Champion Calf Roper in 1966 and 1970.

The other events had their heroes as well, and the Oklahoma cowgirl barrel racers were as fast as they come. And there were good steer wrestlers, bull riders and bareback bronc riders aplenty.

Regular contestants at Cache included several bull doggers from Burkburnett, including 1964 World Champion, C.R. Boucher. Aubrey Rankin from Burkburnett came to haze for many of them. Aubrey owned some good dogging horses and mounted and trained many a good steer wrestler. Sadly, Aubrey was killed when a steer tripped his horse in Dallas. He was usually at the rodeos at Cache but elected instead to make the fatal trip that week. His funeral drew one of the largest gatherings of cowboys in Burkburnett anyone could remember. The next week, we had the rodeo contract at Aubrey's hometown of Burkburnett. Prior to the grand entry on opening night, we led Aubrey's hazing horse around the arena with his cowboy boots tied backward in the stirrups. Mom played "Empty Saddles" on the PA system, and there wasn't a dry eye in the arena or the grandstands. Rodeo had lost a real cowboy.

Many good horses were ridden at Rocking R Ranch rodeos. It was not unusual for any horse that competed in the timed events on the weekends to be used by the owner to gather cattle or do other ranch work during the week. There were also many horses present that were entered in American Quarter Horse Association shows, in both halter and performances classes. Horses, at that time, were bred closer to the foundation bloodlines of the AQHA sires and did not have many of the better qualities bred out of them. This is not to say selective breeding over the decades has failed to produce some improvements, but horses back then generally had sturdier bones, joints, and feet, which allowed them to work harder and have fewer lameness problems. Style of conformation has changed over the decades. However, people like our old friend and well-known equine veterinarian, Doctor T.K. Hardy of Denton, Texas, stated many times, "The specialization of breeders for specific purposes has produced horses with conformation weaknesses and structural flaws."

Dad came in contact with many horsemen during his horse breeding, ranching, and showing days. Most of them would agree, horses of that era were more versatile and had more heart and stamina.

Dad bought and sold lots of great horses, but while we're on the subject of rodeo, I will tell about a horse Dad bought for me which fits the mold of these animals. His AQHA registered name was Cecil Dexter. He was the son of Triangle Hancock, P-23088, by the great horse Buck Hancock, P-1479. On his Dam's side he was the grandson of Dexter, P-193. While bloodlines do not guarantee the horse, any horseman will tell you that good genetics are almost always a vital requirement for an outstanding animal. Certainly, Cecil's bloodline was stellar. Cecil was purchased from Morris Goodman of Apache, Oklahoma, and the three Goodman daughters used him as a barrel-racing horse. It happened more often than not at any barrel race in which the three girls competed, they won first, second, and third place money on the back of this one horse. He was a big, stout bay gelding with plenty of bone and muscle definition, and a deep girth that gave him outstanding lung capacity. Inside his sizeable body lay an intangible but recognizable quality called "heart."

Dad purchased Cecil for me in 1960 when the horse was a four-year-old. We were showing registered horses around the country, and Cecil often won his halter class and as many times was picked as grand champion gelding. He also was an excellent performance horse and won more than his share of events.

When Dad started our rodeo string, I worked as one of the pickup men. Louie Meyers was usually our other pickup man and taught me the job as we went along. Being mounted on Cecil made the job much easier. He could run down any bronc in the arena and never failed to move into position to rescue the cowboy. In the bull riding, we had some bulls that would be stubborn about leaving the arena. Since Dad liked to run a fast-paced show, it was up to Louie and me to clear the bulls by roping them and leading or pulling them out of the pen. Cecil had no fear about getting close enough to let me get my nylon rope on a bull, when many horses simply would chicken out. Not one time did I dally up and have Cecil fail to have the strength to pull any stubborn bull on the other end of the rope.

In August of 1965, after Jim Shoulders had been to the matched bull ridings at Cache, he asked Dad if I could bring a couple of horses to Henryetta, Oklahoma, where he held his rough stock riding school. He needed a pickup man and help dragging bulls. I was happy to oblige and loaded Cecil and a big sorrel thoroughbred horse named Lucky, and made the trip. At Jim's schools, he would sit mounted on his horse in the arena so he could coach the students and keep things moving. He asked me several times if I would sell Cecil to him to use as a pickup horse in his pro rodeos. I wouldn't consider it, even though I was flattered by his continual compliments about Cecil. One afternoon, he said to me, "This next bull won't leave the arena on his own. He bucks okay but usually sets his feet in the dirt, and it will take both of us to pull him out." When the bull bucked the rider off, I roped him. Jim said, "Let me go get my rope and we'll drag him out together." He headed back toward the bucking chutes and the exit gate at the other end of the arena. When he got there I was right behind him with the big stubborn

Brahman bull dragging along behind. I will never forget the look on his face when he turned around and saw what Cecil had done. He smiled and said, "Well, I'll be damned." Nuf said.

Whistle Stop for Wild Willy

Jim "Wild Willy" Windsor lived in the Dallas area and worked for Bill Yale as his rodeo clown. When Mister Yale started bringing stock to Cache, Wild Willy came with him. Over the years, Willy worked the rodeos at Cache and on tour with us. Some of the funniest people in the world are rodeo clowns. They not only work the bull-riding event, protecting the downed riders from the angry toros, but they have lots of time to think up humorous acts to fill the empty time between events. If rodeo cowboys are interested in watching a clown and his antics in the arena rather than go about the business at hand, the clown must be funny. That was the case at our rodeos. Wild Willy would have the crowd, the cowboys, and the announcer in stitches at every show. How he came up with so many new and funny things is difficult to imagine, but often his activity and jokes would bring the show to a stop. Dad liked a fast-moving performance, but Willy would not be denied his turn to entertain.

One season, Willy invented "Sally," a spring-mounted mannequin, to help him attract the attention of the bulls. He buried a heavy weight in the rodeo arena to which a car spring was attached. Sally's plastic body was connected to the spring. When a bull hit her, she popped right back up. Sally had a flour sack dress which Willy's wife, Betty, kept repairing between attacks. Sally also had a bright yellow wig with pigtails. Willie rigged the pigtails with piano wire. When a bull spotted Sally, Willie could tug the wire, causing her pigtails to rapidly flip up and down. Sally was also very well endowed physically. In her former life at a clothing store, she had sported bras for larger-sized women, and Willy often pointed out her attributes over Dad's protest. After all, the rodeo was supposed to be family entertainment.

At what turned out to be Sally's final performance, Mighty Mouse, the bull, repeatedly attacked her and she was torn to pieces. The largest and most recognizable piece of Sally was her ample, plastic breastplate. Willy was almost in tears, but never one to miss an opportunity for a laugh. He slowly walked over, picked up the shattered and

290

bare boobs and simply looked around the arena in dismay. The crowd roared with laughter. It took more than five minutes for Dad to regain his composure and continue to try to announce the rest of the bull riding.

We had most of the same stars and celebrities at the Cache Rodeos that we had at new Craterville. Many of them would perform in the early afternoon during the rodeo at Cache then we would drive them to new Craterville for an early evening show.

Donna Douglas, Ellie Mae of *The Beverly Hillbillies*, was really into the rodeo. She arrived at Cache about one hour before the show began and went around visiting with the cowboys and admiring their horses. When the show began, she climbed up on the fence behind the calf roping chutes and enjoyed the rodeo as much as the fans.

Hank Thompson and the Brazos Valley Boys performed three or four times and big crowds came to see them. On the last date Hank was supposed to appear, he didn't show up on time. The rodeo went on as scheduled, but when the show was over Dad was so embarrassed, he announced anyone who wanted a refund could get their money at the ticket office. About the time the crowd cleared out, Hank showed up drunker than Hooter Brown. We had a dressing room for the stars, and Hank was inside waiting on Dad. He didn't have to wait long before Dad hit the door. Dad pushed Hank up against the wall and gave him a piece of his mind and demanded his $500 deposit money back. Hank apologized and pulled out a big wad of one hundred dollar bills and peeled off five. We still love Hank's music, but it was the only time Dad ever failed to give a show as promised.

Dan Blocker (Hoss Cartwright) might just have been having a bad day, but he was opposite in real life than he was on TV. He acted like he didn't want to be there. He flew into the Lawton airport, and we picked him up in Mom's Cadillac. During his personal appearance, some Indians presented him with a beautiful Indian blanket and made him an honorary tribal member. It was a big deal for the Indians, and just like you would expect from Hoss, his big trademark smile showed pleasure in the gift. When we took him back to the airport after the show, the blanket was in the rear seat of the car. Thinking he was just overlooking the gift, I said, "Oops! Don't forget your blanket." He grabbed his costume and his traveling case and said, "Keep it, I don't want that piece of junk."

The incidents with Hank and Hoss were exceptions. The special appearances by the stars, the excitement and professionalism of the events, and the people who helped run the rodeo were first-class, but remember, it was a rodeo and outstanding rodeo stock was also a requirement.

The rodeo stock was pastured and well cared for on the Rocking R Ranch at Meers. Scenes at the ranch often included the unusual sight of rangy bucking horses, mixed breed bucking bulls, and lean Brahman roping calves, grazing alongside sleek registered Quarter Horse mares and stately Hereford cattle.

38. The Rocking R Ranch at Meers

The business card of Frank Rush
with a puzzle that Dad enjoyed on the back.

In 1956, as old Craterville was shut down, new Craterville was being built at Quartz Mountain. The Indian Store and rodeo grounds were under construction at Cache, as well. Dad was looking for a place for Mom, Suzy, and me to move. Lucius Long owned a three thousand, two hundred acre spread about fifteen miles north of old Craterville near Meers. Mister Long let it be known the ranch was for sale, and Dad asked a real estate man to negotiate a deal.

Every rancher had a brand that was as meaningful as a name, address, or phone number, and Dad had chosen the "Rocking R" for his brand. There were other Rocking R brands registered with Oklahoma Cattlemen's Association; however, the location of the brand on the animal's body was also a part of the identifying message. The message was, "Don't steal this animal!" Dad registered his brand on the left shoulder of his cattle and on the right hip of his horses. Livestock men and brand inspectors associated a man's brand with his land, stock, equipment, and reputation, good or bad. Dad and Mom rejoiced in naming our new home the Rocking R Ranch.

There was a big two-story ranch house, a horse barn, and another home on the place. In absence of the mountains, the property would have been beautiful, but with the Wichitas serving as the backdrop, the view was magnificent. Mount Sheridan and Tarbone Mountain were among the tallest in the range and lay directly to the south. An unobstructed view of Mt. Scott could be seen to the southeast. The big game fence around the refuge joined the ranch on the south and west borders. The Joe McDonald Ranch joined us on the north and the Wayne Rowe Ranch joined us on the east. All of the larger ranches on the north slope of the Wichita Mountains were productive and picturesque, including the Haley Ranch, Thomas Ranch, and Ketch Ranch. The neighborhood fit Mom and Dad like a pair of hand-made cowboy boots as they began to adjust from being uprooted from old Craterville.

Medicine Creek wound through almost every pasture of the Rocking R, and its deep pristine pools along the way provided water year round. There were several farm ponds on the property brimming with fish. The oak trees on the hills and pecan trees along the creek produced an abundance of acorns and pecans for wildlife.

Deer, fish, quail, turkey, dove, and elk made the ranch a paradise for any sportsman or an eleven-year-old lad such as I. There were bobcats, coyotes, all kinds of critters, and plenty of diamondback rattlesnakes to keep you alert. The native grasses provided rich nutrition for Dad's Quarter Horse and Appaloosa horse herds, and Dad's Hereford cattle thrived there as well. For all of us, the ranch was paradise.

This family photo taken in front of the ranch house at Meers shows some of the ranch pastures and the beautiful Mount Sheridan in the background.

39. Hollywood Visits the Rocking R Ranch

In 1958 and 1959, Walt Disney was producing a television show called *The Saga of Andy Burnett*. The show ran for several weeks as a serial, depicting the life of a pioneer who traveled from Pittsburgh to the Rockies.

A location scout came to the area and looked at the Wichita Mountains Wildlife Refuge and herds of buffalo, but there were some problems with filming the action scenes. Panoramic scenes of the buffalo were acceptable in the refuge; however, the need for stunt work and depictions of Indians killing the buffalo were out of the question. The scout came to the ranch to talk to Dad about leasing his privately-owned property on which the buffalo hunt could be filmed. The scout liked the looks of the location with the mountains in the background. Dad set the price, and a deal was made.

The film being shot did not contain much dialog, so not all of the main actors came to Oklahoma. The second unit film crew and stunt doubles, along with several film trucks filled with equipment, were sent to do the job. Actor Iron Eyes Cody portrayed Mad Dog, the film's Indian chief, but he was not at the ranch. Iron Eyes Cody's stunt double on the second unit was Buddy Heaton from Kansas.

Yakima Canutt was famous in Hollywood for his portrayals of cowboys in Western movies, as well as his stunt double work. During his long career, he appeared in hundreds of films, including John Ford's *Stagecoach* and *Ben Hur*. On this project, Yakima was working as the second unit director. Yakima was in charge of the operation but had time to visit between takes. The local cowboys really took to him and his gift for telling stories about his movie career.

A herd of buffalo, about thirty animals, was leased from a private herd in New Mexico, and trucked to the Rocking R Ranch. The scenes

a simulated stampede scene. Frank Rush's "Rocking K Ranch," near Meers, also will be used as a location for the TV show, scheduled for release next year. See photos Page 22. (Photo by Bill Dixon)

VOLUME 56—NO. 77   (AP)   (UP)   AP WIREPH

Wichitas Scene Of Andy Burnett Film
Cowboys, Indians Swap TV Roles

By BILL CRAWFORD
Staff Writer

An excursion to a TV film location can sure become confusing at times to the average home video fan.

Cowboys are Indians—and Indians are cowboys. You can't tell se from the other.

Such is the case with the "Saga Andy Burnett" episode being 'med (color TV) by the Walt isney Productions in the Wichita Mountains Wildlife Refuge and Frank Rush's "Rocking R anch," near Meers.

For example, Freckles Brown, awton's championship rodeo perormer, is one of the "star" Inians appearing in several seuences in which the refuge's uffalo herd—largest in the world is used.

Freckles, decked out in buck-skin, black braids and a heavy layer of grease paint, looks like a sure enough Red Man. His only props are a paint horse and bow and arrows.

Another cowboy, who gets a jolt out of hamming it up before the Disney cameras, is Buddy Heaton of Clayton, N. M. The 26-year-old rodeo man, who was injured on location this morning, also is owner of several head of buffalo on contract for the TV film.

His buffaloes, who call a New Mexico range home, are to be used in closeup scenes since they have performed in rodeos and are "easy to handle."

The Indians? Most of them on the refuge location Tuesday afternoon were acting in the capacity of cowboys herding the buffalo in camera range.

However, there really isn't need for alarm at the artificiality of the Indians in the TV movie. Some "real-live" Indians, including Truman Ware and Bobby Ahboah of Anadarko, are present to add authenticity to the color TV episode.

After all the ruddy-complexioned cowboys (many of them are from Cache, Indiahoma, Fort Cobb and Meers) make a crew of good-looking Indians atop their well-behaved ponies. And the typical TV viewer apparently won't notice the difference.

Giving a professional acting touch on the location for the close-ups is Hollywood actor and "double" A. C. Hudkins, who plays the part of an Indian.

Hudkins looked so real or area cowboy-like Tuesday afternoon that this reporter attempted to start a conversation with the handsome "Indian" actor about the Meers ranching activity.

Director Yak Canutt, veteran Hollywood movie stunt man, is well pleased with progress being made by the Disney crew here—considering the weather. A few

A news photo of the buffalo herd being filmed for the Andy Burnett series was featured in the *Lawton Constitution* newspaper.

called for a buffalo hunt, a stampede, and a shot depicting the trampling of a buffalo hunter, played by a stunt double and a lifelike dummy. A big pit was dug for one of the cameras, and the buffalo were herded over the covered pit for a ground level view of the oncoming stampede. The stunt double was filmed taking shelter behind a fallen tree trunk to avoid being trampled. The buffalo charged as the stunt double dove for cover. The dummy was then substituted, and raised to its knees with concealed wires. It appeared that the buffalo trampled the hunter. Close-up shots of their hooves mashed the dummy into the ground. The whole depiction looked real when edited.

In the next scene, another camera panned up the ridge where Chief Mad Dog, Buddy Heaton, looked on and took some pleasure in seeing the buffalo take a measure of revenge on the white hunter.

Several other scenes were filmed. One included a buffalo hunt, showing Indians firing arrows into the buffalo. Again, it all looked authentic in the final product. No one could tell the Indians were actually local cowboys in costume, bull rider Freckles Brown included. Also, no one could detect the fact that no actual arrows were fired from bows of the would-be Indian actors. The arrows were drawn in later at the Disney studios in California.

The whole thing was scheduled for three days of filming, but two mishaps slowed progress. The first problem could have caused injury to a cameraman. Most of the stampeding buffalo jumped the camera pit, though one buffalo tripped, fell, and rolled into the pit. The cameraman got the shot, jumped out of the pit and ran for cover. The buffalo was not much the worse for wear, but when the movie was released, the animal's few seconds of fame made the final cut.

Yakima barked instructions, the grips moved the props, the wranglers drove the buffalo over the camera pit again and again until the director yelled, "It's a wrap!" Buddy Heaton, standing in for Iron Eyes Cody as Mad Dog, did a masterful job with one exception. The film was "in the can" in movie lingo, until a technician and the continuity director were reviewing the film and noticed Buddy had been wearing sunglasses during the final shot. Yakima was outraged and rued the whole scene would have to be filmed again because of Buddy's "damn' fool mistake." The sun was too low to provide good light for the retake

This photo, taken by Frank Rush, depicts an Indian actor in the process of firing an arrow into a running buffalo. There were no arrows actually fired and the buffalo's fall into a well-plowed patch of ground was the result of a trip wire. The flying arrow was drawn into the film by the animators at the Disney Studios in California. The buffalo went unharmed.

that day, so a fourth day of filming was needed, at no small expense to the production company.

Buddy was considered a wild and crazy man by most anyone who knew him. His antics as a rodeo clown, actor, and cowboy were notable in Western movie circles; nevertheless, he was a professional, and this was apparently an amateur mistake.

Buddy apologized to Yakima at length, and then rode his horse over to the corrals where Dad and the local cowboys were unsaddling their horses. Everyone was feeling kinda bad about the mishap until Buddy said, "Men, these Hollywood boys got lots of money, and I figured these sunglasses would make us all another good day's pay. You guys don't owe me anything for my little screw-up, but I wouldn't mind if someone would unsaddle my horse, and buy me a drink and a steak in Lawton."

I understand several of the local cowboys showed Buddy a pretty good time in town that night. It was also noted that Yakima and the film crew joined the party.

ITUTION-MORNING PRESS, Sunday, Nov. 24, 1957

DIRECTOR AND SONS. Director Yak Canutt, veteran movie s t u n t man, isn't describing the fish "that got away," but instead is expressing his approval of the Wichita Mountains as a perfect location for a western movie. Standing beside their father, who has been in Hollywood since 1919, are Joe Canutt, left, and Tap Canutt. Joe is a double for "Slim Pickens" and Tap is Andy Burnett's "double" in Walt Disney's "Saga of Andy Burnett," on location in the Wichitas. The movie crew is expected to finish filming the color TV episode here about mid-week.   (Staff Photo)

Yakima Canutt poses for the news photographer and explains the scene to be filmed to two of his actors.

40. Home on the Range

From Hollywood to hunting, from ranching to rodeo, Dad kept everyone around him busy. Adding to the activity in 1959, Dad decided to build Mom a new house, but there was one small problem. The two-story house that was on the property was located on what was obviously the most ideal site. The site had a commanding view of the mountains and a large part of the ranch pastures. Dad decided to move the old house to a different location. The old house was too good to destroy, and it would provide a place for us to live during construction.

Dad's friends and carpenters, Jesse and Red Robertson, were hired for the construction, and work got underway in the spring of 1960. It was a magnificent house plan. Each bedroom, the spacious living room, dining room, and kitchen shared the view looking south. Large picture windows looked out on the lawn with a new swimming pool and the pastoral scenery beyond. The exterior of the new structure would have the familiar log appearance, and sandstone and native rock would accent a style befitting the Wichitas.

One would walk into the living room, and in any season the experience was breath-taking. The living room included a fireplace large enough to burn logs five feet in length, and there were leather couches and several leather chairs arranged around the space. Mom ordered an oversized brown leather couch long enough to seat five people comfortably; when it arrived, she was thrilled. After the room was arranged, the new furniture did not completely fill the ample space, so Dad ordered another oversized couch exactly like the first one. Mom protested, but it did look very impressive, so she let Dad keep both couches.

Each room was paneled with knotty pine and stained to match the décor. Suzy's room had a pale pink stain, and Mom and Dad's bedroom and sitting room had a light turquoise tint to the wood. I had seen some pine that was sandblasted to look like old lumber in ranch baron Paul Waggoner's home, the Knott Inn, in Vernon, Texas. Mom had my room finished with those horizontal pine boards, and it looked a little like a horse stall. The room was perfect for a boy.

Mom and Dad outdid themselves on the house, but they loved to share it with family and friends. By today's standards the house, thirty-five hundred square feet, was not huge. But with that fabulous view and architecture, it was quite a showplace.

During the construction of the house, the foundation work ran into an underground rock. The men tried to dig it up, but is must have been the top of a buried mountain peak, so they were not successful. If the rock could not be moved, the building would need to have the plans changed considerably, so Jesse, Red, and Bob had a dynamite idea. No kidding, we're talking TNT here. No one knew how much to use, but more seemed like a better choice than less, so a blast hole was dug into

Genelle and Frank Rush, along with Hank the birddog,
stand in front of the newly finished ranch house.

the rock and two sticks of explosive were loaded. The fuse was lit. We all ran about two hundred feet away and hid behind some big boulders, thinking we would be safe. Wrong! The explosion sounded like a howitzer at Fort Sill had gone off; after about three seconds, we peered out of our hiding place to see what happened. It looked perfect, and the rock in question was gone. Gone straight up in pieces, that is. It started raining rocks! Some were as big as basketballs. Some were as tiny as the brains that thought up the idea. Outside of damage to the roof of the barn and a few egos, no one was injured, and the construction of the house continued.

Construction of the house did not detract from the operation of the ranch. Dad bought some excellent quarter horses, mostly from Doctor W.C. Tisdal's Lazy T Ranch in Hallett, Oklahoma. Jimmy Tis was one

The ranch house and swimming pool at the Rocking R Ranch.

A view from the front porch of the ranch house looking
toward Tarbone Mountain to the south.

of his stallions used for breeding our mares and some outside mares as
well. Jimmy Tis won several big Oklahoma Quarter Horse Association
shows and was recognized as the "Top Stallion Of The Year" for
Oklahoma at Pawhuska in 1958. He was a son of Paulo P-1147. Paulo
was a double grandson of Little Joe by Traveler and a half brother to
the widely-known stallion, Hobo, so Jimmy Tis came with great blood
lines. Another stallion that Dad purchased from the Waggoner ranch
was Dun Star King, own son of King P-234. Between those two studs
and a herd of eighty well-bred mares, the Rocking R Ranch quickly
gained notoriety.

The living room at the ranch house was the site for a neighborhood party.

Dad also still had his Appaloosa mares with Dan Coates' colorful stallion Quanah as the principal sire. There were about thirty good Appaloosa mares in that herd, including Belton, a mare that had foaled many great colts for Dan and Dad.

Suzy became interested in registered Shetland ponies. Dad's friend, Vern Brewer from Gainesville, Texas, had registered Shetlands with the most popular bloodline. Dad and Suzy paid the handsome fee of $6,000 for a Shetland stallion named Larigo's Topper. Mom thought Dad had lost his mind, but they sold two colts out of the stud the following year for $4,500 total, so she had to eat crow. The Shetland pony market faded a bit over the next few years, but it turned out to be a fairly profitable enterprise.

Dad maintained a herd of about one hundred registered horned Herefords of Zato Heir and Hazlett breeding. He had been very successful with these bloodlines over the years. The registered cattle market in the late '50s and early '60s was very volatile, but Dad had been wise and lucky enough to sell when the price was good and increase his herd size when the market was soft. We had some trouble with the coyote packs trying to kill the young calves, but the Hereford cows knew how to use their horns and were very protective mothers.

This group of quarter horse mares were anxious to get back to grazing after leaving the corrals at the ranch.

The family at work gathering cattle in Tarbone Flat.

Suzy and Frankie display Jimmy Tis and his little sister Jimmy Sis.

Frankie on Quanah's Tomahawk and Suzy on Quanah's Warrior
visit with ranch foreman Don Goodin.

There was plenty of ranch work to keep us busy, and we had some good horses to ride on the rocky country. Dad had kept the best of the horses from Craterville, and moved them to the ranch. Everyone had his own favorite horse. Beans liked a little stout sorrel horse named Junior. Don Goodin, another ranch hand, could ride any horse and school it in the process, so he usually rode anything that needed some work. Big Tom usually rode a horse named Dunny, and that left James Rhoads to ride Willard. I had a big yellow horse named Buck that had a bad fistula scar on his withers, but he was solid for any job.

Dad rode a big bay named Bill. Bill was a super ranch horse with plenty of bone, good feet, and lots of heart. Bill had only one problem not uncommon to horses raised in snake country. When a rattler gave his warning or if Bill was within two hundred feet downwind of a snake, the rider was faced with two choices. First, one could either attempt to land on a soft spot when Bill bucked you off, or you could vacate the area with Bill. The first option meant you might be bucked off onto the snake. The wiser choice was to depart to a distance at which Bill calmed down and take another route to the destination. Dad and Bill were both strong-willed, but usually they managed to deal with the snake situations to the satisfaction of both.

Dad started taking Suzy, Big Tom, and me to Quarter Horse shows for enjoyment, as well to build a reputation for his herd. Jimmy Tis and Dun Star King were shown in the stallion classes. We hauled Jimmy Tis and Suzy's great blue roan mare named Pauline Bee, along with some other mares, to exhibit in the mare classes. I showed Cecil Dexter in the gelding class. We also hauled four or five stud and filly colts that would either be used in our breeding program or sold in the annual sale. As often as not, we not only won the respective class, but our horses were selected as the Grand Champions of their division. They had classes for Produce of Dam, in which a mare and two of her colts where shown together, and a class for Get of Sire, in which a stud and three of his colts were shown together. We won many of those classes because of the fine overall genetic quality of the herd. In performance classes, I rode a little horse called Peppermint Joe that was outstanding in reining, Western pleasure, or any other performance class. Suzy rode Pauline Bee for her performance horse.

We needed to haul eight to ten head of horses to each show, which was difficult because there were not trailers available of that size. Dad found a used Diamond T racehorse van in Pampa, Texas. Big Tom got the privilege of driving the truck home the first time and made me ride with him on the overnight journey. We thought Dad had made a mistake in buying the van because it was in bad need of work and paint. When we finally got home about daylight, Dad went right to work having the engine and cab rebuilt, new horse stalls installed, and a fresh coat of paint and "Rocking R Ranch Show Horses" painted on the sides. To be sure, when we pulled up to a show, they knew we were there. That big van got attention and our horses did as well.

Dad started having ranch production sales in 1960. He would sell forty to fifty colts from his Appaloosa and Quarter Horse herds, eight or ten brood mares, some saddle horses, and usually two or three good stud colts that we had proven in the show ring. Paul Waggoner of the Waggoner Ranch in Vernon, Texas, usually consigned a dozen or so colts to the sales as well.

We put up a big tent with an auction ring. There was a viewing of the sale animals the day prior to the event. We exhibited calf roping and other working horses the morning of the sale, then a barbecue meal was served to all who attended. The auctions were conducted by Colonel Walter Britten from College Station, Texas. Several hundred people attended, so it helped get publicity for the ranch and the horses.

After three successful annual auctions, Dad decided enough buyers were available for the annual colt crop to be sold at private treaty. After 1963, buyers would call or visit the ranch to purchase horses. Without the expense of the auction, the net gain was to his advantage. For many years, you could see the Rocking R brand on the shoulder of horses at rodeos, horse shows, and anywhere else horsemen gathered, and they always represented their owners well.

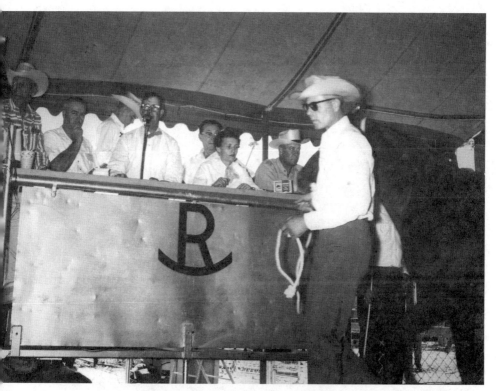

The action of the auction in the sale arena at the ranch with Col. Walter Britton calling the sale. Frank Rush is shown second from left.

The front and back cover of the 1960 sale catalog.

An advertisement flyer for a Rocking R Ranch sale.

A 1961 horse sale advertisement.

Whistle Stop for Merle

A lot of notable people showed up at the horse sales and bought horses or just came for the barbecue and socializing. One buyer who would become a lifelong friend of our family, was Merle Frazier from Jackson, Mississippi. Merle bought a couple of horses, but the lasting consequence of his visit was the friendship he and Dad developed. Merle was one of the most sought-after motivational speakers in the nation. His gift of encouraging people to work hard and make something out of their lives was inspired by his strong religious beliefs, and delivered with a style of a southern gentleman with class and good looks to boot. Merle's self-examination of his speaking success includes accepting the simple truth that every person can achieve goals and improve his or her life. His full-speed approach to daily living, friendships, work, or any challenge he faces is contagious. These characteristics were right down Dad's alley, so Merle became one more of Dad's close friends.

One of the horses that Merle bought from Dad was a beautiful Appaloosa stud with a characteristic blanket of spots over his rump. Merle loved to tell the story of the animal and tease Mom about her involvement with the horse. The story goes back to the time when Dad used to turn the horses out during the day to graze around the ranch house. The grass in the back yard was green and lush. Mom also had a clothesline there to sun-dry her sheets and clothes. One day, Mom finished hanging out two or three loads of wash to dry and went back for another load. The Appaloosa stud saw an opportunity for fun so he systematically pulled every article off the clothesline. He also did a fine job of getting everything dirty. It would be a gross understatement to say that Mom was a mad little woman. She shooed the horse away with a broom, at which point he backed his ears and chased Mom back into the house. Mom got her shotgun out of the gun case, and loaded a shell containing birdshot. She hit the back door and gave the horse one more chance to retreat, an opportunity of which he, unfortunately, did not take advantage. Thinking that the animal was far enough away

315

that the pellets would do no more than sting, she waited for the animal to face away from her, then kaboom! The stud bucked with fright and pain and made a dash for shelter on the far side of the barn. Mom quickly realized that if Dad got home and the colt was dead, or at least seriously wounded, he would be furious.

Dad and I arrived home to meet Mom in tears, standing in the driveway. If you flipped a coin to see if she was more irate or more scared, it would have come down on its edge. Dad calmed her down, and he and I went to tend to the victim. There were red streams of blood from about twenty dimples in the horse's hindquarters. Dad, being one to see the humor in about anything, noted, "I've never seen an Appaloosa with that much color." The horse recovered but never ventured close to Mom's clothesline again.

Years later, when Merle was inspecting the same horse before the sale, he was compelled to run his hand over the beautiful spotted blanket of the animals rear end. He wondered aloud, "What are those little bumps under his skin?" After Mom, Dad, and Merle became even closer, the truth came to light. He still laughs when he tells the story about how Mom motivated and educated the horse for the low price of one shotgun shell.

Merle would cross paths with our family many times over the next several decades. He later moved to Dallas while we were at Sandy Lake Park and even ran a dude ranch as one of our competitors. That never affected Dad's friendship with Merle.

Any person Merle knew on a personal basis received a birthday card and an anniversary card from him, without fail, on each occasion. It became an expected event to get your card from Merle, usually on the exact date of the event. Merle mailed thousands of cards each year until he retired this practice in 2003. The expense and time consumption became too great, but while it lasted, it was a wonderful gift of love.

41. Horsing Around

Dad was a member of the American Quarter Horse Association and a director in the Oklahoma Quarter Horse Association. He attended the annual board meetings usually held in Tulsa. Dad was a certified American Quarter Horse Association judge for many years. We did not enter the shows he judged, but he did travel quite a lot judging other shows around the state. He was also Horse Show Superintendent for the State Fair of Oklahoma for several years. Dad knew everyone in the horse business in Oklahoma and North Texas, and his management skills did a lot to improve the state fair horse shows. Dad also joined and judged horse shows for the American Paint Horse Association.

Dad was hired to judge a big APHA horse show in Canton, Ohio. He and Mom flew up to Canton and really enjoyed the event, even though Dad had to work. The show was Dad's first and last national level event; however, he judged lower-level shows around Oklahoma for several years before and after Canton.

In any rodeo, horse show, or other type public event, Dad preferred a fast pace. He always said, "Most paying customers get tired of watching anything if it runs too long, even when they enjoy the event." He had several halter classes to judge with lots of animals in each class. He recalled how he would walk into the middle of the arena as the horses were being led around the fence and pick out the animals from last to first place. After they lined up in the middle of the pen in selected order, he would quickly walk the line and review his placing. Dad might move a horse up or down a slot or two if he saw something on closer inspection that caused him to change his mind; but in general, he went with his first impression. He said, "When you look at a horse too long, you might start second guessing yourself and get confused." Dad knew good horseflesh, and he had the ability to rate conformation, overall appeal, and defects and choose horses in order of their total appeal. Dad's judging style apparently gave the impression he didn't give the

317

horses adequate consideration. It takes some judges longer than others to make up their mind, but to most judges, time is not critical. A satisfactory result is the issue.

In keeping with his philosophy of first impressions and keeping things moving along, Dad finished his judging chores a good bit earlier than the Canton Horse Show chairman was expecting. He called Dad into the office later and questioned him about the speed at which he had judged the classes.

Dad asked him, "Do you or your committee disagree with the way I placed the classes?"

The chairman answered, "No, not at all."

Dad told him, "It doesn't matter if I'm being paid by the hour or by the day. Either way, the best horse in each class would have still won the blue ribbon, and the sorriest horse in the class would have been at the other end of the line."

Dad joked about getting fired from the biggest horse show he ever judged. It wasn't true, but he didn't get invited back either. He probably wouldn't have gone anyway. He didn't particularly like the idea of people telling him how long it should take to select a winning horse.

:

Whistle Stop for Big George, Pete, Punk, and Bill Hill

Dad loved unusual animals, and he found and purchased a giant, spotted trick mule named Big George. In the winter, Dad would bring Jimbo, his giant steer, to the ranch to relax and enjoy some time off from his exhibit at Cache. Oddly, Big George and Jimbo usually kept close company in the pasture. We wondered if they were attracted to each other because of their unusual size.

Like Jimbo, Big George was a seldom sort of creature. Big George was nineteen hands tall (seventy-six inches) and had a white coat with grapefruit sized brown spots all over his body. Each spot was circled by a dark ring and his ears were as along as a man's arm from elbow to finger tip. We didn't take him away from the ranch often, but we did take him to parades and other places to advertise the rodeos. He got plenty of attention wherever he was. He also was trained to perform circus tricks, not many, but enough to do a rodeo.specialty act. Dad got an offer for Big George from a rodeo clown in California, which he later regretted accepting.

After Jimbo died, Dad bought two big Holstine/Bramahn cross steers that weighed about three thousand pounds each, named Pete and Punk. They weren't as big as Jimbo, but the pair of them was large enough to brag about and merit a twenty-five cent admission fee for a look-see.

When Dad was the horseshow superintendent at The State Fair of Oklahoma, he hired Bill Hill to work for him. Bill was a self-titled traveling promoter. He traveled to keep out of trouble, and he promoted about anything to make a dollar. Dad rented space across from the horse barn at the fair grounds. He put up a tent and a painted front wall to "ballyhoo" an exhibit for Pete and Punk. Bill acted as the "barker" for the exhibit and did quite well, considering his convincing manner. The first year Bill and Dad split a small profit, but the next year Bill had a better idea. He persuaded Dad lease space for two tents and two ballyhoo fronts. He could hire another barker and put Pete in one exhibit and Punk in the other. The idea gained Dad's permanent

319

Big George ridden by Frankie.

respect for Bill. Not only did people pay twenty-five cents to see one steer, they paid an additional twenty-five cents to see the other. Every few minutes Bill and the other barker would fake a dispute over which steer was the biggest. People would actually spend several quarters going back and forth between exhibits trying to satisfy themselves as to which steer deserved the title. Dad and Bill made a lot more money

320

on the steers than Dad was paid for being the horse show superintendent. So far, so good for Bill, but his sometimes questionable business
sense occasionally emerged.

Bill got Dad in trouble at a rodeo in Hollis, Oklahoma. Bill knew
little about rodeo, but in his quest to make money, he wanted to sell
bottled drinks in the grandstands during the show. He had a full case
of drinks slung to a strap over his neck. The drinks were one dollar
each, and Bill did not have change for one customer's $100 bill. Bill
took the C note, set the whole case of drinks in the man's lap, and
promised to return with his change; but he didn't come back. After the
rodeo, the man located Dad and demanded his $99 in change. Dad
made it right by giving the man his money, but we didn't see Bill for
ten days. By that time, Dad had enough fun telling the story that he let
Bill off the hook.

Bill started helping Dad book his Santa Claus sleighs. He was
very good at going into a small town with some window cards and
going door to door with a sales pitch about the sleds. He would collect
ten, twenty, or fifty dollars from a merchant and leave them a custom-
printed window card announcing "Free Sleigh Rides on Santa's Sleigh
Courtesy Of This Local Merchant" and a big stack of complementary
sleigh tickets. As often as not, Bill might be able to collect two or three
times the daily fee Dad charged on contract with the TG&Y stores.
Dad would add the town to the schedule and one of the sleighs would
give rides up and down Main Street for a six-hour period to the delight
of kids, parents, and merchants alike.

Bill and Dad parted ways over Bill's unprecedented success. Bill
was so good at his trade that he began collecting money for two or
three towns on the same date for the same sled. Bill assured Dad that
it was an oversight, but Dad had to refund a lot of money and eat a lot
of crow. As usual, Bill had to travel on down the road to promote other
enterprises.

To this day, when some strange business deal crops up and one of
our family members refers to it as "a Bill Hill deal," we all understand
the deal might have some questionable characteristics.

Pete and Queenie, a dwarf cow, that
accompanied Pete and Punk while on exhibit.

Pete and Punk.

42. Meers Store

Like Dad's collection of unique friends and activities, our home community of Meers, Oklahoma, was an interesting mix of people and events. In one way, Meers was typical of most small communities. You couldn't do anything that missed the attention of the regulars at the Meers store. There were only two people who owned and inhabited the whole "city." Gladys and Lee Meyers were the proprietors of the only building between the two city limit signs, and they presided over the activities each day as the locals came in for grilled hamburgers, a Virginia Dare soda, and homemade pie. At one time, there had been a larger town with an economy based on mining and cattle. During the late '50s and early '60s, when we lived at the ranch, the store was the only structure remaining. Not to say that the old store didn't offer a wide range of services including a gasoline pump, a post office, groceries, café; and some farm, hunting, and fishing supplies. Mostly it was a forum for running conversation and friendly social life, which helps make any community a good place to live.

Lee was the target of many a harmless prank; and the more he let someone get under his skin, the more he clapped his false teeth. The habit was only slightly irritating, but it was considered a gauge of Lee's gullible nature and resulting agitation.

Dan Coates was clued in on Lee's temperament prior to his first visit to the store. Lee didn't know Dan from Adam when he walked in at noon one day with a briefcase and an order form in hand. About a dozen local cowboys were sitting at tables eating lunch when they overheard Lee inquire about what Dan wanted. Dan replied, "I'm taking orders for the power company on how many packages of electricity the store will need." Lee took the bait and swallowed the hook. The cowboys understood immediately that Lee's leg was being pulled, so they just kept eating and trying to stifle their laughter. Lee inquired, "What in the world is packaged electricity, and why do I need any?" Dan had his

The Meers Store has changed little over the decades. This postcard photo is reprinted courtesy of the current owners, Marjorie and Joe Maranto, and Praire Production Company of Tulsa, Oklahoma.

story ready and explained that the power lines were going to be rebuilt. Unless the store had a generator, his estimate of three packages of electricity per week would be enough to get by on. Lee said, "Well, I guess I haven't got a choice, but how much does this cost?" Dan explained, "The packages are free, as long as you promise to return the empty containers and agree to buy electricity from the power company after the lines are rebuilt." Lee inquired, "Where else could I buy it?" Dan said, "Mister Meyers, after you use this packaged stuff, you may like it better than the other kind, so we just want to make sure we'll have a customer later." Lee signed the ticket, Dan left the store and came on up to the ranch to spend a couple of days.

Everyone in the community except Lee knew about the joke, and for weeks Lee kept telling everyone they better sign up for packaged electricity. Later, when Lee discovered the scam, his teeth rattled at a record pace.

Today, Meers is still operating, but under new management. The dinner-plate-sized hamburgers (big enough to feed four people) are still being served. Long lines of customers drive for miles to enjoy the food, the beauty of the Wichitas, the running conversation, and the social life.

Whistle Stop for E. Paul Waggoner

Dad always invited business associates and friends to come hunting during deer season at the Rocking R Ranch. During the early 1960s, the deer population was at a peak, and we had plenty of room to hunt. Dad would have Big Tom and me guide the hunters and make sure they got a trophy buck. Some couldn't hit the broad side of a barn so Big Tom or I would help them out with our rifles. We would then have to dress and skin their deer in preparation for the trip home. One year in a five-day season, Big Tom and I processed forty-three deer for hunters at the ranch. We got pretty good at the task, and the experienced hunters and the city dudes always went home happy.

E. Paul Waggoner, owner of the legendary Waggoner (Three D) Ranch near Vernon, Texas, was invited to hunt at the ranch. Fagon Miller worked for Mister Paul at Vernon after he finished working for Dad at old Craterville and had introduced Dad to Mister Paul in the early 1950s. Mister Paul and Fagon came to Meers to hunt, and in return we were invited to hunt with them on the Waggoner Ranch. As a result of these hunts, Dad and Mister Paul enjoyed their business and personal relationships more than ever.

The Waggoner ranch was filled with game, livestock, and oil wells. It contained five hundred, twenty thousand acres and was known as the largest ranch in the country under one fence. The ranch was equally famous for its fine Quarter Horses, Poco Bueno in particular. Dad bought some Waggoner Ranch mares and also let Mister Paul consign some horses to the annual production sale at Meers.

Fagon was the manager of the horse division of the ranch and was largely responsible for creating a stellar reputation for the Waggoner horses. Fagon and his wife, Ruby, had two sons, one named LaDon and one named Paul after Mister Waggoner. LaDon was about my age, so I was invited to come with Dad to hunt. Fagon and his family lived near Mister Paul at the Santa Rosa rodeo grounds just south of Vernon.

Mister Paul had several houses on the ranch, but the "Knott Inn," his home at Santa Rosa, was the place he hung out with his cronies. Gambling, drinking, hunting, and fishing were common occurrences with the group. He also had a lot of well-heeled business friends who visited him. There was no question in my mind, even at the age of twelve, there was a lot of whiskey and poker chips being passed around at the Knott Inn. Mister Paul drank Jack Daniels like water and so did most of his buddies. Dad would never drink or play cards with the bunch, perhaps because I was with him, but probably because he didn't enjoy either one. I always understood that Mister Paul respected Dad, and he never pressured Dad to indulge.

Mister Paul hired his own game wardens on the ranch, along with a large crew of ranch hands and foremen. He would invite twenty or thirty other guests to accompany him on goose hunts at one of the big lakes in the Zacaweista section of the Ranch. The hunters would take up positions in blinds along the shore of a lake. In a nearby wheat field containing thousands of acres inside one fence, there would be tens of thousands of geese grazing on the green, winter wheat a mile or so away.

Mister Paul drove a big, new Lincoln Town Car that he actually called his "hunting wagon," and he used a .22-250 rifle to assist in scaring the geese from the fields. As his Lincoln made a wide circle to get behind the geese, you could see the dust boil up behind the car in the distance. When he got in position, he would gun the car to sixty or seventy miles per hour and fire the rifle out of the window to the dismay of the geese. The big Canadian geese flew overhead toward the security of the lake and directly over the hunters, but not all of the geese made it. Those goose hunts, not to mention Mister Paul's eccentric personality, were very exciting for Dad and me, and we enjoyed our hunts together. Mister Paul's unorthodox methods of goose hunting may not have been a widely accepted practice, but he had more fun than anyone.

When Mister Paul, Fagon, and LaDon were invited to the ranch at Meers to hunt deer, Mom would cook a big breakfast about 5 a.m. as we made plans for the day's hunt. Dad let me guide Mister Paul on his visits. On the occasion of their first hunt, I had already located a huge buck, and I wanted to try to get Mister Paul a shot at the animal. When we left Dad's office, Mister Paul picked up Fagon's .30-06 rifle and started out the door. Fagon said, "Paul, you've got the wrong gun." Mister Paul carried a .270 deer rifle and after a brief set-to, was convinced he had made an error. Mister Paul said, "Fagon, give me your pocketknife," at which point he carved his initials "EPW" on the wooden stock of the beautiful gun. Fagon protested, but Mister Paul said, "It's my damn' gun, and if I want to mark it up a little, it won't hurt. Besides, I won't get it confused with your gun anymore."

The rifle also had an unusual Redfield scope with a "post and cross hair" type sight inside. We all admired the rifle and noticed the odd sight style, an event that would have meaning many years later.

I got to know Mister Paul and learned a lesson about his personality, which would be useful when I guided him on future hunts. I had worked hard to get him within range of the big twelve-point buck. He was in a perfect position, about ninety yards from the monster, to make a clean kill. He took the safety off his rifle, looked through the scope and said to me, "Do you think I can get him from here?" I whispered, "Mister Paul, you will never have a better shot than this, just take a deep breath and squeeze the trigger, easy like." Seconds passed. The buck began to get nervous. More time elapsed while the buck wandered off into the woods. Mister Paul thought out loud, "I could'a got him easy." I began to understand that it wasn't the kill that interested him. It was more about a successful stalk and satisfaction in knowing he could do the job if he was so inclined.

I guided Mister Paul on a few more hunts in the following years with the same result. He never actually killed a deer, but he always got his sights on one, and for him, that was enjoyment enough.

Dad and I were having lunch with Mister Paul and a group of cowboys at the Knott Inn on one of our hunts. Like Dad, Mister Paul collected a lot of Western pictures and keepsakes in his office. There was a pair of horse bits hanging on the wall. The shanks were made from a fancy .45 pistol that had been sawed in two with a mouthpiece welded in place and rings for the bridle and reins. The gun had ivory pistol grips with ruby inlays for eyes on a hand-carved Longhorn head. It was obviously an unusual object but also had been used on the horse that Mister Paul rode during the grand entry at his annual Santa Rosa Round-Up Rodeo. Dad told Mister Paul he thought the bit was a real collector's piece. Mister Paul reached up, took the bit off *the wall, and handed it to Dad. He said, "I won those bits in a poker game a few years back and have just about worn them out. Why don't you keep them for me, if you think they're so damn' pretty." I would have expected Dad to decline the honor of the gift, but instead he said, "Yep, that's a good idea, you might get broke and lose them in a poker game." Mister Paul roared with laughter about Dad's acceptance remark.*

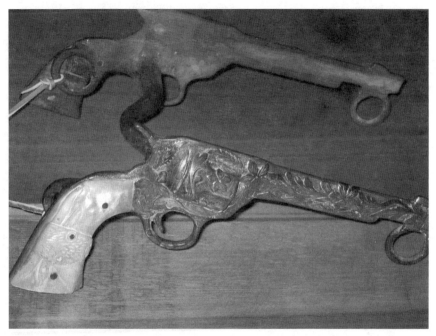

The pistol bits were a gift to Dad from E. Paul Waggoner. Dad later gave the bits to Tom F Self. Notice the fine filigree gold and silver engraving.

Coincidences sometimes make a long journey before they come to pass. A few years later, Dad was in Arlington Memorial Hospital to have gallstones removed when he made friends with his roommate Aubrey Mayfield of Arlington. Mister Mayfield owned a big lumber company in Arlington and a lot of farmland to the south of the city. As development took over, Mister Mayfield had become wealthy. If you travel in southwest Arlington today, you might notice Mayfield Road named in his honor and where his farms were located before progress claimed the land. Mister Mayfield and Dad became very close friends and enjoyed many evenings visiting together with Mom and Mrs. Mayfield in their home. Mister Mayfield loved to hunt, and he had quite a nice gun collection in a beautiful gun cabinet in their house.

Many years later, before Mister Mayfield passed away, he instructed his wife to give Dad a certain gun from his collection. A few weeks after his passing, Mrs. Mayfield called Dad and asked him to come over for the gun and leather case it was in. Dad was honored by the gift and brought it back to Sandy Lake Park without really looking at it closely. Dad called me into his office to show me the keepsake. I said, "Dad look at this case!" Tooled into the leather was "G. T. Arlington, Tx." It also had "Oliver Saddle Company, Vernon, Tx" engraved in the leather. Dad was looking more closely at the leather tooling of the case while I removed the rifle. The hair on my neck stood straight up when I raised the rifle to my shoulder and looked through the scope. As my eye focused, I recognized the old familiar "post and cross hair" sight in the scope. I took the rifle from my shoulder and looked at the side of the stock where the initials "EPW" had been carved years earlier at our ranch in Meers. Dad and I were both in a state of shock: The odds of this rifle coming back to us were huge. We found out later from Mister Mayfield's son, Cecil, the rifle had been a gift from Mister Paul to Mister Mayfield. Rather than give the rifle to a museum, it had been Mister Mayfield's wish that Dad receive the rifle. I am sure Mister Paul would have agreed. Cecil was also unaware of the story of the "EPW" carving on the gun, which added to our enjoyment of the rare luck involved with this gift from old friends.

The rifle's case was a mystery, since I did not know who "G.T." was until August of 2005. Paul Miller, who still lives in Vernon, was visiting us. Being named after Paul Waggoner and knowing a great deal of his history, Paul believes the rifle case belonged to Glenn Turpin of Arlington. Mister Turpin was the manager of Arlington Downs, the racetrack the Waggoner family had founded in 1929. The track was torn down in 1958, and by another coincidence, Arlington Downs was located where Six Flags Over Texas now stands, and where we performed the Wild West Show.

The hunting stories about Mister Paul are typical of so many friendships and experiences that were cultivated and relished by Dad.

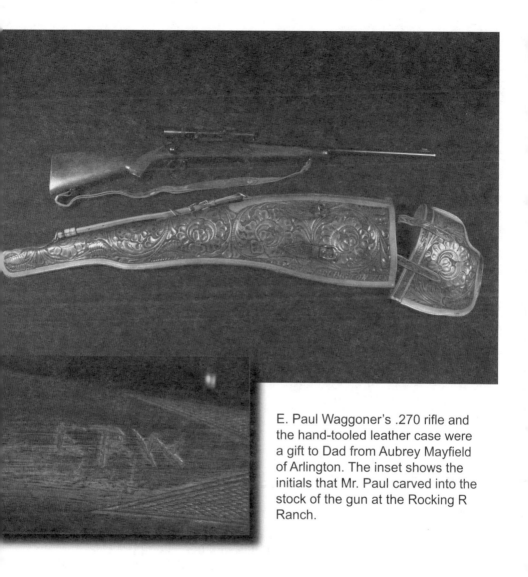

E. Paul Waggoner's .270 rifle and the hand-tooled leather case were a gift to Dad from Aubrey Mayfield of Arlington. The inset shows the initials that Mr. Paul carved into the stock of the gun at the Rocking R Ranch.

43. Meanwhile, Back at the Ranch

Suzy graduated from Cache High School in 1961 and started attending college at Cameron in Lawton. I had attended school through the ninth grade at Cache and was interested in Vocational Agriculture and the Future Farmers of America. Bob and Betty Roundtree were teaching in Cache, where they had become close friends with Mom and Dad. Sometime prior to 1961, they had taken jobs with the Lawton Public Schools but still visited often with my folks at the ranch. On one of their visits, Dad expressed his concern about of the Vo. Ag. Program at Cache, and Betty gave him an idea. There was a teacher at Lawton High School named Mister Marvin Bicket. Mister Bicket had a stellar reputation as heading the most outstanding Vo. Ag. program in the state and possibly the nation. It was possible to transfer school districts, providing an application was accepted by the district. With Betty's introduction, Dad and I went to meet with Mister Bicket. That meeting would prove to have a profound influence on my education and my life.

I wasn't old enough to drive, at least legally, but Suzy was commuting to Cameron College so we could ride to Lawton together on most days. I enrolled at LHS and started class in the fall of 1961. My first hour was spent with Mister Bicket in Vo. Ag. All was well, although when I went to my second hour of class, it was quite a shock to walk down a hall of a school with two thousand, one hundred upper classmen. I had come from a school that had only twenty-four students in my whole class and felt a little overwhelmed the first day.

Later in the week, I went by Betty Roundtree's office to say hello and report on my first few days of school. Betty was a counselor at LHS, and she had a student secretary in the front office. As soon as I walked in, I realized that the secretary was the prettiest girl I had ever seen. I waited a few minutes for Mrs. Roundtree to finish a meeting, and the pretty secretary said to me, "Aren't you Frankie Rush?" "Yes," was my surprised response. She told me her name was Vickie Foster and her sisters, Lynn and Joan Foster, had worked for Dad at new Craterville a few years earlier. "Well, I'll be! I didn't even know they had a little sister." I mumbled. Vickie told me that her folks, Thad and Genevra Foster, had moved from Granite to Lawton in 1960, and he became principal at a local grade school.

Vickie and I had three or four dates that year with Big Tom and Suzy driving us to the movies, but we didn't date again until January of 1966 when Vickie transferred to Oklahoma State University where I was attending school. In 1967, I married that pretty little thing. Between starting school under Mister Bicket and meeting Vickie, the first week at LHS was very lucky for me.

44. What Would Mr. Bicket Do?

I studied under Mister Bicket for three years, but prior to that, Dad had encouraged and allowed me to show steers and heifers for my 4-H projects. Between Mister Bicket and Dad, I was able to start my class project raising Hereford cattle and quarter horses.

Mister Bicket, Dad, a few other Vo. Ag. classmates, and I traveled to several ranches looking for show calf prospects. Roy Turner of the Turner Ranch in Sulphur, Oklahoma; Doctor Paul Bassell of the Bassell Hereford Ranch in Texas; and W.R. "Budd" Thurber of the Bridwell Hereford Ranch in Windthorst, Texas; were the well-known breeders we visited to purchase heifers and show steers. Mister Bicket and Dad both were acquainted with these men and their cattle, so we got to choose from excellent stock. The students with cattle projects stayed busy with preparations for the school livestock show string and breeding projects.

The livestock show at the Tulsa Fair fell on my birthday, October first. Mom and Dad made the trips to act as sponsors and to help Mister Bicket with the students and our animals. Mom always managed to bring along a birthday cake that everyone enjoyed.

I recall my first year in Tulsa in 1961. Mister Bicket got us up at 4 a.m. to wash our steers and get ready for the first class, scheduled to start at 8 a.m. An early cold spell had set in the day before, and the temperature was about twenty degrees. When we came in from the wash rack, the rinse water had frozen on our steers' hair and each of the students, myself included, was freezing as well. Mister Bicket and Dad were standing in the aisle of the show barn visiting and inspecting the steers. Mister Bicket reached under the flank of my steer and found some soap that I had failed to rinse off. He said, "Frankie, wash him again, and be sure to get the soap out next time." I said, "Do you mean rinse him again?" Mister Bicket said, "No, wash him again with soap and be sure and rinse him better next time." Any thoughts of an appeal on my part quickly disappeared. Dad overheard the reprimand and nodded his support for Mister Bicket. I never again cut corners on any project for Mister Bicket, but I did have second thoughts about owning my own show string when I grew up.

Dad had also allowed me to own some of my own Quarter Horses prior to going to school in Lawton, so I had two livestock projects. As

Mr. Marvin Bicket, Frank Rush III and Frank Rush admiring
Cecil Dexter from the corral fence at the Rocking R Ranch in 1963.

a senior, and while I was president of the FFA Chapter, Mister Bicket submitted my name for the honor of Junior Master Farmer Award in FFA. Between my horse and cattle projects, as well as all the other FFA activities I was involved with (such as speech contest, livestock judging and agriculture demonstration teams), I had a good JMF application. Students applying for the title also had to submit a project report book in which all records were maintained. Mister Bicket was very strict about each individual maintaining his own record book, just as any businessman would. Another important requirement was a scrapbook. Suzy helped put together an outstanding presentation in my scrapbook. The material was then submitted to the state committee. In March of 1964, at the State FFA Convention in Stillwater, I received my Junior Master Farmer Degree, and in addition, was awarded the Southwest District Star Farmer Award. My Star Farmer Award was the first state degree awarded in FFA with the primary student enterprise being Quarter Horses.

Lawton High School FFA was always well represented at the local livestock shows as well as the Tulsa Fair, the Oklahoma State Fair, and other statewide agriculture-related events. Mister Bicket was a master at fitting, preparing, and showing cattle. He was also a master at teaching other agriculture-related skills and many life lessons as well. I cannot over-estimate the value I place on my education under Mister Bicket. Many people are blessed to have one or two teachers who touch and change their lives. Mister Bicket not only taught me a great deal in class, he taught me even more about making good decisions and living each day trying to live up to his high moral standards.

An example of Mister Bicket's influence, even on other adults, is one of my cherished life lessons. One day during my high school years, Dad and I had a difference of opinion about some issue. The subject of the incidental disagreement is not important, but what Dad said to me is. After trying to convince me to see things his way Dad said, "Son, what do you think would Mister Bicket would do?"

I take the liberty to include this Mister Bicket story as part of the Frank Rush story because these two men had a positive influence on many young people. Mister Bicket passed away in June of 2005. At his funeral in Lawton, Oklahoma, was a host of former students, all of who had been greatly influenced by him. To this day, on the many occasions in which I have had to make a difficult decision or face a hard issue in life, I rely on Dad's words to help me: "What would Mister Bicket do?"

Whistle Stop for Herschel Boydstun

Herschel Boydstun came to Cache to teach Vocational Agriculture in 1939. He visited old Craterville and made friends with Dad. The two of them, along with Mom and Herschel's wife, became close friends. They played cards together, went to the movies, and Dad and Herschel hunted every chance they got. Herschel would go on to teach at some other schools and work for the Oklahoma Game and Fish Department, but he and Dad remained close. In 1949, he got a job in the School of Agriculture at Cameron College, in Lawton, under Dean James Taylor.

Herschel, like so many of Dad's friends, was gifted. He had a reputation of fitting and preparing show cattle for the ring along with many other livestock-related skills, and he was also a fine educator.

While at Cameron, Herschel excelled in teaching agriculture, especially in the area of beef production. He followed Dean Taylor to the College of Southern Idaho in February of 1965 to head the agriculture department and began to apply his skills and knowledge to the commercial production of rainbow trout. He invented new ways to feed young trout in fish hatcheries, so that they would grow faster, and all weigh almost exactly the same when they were ready for market. He also is responsible for improvement in selective breeding of trout, drawing on his knowledge from the beef industry for new applications.

One day in the late 1970s, Herschel called Dad and asked him if he still had the branding irons which had been used to brand the horns of Dad's registered Hereford cattle in Oklahoma. Dad told him he did, and, having no need of them, sent them to Herschel. Horn branding irons are a set of numbers zero through nine. When heated, the irons would be used to painlessly burn the individual cattle's registration number into their horns.

Herschel needed a way to identify individual trout for selective breeding and realized the brands would work. Obviously he could not use heated irons on the fish, and bio-chip technology was not yet avail-

338

Frank Rush and his longtime friend Herschel Boydstun visit at
the fish hatchery at the University of Southern Idaho. c 1992.

*able. Tagging the fish by any other means was not possible. Herschel
used nitrogen to freeze the irons and "cold brand" the fish without
harm but with the desired result. His idea revolutionized selective
breeding in the commercial trout industry.*

*Herschel bred the "House Creek" strain of foundation fish that is
known in the fish industry as being exceptionally high-producing, dis-
ease-resistant, and meaty. His innovations in education and research
are exemplary. In fact, he has bred the largest trout (twenty-nine
pounds) ever raised in commercial production.*

*Herschel and Dad were always close friends, partly because both
of them thought outside of the box when it came to their chosen fields.
They hunted and fished together over five decades. They talked endless hours on every subject. Most of all, he is Dad and Mom's life-long
buddy.*

Mom and Dad holding an impressive stringer of trout caught near Twin Falls, Idaho, with Herschel acting as fishing guide.

45. Making the Grades

Suzy continued her college education at Southwestern State College in Weatherford, Oklahoma. She commuted from the ranch at Meers, and was engaged to and married Big Tom in 1962. Their wedding was held in the chapel at the Holy City in the Wichita Mountains Wildlife Refuge; and Dad, Mom, and Big Tom's parents, Dick and Dorothy Self, hosted the reception at the ranch in Meers. The evening of their wedding was beautiful, and the big ranch house that Dad and Mom enjoyed so much never looked better.

The wedding didn't alter Big Tom's schedule much. He was teaching school on weekdays, hunting with me and working cattle and horses at the ranch on weekends, but he no longer had to go home at night.

I attended college at Oklahoma State University in Stillwater after I graduated from Lawton High School. On weekends and during the summer break, I was home working at the ranch, rodeos, or new Craterville. Vickie transferred to OSU after three semesters at Cameron College in Lawton, and it wasn't long before we started dating again and fell in love. Vickie and I were married in the Spring of 1967 and had one more year of college before we graduated, she with a degree in Elementary Education and I with a degree in Vocational Education.

After we graduated, we taught school for one year in the Lawton Public School system. Vickie was an outstanding teacher with good guidance from her mom (Genevra Foster), Wilma Davis, and Thelma Talla. Vickie's parents were teachers, so she drew from their experience and help while teaching. I taught science on the junior high school level at Tomlinson Junior High. Big Tom's mother, Dorothy Self, taught with me at Tomlinson and was a great deal of help and support for me.

Dad and Mom were busy running their various enterprises. Things began to turn down for Dad. The cattle market cycled and prices fell. New Craterville was gaining an increasing attendance from migrant farm workers, and in the '60s there was a great deal of ethnic discrimination, so overall attendance suffered. By the time Dad finally realized the Corp of Engineers would never make good on their word about further compensation for the condemnation of old Craterville, he was in deep water financially. Dad was a tireless worker and had good people working for him; however, the cost of doing business was starting to pile up.

Dad sold new Craterville in an effort to return to a positive cash flow, and it was just a matter of time until the same fate would befall the ranch at Meers, and the Indian Curio store and rodeo operation at Cache. The resulting dispersal was barely a breakeven proposition, and Dad was looking for a way out.

46. Take Us to Texas

As if on cue, Uncle Fred Tennant, Dad's old friend in Texas, called with a proposition that was just what Dad was looking for. Uncle Fred's friend, Angus Wynne, had developed and owned Six Flags Over Texas, which opened in 1961. Uncle Fred told Dad that Six Flags had a circus as part of their live show entertainment, and Mister Wynne was looking for a replacement for the show. Mister Wynne wanted a Wild West Show, and he wanted it to be first class. The arena where the show would be staged was ideally located in the "Texas Section" of the Park. The concept seemed a natural. Uncle Fred, knowing of Dad's experience with rodeo, Indians, and entertainment, recommended Dad and asked him to come to Arlington for a powwow with Mister Wynne.

Dad and I arrived at the corporate offices in January of 1967. Uncle Fred and Mister Wynne were very cordial, and after a couple of hours discussing details and logistics, Mister Wynne said, "Frank, you're hired."

Dad had only one request. He said to Mister Wynne, "You be my boss. If you have a problem let me know. If I have a problem, I'll come see you, but I don't want any middle men." Mister Wynne shook hands with Dad and said that was the way he liked to deal.

The show was scheduled to open on Memorial Day weekend, and in the meantime Dad got busy moving us to Texas. The ranch at Meers was still in Dad's possession until it was sold in December of 1967, so we did have a place to leave some of our horses and equipment. We didn't have a place to live, but Mister Wynne offered to let us put four trailer houses to house the performers on the back lot of Six Flags in a location near the arena where we would perform. In early April, we crossed the Red River, heading south towards a new life.

Dad started putting together the Wild West Show, selecting the acts and designing the props for the show. Mom helped him with the music and costumes, and everyone else was busy doing their part to stage the show. Jerry McClung from Lawton was writing the script for the show, and Dad had conceptual drawings made, depicting how he wanted the show to look.

Dad hired a family for the show headed by Denny Peterson from Ogallala, Nebraska. Denny was an accomplished trick rider and Roman rider. He and his wife, Charlotte, acted as parents for his three younger brothers, Levi, Dennis and Rex, and one sister, Shelly. The four younger Petersons could hold their own in the arena, and crowds loved to see them perform their tricks from the backs of running horses. The whole family had good horses, beautiful costumes, and proper equipment. In mid-August, 1966, as per the original agreement, the Peterson family had to meet previous obligations and could not finish the Six Flags engagement.

Alan Cartwright of Benbrook, Texas, was twelve years old at the time and his parents, Aubrey and Carolyn, had been acquainted with Dad and Mom for years. J.W. Stoker had taught Alan to trick ride and Roman ride, and his performance was sensational, especially considering his age. He'd been raised on horses, and his ability as a trick rider, a Roman rider, and horseman could be expected only by more seasoned performers. Because Alan was such a hit, Dad asked him to return to the show for the entire second season. Alan loved the business, and as an adult, he and his family have staged Wild West Shows on their own, including a featured show at the Ft. Worth Livestock Show. Alan and J.W. Stoker did the stunt double work in Clint Eastwood's *Bronco Billy* movie. In 2001, Alan returned to Six Flags to stage a smaller version of the Wild West Show for the Park's fortieth anniversary season.

Dad and Mom's old friend, Howard Morris, from Jackson, Mississippi, had a daughter, Wendy, who owned a big, black dressage horse named Midnight. Dad called on Howard to audition Wendy. Dad had met Howard when he was stationed in the horse-drawn artillery at Ft. Sill years earlier, and Howard had taught Mom to ride her show horse, Ace of Spades, thus Wendy's act was reminiscent of Mom's. Howard was also the coach for the U.S. Olympic Team for many years, so Wendy knew how to put her horse through an impressive exhibition of dressage and English riding.

Big Tom and I performed with a pair of liberty horses. Liberty refers to the fact that the horses were turned loose in the arena to do their tricks. The horses did a few basic tricks, but they were also excep-tional jumpers, and the act was staged around their ability to jump ever-taller hurdles. Big Tom's horse was named Texas Cow Pony (TCP for short) and my horse, Alaba, represented the flag of France. The crowd always favored TCP, and he almost always won the jumping contest. After all, we were in Texas.

Dad called on and tried to hire Montie Montana, the famous showman and movie star from Hollywood, to work the show. Montie was occupied in California working on movies and making personal appearances, but he did have a great recommendation. Frank Dean of California was considered the dean of trick roping, bullwhip popping, and target shooting. Frank wrote numerous books and articles about the techniques of his profession. His writings taught the technique of trick roping as well as how to present a performance in the arena and on Hollywood movie sets. His legendary skill and artistry is considered to be the defining method for Western specialty acts. Frank and his wife, Bernice, were glad to have the opportunity to work with Dad, and they added a great deal to the show.

One resource Dad depended on was the service of some of his Indian friends from Southwest Oklahoma. The Palmer family had the most beautiful costumes and skilled dancers, and they were delighted to spend their summer working for Dad. George Palmer was an accom-plished drummer and Indian singer, and with about twelve or fourteen dancers in full dress, the group made a colorful and compelling addi-tion. Dan Coates, rodeo announcer and family friend from Ft. Worth, emceed the show with expert ability and a voice to match.

Clyde Ashworth and his family lived in Arlington. Mister Ashworth was an attorney in the area and would, in later years, become a judge of much notoriety. He and his wife had two sons, Mark and Bobby, and their cousin, Frank, who were accomplished musicians. Mark played drums, Bobby the organ, and Frank played the trumpet, and between the three of them provided live themed music for the show.

The troupe performed a fast-paced, forty-five minute show. After an opening medley by the band, Dan Coates introduced Dad mounted on his beautiful parade horse with a silver saddle in the style of Wild West Show producers Buffalo Bill and Pawnee Bill. A grand entry led the show with twelve mounted riders in costume and carrying two sets

Frank Rush taking an introduction at the
Six Flags Wild West Show in 1967.

of flags representing Spain, France, Mexico, The Confederacy, The
Republic of Texas, and the USA. The Indian dancers followed next.
The Indian portion of the show celebrated "Our American Heritage"
prior to the appearance of the white man. The next six acts were
themed representing the flags including: France, Denny Peterson
Roman Riding; Spain, dressage riding by Wendy Morris; Mexico, trick
roping and bullwhips by Frank Dean; Confederacy, stagecoach holdup
and rescue; Texas, trick riding by the Petersons. The finale, representing the United States of America, was a kaleidoscope of color, action
and patriotic music as the entire troupe entered the arena for a final
bow. At the conclusion of the show, the audience was invited to see
the horses and visit the performers in the stable area adjacent to the
arena.

The cast of the Wild West Show including Clark Schultz's bucking Ford and Dad's stagecoach.

The show was scheduled for three performances a day with an expected run of one hundred days. Six Flags had an extensive exit poll program to learn what Park guests participated in while at the Park and which shows they enjoyed the most. Our show quickly outpaced the other live shows in the Crazy Horse Saloon and other venues around the Park. Some department managers had their feathers ruffled because they felt their territory was being infringed on. There was no out-right hostility on the issue, but we came to learn they were not altogether happy about the popularity of our show. They felt Mister Wynne had overridden their authority and position by hiring Dad on his own. Occasionally, some supervisor would approach Dad about some aspect of the show, and Dad would tell them if any changes were needed Mister Wynne would let him know.

Mister Wynne did indeed have a change of plans. He asked Dad to change to four performances a day and extend the season for a couple of weeks. The show closed in mid-September, and Mister Wynne extended our contract for the following year.

While we were still at Six Flags the first year, Dad started thinking about the show line-up for the following year. The Petersons and Frank Dean were not able to return for another season, but the rest of the troupe could remain pretty much intact.

Frank Dean started training Suzy to shoot like Annie Oakley from the back of a running horse. The first order of business was to teach Suzy how to hit a flying target. A BB gun and a tin can would suffice for lesson one. Suzy used up several ten-pound boxes of BB's and Big Tom's arms became conditioned to toss bean cans in the air for a target. She then graduated to a .22 rifle and started shooting helium balloons, bean cans, and about anything else that could be tossed in the

Indian dancers warming up the audience with the announcer's stand and the bandshell tepee in background.

348

air. Mister Dean's practice regimen included shooting hundreds of .22 rounds a day. Later, she started riding in a circle horseback and hitting the targets thrown by Big Tom from the back of a leading horse. Her skill developed, first at a walk, and then at a gallop. She practiced daily through the fall and winter. When spring arrived, she was deadly accurate and ready to perform.

Jay Brown, his wife, Dorris, and his three daughters, were our former neighbors from Mountain View, Oklahoma. Dad bought trick riding saddles for the girls and arranged for them to have trick riding lessons. The three girls were already accomplished horsewomen, and over the period of a few months they became skilled trick riders. The Brown family moved to Texas and to fill the vacancy left by the Petersons.

Clark Schults was a famous rodeo clown. He and his wife and daughter would add a new and hilarious act for the second season.

Denny Peterson speeding around the arena Roman style.

Clark's act was framed around a Model T Ford car that had been modified to buck when the accelerator was pushed to the floor. The car's rear axle had been moved forward to a point just behind the center of gravity causing the front wheels to come off of the ground by about four feet. The rear end of the old jalopy, where Arlene sat in the back seat for added weight, would drag the ground. When the car's front tires were off of the ground, Arlene could steer the contraption by brakes on the rear wheels. Clark and Arlene were a riot in the arena. Kids shrieked with excitement when the car reared up. Senior citizens connected with the humor of the old couple fussing over the operation of the vehicle, and the men in the audience all wanted to know how it worked so they could build one like it. Clark and Arlene had a teenaged daughter who helped with the show and a younger son who had a birth defect that necessitated daily physical therapy. Five people were required to "pattern" the movement of his neck and limbs several times daily. There was never a shortage of volunteers to help the young boy. The therapy not only had a positive result with the lad, it seemed to bind the show people together.

Alan Cartwright returned as a permanent member of the cast. He took on a larger part in the show, and his youthful good looks, skill, and showmanship blossomed.

The second year of our Six Flags run was even more successful than the first. We had done more than three hundred and fifty performances in 1967, and Mister Wynne increased the number to about four hundred and twenty the following year. Mister Wynne would come down and watch the show with enthusiasm from the grandstands every few days, and he liked to bring VIP visitors with him.

An example of Mister Wynne's personal confidence in Dad arose shortly after the show opened. Mister Wynne's daughter, Temple, worked at the Park in a Sno-Cone booth located near the Wild West Show arena. He came over to Dad one day to introduce her, and in private, told Dad that he was seriously concerned about her safety. I am sure he thought she might be an easy target for someone to abduct and hold for ransom. Mister Wynne told Temple if she ever felt unsafe to leave her booth and come straight to Dad or any of the show people. That never came to pass, but we all kept an eye on her.

Dan Coates emceed the action in the arena.

Dad's Six Flags Wild West Show was professional, entertaining, and packed with talent. It was a true crowd-pleaser.

In the fall of 1968, Mister Wynne sold his interest in Six Flags to the Pennsylvania Rail Road Corporation. When Mister Wynne moved on, Dad did not want to continue the show under another manager and

Suzy Self taking aim at a target tossed by Big Tom, also on horseback. The target can be seen high above the arena.

decided to turn down a contract that was offered for the third season. Some of the performers got together and produced the show on their own, for the third and final season. Later, the show arena was razed for redevelopment of the Park.

Driver Big Tom Self may be wounded by a band of
marauding Indians in the live action stagecoach holdup.

Rope spinning master Frank Dean spins a
giant well rope as part of his routine.

Indian singers George and Gus Palmer provided the
authentic background music for the Indian dances.

Clark Schultz's bucking Model T Ford was always a crowd favorite.

Whistle Stop for Mr. Hunt

One day, during the second year of the Wild West Show, Uncle Fred Tennant told Dad that he wanted to bring a special guest with him for a day to see the behind-the-scenes action. Uncle Fred showed up the next day with H.L. Hunt. All of us were surprised to meet the richest man in the world, but after introductions, everyone pretty much went about their business of preparing for the daily shows. Mister Hunt made himself at home and sat around in the stable and green room visiting with the cowboys and Indians. After the 11 a.m. performance, Mister Hunt said he was hungry and asked Dad what was for lunch. Dad said, "Mister Hunt, Genelle makes sandwiches at noon and you're welcome to come in the trailer house and eat with us." Mom had ham, turkey, and bologna along with a pretty good spread of extras and a homemade cherry cobbler. Mom was embarrassed because all she could offer was a sandwich, but Mister Hunt insisted on putting his own together with two slices of bologna. He tried the cobbler and said to Mom, "When I was wildcatting in east Texas, I could make a great cherry cobbler myself." He said he hadn't baked one in years and would like to try it again. Mom said, "Well, Mister Hunt, I've got everything you need, so just get busy." That old man was so tickled that he and Mom missed the 1 p.m. show so they could bake another cobbler.

Mister Hunt stayed until all four shows were over, and finally Uncle Fred told him he had to get back to Dallas, so they departed, happy as a couple of kids.

For the next few years, Dad would visit Mister Hunt in Hunt's office in the old First International Bank building in Dallas. He would go past the receptionist, through the office of Mister Redwine, Mister Hunt's attorney, and straight into H.L.'s office. There they would sit and eat peanuts out of the shell and tell old stories to each other. The waiting room out front was filled with important people wanting an audience with Mister Hunt, but the old man always took time out for the bull sessions with Dad.

357

After the Six Flags Show closed, we needed to move on. Dad had located an acreage owned by a J.T. Stevens about two miles north of Six Flags on Baird's Farm Road. Mister Stevens lived on the property, but there was room for our horses and trailer homes, a big horse barn, and another building for storage.

The land was located just across the fence from the Baird's family farm, which they used for weekend recreational purposes. Dad made friends with the whole family and learned that they owned Mrs. Baird's Bakery. Dad realized they were likely clients to sponsor his parade wagons. As it turns out, Mrs. Baird's Bakery has sponsored wagons for us in scores of parades over the years.

During the fall and winter of 1968-69, Dad, Mom, Suzy, and Big Tom lived on Mister Stevens' property. Dad continued to book his Santa Claus sleighs and wagons for special occasions, parades, and shopping centers.

During that same period of time, Vickie and I graduated from Oklahoma State University in the spring of 1968, then taught school one year in Lawton before making a permanent move to Texas. After our move, Vickie taught in Arlington.

Tom and Suzy also taught school in Arlington, and Tom worked part-time at a pawnshop owned by Cotton Powers. Cotton and his wife, Wanda, became close friends of our family. Cotton, like so many of Dad's friends, has an energy and spirit that makes him a fun person just to be around.

The Frank Rush Production business was keeping Dad busy. He approached the El Chico Corporation for sponsorship of parade floats and in the process became acquainted with the Cuellar brothers, owners of El Chico. The friendship lasted many years, even though most of the older generation, including Frank Cuellar Sr., passed away. During those years, Dad was often invited to attend their regular Friday family business lunches at one of their restaurants. These gatherings were open only to the family and very close friends. Dad considered it an honor to be invited, even though Mexican food was not his favorite fare. An interesting family keepsake was given to Dad years later after the passing of Frank Cuellar. The El Chico Corporation had been awarded the American Restaurant Association, Restaurant of the Year Award of Excellence. A miniature Statue of Liberty, about ten feet tall, was the trophy. Frank Cuellar, Sr. had the statue in the backyard of his home in north Dallas and instructed his son to give it to Dad after he passed away. The statue still stands guard near the entrance of Sandy Lake Park.

A long line of new friends and business acquaintances were coming into Dad's life, and he kept on booking the stagecoach and Santa's sleighs as much as possible. Frank Rush Productions kept beans on the table. We all had jobs and things were okay, but life was sure different in Texas. The family was back together again, and things soon started looking up. We were continuing along the tracks of our exciting adventure.

47. Going Once, Going Twice, Sold!

Years earlier, Dad had taken interest in a real estate auction company from Rome, Georgia. He had kept in contact with the owner and made friends with a broker who worked for him in Dallas, by the name of G.C. Walters. G.C. invited Dad, Big Tom, and me to come over to his office on Central Expressway at the Knox/Henderson Exit and visit about an opportunity to join his firm. Big Tom and I were already working on obtaining real estate licenses because Dad felt like there was a good market in ranches and farms in the North Texas area. Dad didn't want to work for G.C. right away, and Big Tom was still teaching year round, so he wasn't ready to commit full-time either. I was looking for something to do when I moved back to Texas, so I took the job offer.

G.C. put me in charge of sales brochure production, the mailroom, and lead development while I was learning the trade. A short time later, Dad moved his real estate license to the office, and Big Tom soon followed suit. Before long, we were knee-deep in finding and listing properties to be sold at auction.

The real estate auction business has always been big in the South. People in that part of the country accept the method of a public auction as an honest and fair way to sell land, settle estates, or trade property. Auctions can move land quickly and at fair market value.

Once in a while, an auction would "catch fire" and bring the sellers a premium price, especially if the property had unusual characteristics. Our approach was to sell unique properties rather than houses, apartments, and the like.

Ralph Segars actually called the auctions. Along with Ralph, three other salesmen and Dad, Big Tom, and me, sales were put together in rapid succession. We usually had more than one auction every week. The salesmen would help each other with the various aspects of the sales, so for over two years while we worked for G.C., we learned a lot about real estate. Most of the sales were in Texas, but we traveled to

Louisiana, New Mexico, and Colorado on occasion. We had some good and some not-so-good experiences.

On one hand, G.C. was a real estate genius, but on the other hand, he was such an unusual character people had difficulty dealing with him. He knew land prices and what any type of property would bring at auction. He also had the ability to convince people to sell at auction. He could appraise a prospective piece of property and tell you how many acres or square feet were in the tract, what the property would bring, and what the total would be without the aid of a calculator or a pencil. Once the land was put under contract and the auction was complete, his appraisal would prove to be accurate beyond any estimate of a less knowledgeable person.

Real estate tycoon O.L. Nelms would occasionally let Ralph Segars clear out some of his extensive real estate inventory. Nelms was famous for having scores of semi-truck trailers sitting around Dallas with big signs on the side stating, "Thanks for helping O.L. Nelms make another million!" To say Nelms was eccentric is an understatement, but we did have some big auctions on his behalf.

Colonel D. Harold Byrd, brother of Admiral Richard E. Byrd of polar exploration fame, had auction sales with the firm from time to time. As compelling as Colonel D. Harold Byrd was, his rank, unlike that of his famous brother, was honorary. The walls in Colonel Byrd's office were fitted with memorabilia collected by him and his more-worldly sibling. One interesting artifact was a small, silk American flag framed with an engraved plaque stating, "This flag crossed the South Pole and the North Pole on expeditions of Admiral Richard E. Byrd, 1926-1934 and was carried on Apollo 8 in December 1968." Dad tried to trade him out of the artifact, or at least put the artifact in an auction, but Colonel Byrd wasn't that hard up for cash at that moment.

From time to time, Colonel Byrd got into a fiscal squeeze, causing the liquidation of some of his property. He owned a building called the Texas Schoolbook Depository. President Kennedy had allegedly been assassinated from the fifth floor of the building, but it had not only fallen into disrepair, it was considered a thorn in the side of the reputation of Dallas. The auction of the building was advertised in the *Wall Street Journal, Miami Herald,* and *Los Angeles Times,* but the media picked up the story and created a great deal of free publicity. The auction was held in the Holiday Inn North ballroom on Central Expressway in Dallas, and the room was overrun with reporters, curious onlookers, and prospective buyers. Walter Cronkite ran a story about the sale on the CBS national news.

There were other parcels of land sold as a warm-up to the main event, but there was little doubt the excitement was about the infamous building. Dad, Big Tom, and I, along with the other sales staff, worked the floor. G.C. was chewing his big cigar and working the bidders with his usual nervous flourish. Segars was warming up the crowd with good humor mixed with his professional skills of calling the action. When the dust settled, a man from Tennessee named Aubrey Mayhew wrote a check for $600,000 and became the new owner. Mister Mayhew soon let it be known he was going to tear the structure down and sell the bricks, one at a time, along with a certificate of authenticity. There were well in excess of two hundred thousand bricks, and at $10 for each souvenir, there was little doubt that he would show a big profit and still own of a prime piece of land to boot.

The Historical Society became the Hysterical Society after they realized that the structure would be torn down. The building was, after all, as infamous and historical as Ford's Theater in Washington, DC., site of the Lincoln assassination. Within a few months, the group arranged a deal to buy the property from Mister Mayhew at a much higher price, but they saved the structure in the process. Mister Mayhew had played a smart game of poker, and he came up with the winning hand.

Just prior to going to work for G.C., Dad had also been the real estate agent for the sale of Sandy Lake Park to Jerry Hicks. This transaction points out that not all of the land deals were sold at auction. Even when we worked for G.C., several deals were made at private treaty, as this was the more common method of selling property.

During my research for real estate leads, I came across an interesting ad for a sixteen-hundred-acre ranch near Kaufman, Texas, and brought it to Dad's attention. After further research, we located the lady who owned the ranch and her representative, Bob Folsom. Mister Folsom also happened to be the owner's nephew. His office was at 2001 McKinney Avenue near downtown Dallas, and Dad dropped in to discuss the Kaufman ranch. While Mister Folsom had an extensive staff of real estate agents, their specialties were focused on commercial property, and they had little interest in rural real estate. Mister Folsom told Dad his aunt had been problematical for him because she was anxious to dispose of the property, and he had no success to date. Dad suggested an auction; however, before the scheduled date of the sale, we sold the property at private treaty. The aunt was happy, and so was Mister Folsom. Mister Folsom didn't forget Dad's accomplishment. The sale was a good deal, a fact that would later be to our benefit when we became interested in buying Sandy Lake Park.

We also found some good properties in Colorado. We sold the Great Northern Hotel in Ft. Collins, and some large tracts for subdivision to an investor from back east. Ralph Seagers located a motel complex in Alamosa, as well as a subdivision development in Silver City, New Mexico, complete with lots located on a high-class golf course. We also listed a big ranch near Houston, Texas, where the owner had committed a homicide. The details were written in a best-selling book, and the whole incident had received lots of notoriety. We got the land ready to sell, but the estate sold the ranch at private treaty the day prior to the auction. We collected a fee for our work but missed the chance to add to the story of the infamous ranch.

Dad had made the acquaintance of Marvin Bittick, who lived just west of Six Flags near the old ballpark. Marvin owned the Post and Paddock Stables north of the DFW Turnpike, and he and Dad traded horses and horse stories. Marvin also owned several acres of land that he had tried to sell during the development boom in Arlington. Dad approached him about having an auction, but before auction arrangements were complete, Dad helped Marvin sell the land to a private buyer. Today, the parking lots of Ameriquest Field in Arlington and the restaurants and businesses that thrive nearby occupy the property. The commission on that particular sale helped us get started at Sandy Lake a short time later.

We spent a lot of time traveling out of state. Big Tom's son, Tom F, and my son, David, were just toddlers, and we didn't like the idea of being on the road all that well. After a couple of years and a lot of education in the real estate auction business, we began to realize our future with G.C. was limited.

G.C. occasionally overworked a prospective land sale to the point it cratered, and in some instances, he failed to follow through to complete a deal. He could make an impossible deal work, or he could just as easily mess up a sale that seemed like a sure thing.

A case in point came when we listed a thirty-two thousand acre ranch near Kim, Colorado. Doctor James Donley of Trinidad, Colorado, was the owner. The ranch was in the southeast part of Colorado, and not at all what the public image of the state's mountain country would bring to mind. The ranch did, however, have productive grassland, plenty of water and lots of game. G.C. and I traveled to Trinidad in a blizzard during the winter of 1969 and signed an auction contract with the old doctor. The agreement included a clause stating a ten percent commission would be paid on the highest bid, regardless of whether the owner accepted the bid or not. This was called a "cut loose contract," and a sale looked like a sure thing. Come the day of the sale, we had several interested buyers, including Keith Barnett and his wife, Mariam. Mariam had inherited the Seagram's 7 estate, so there was little doubt they had the means to buy the ranch. While the sale was in progress, and when the high bid by Keith's wife was well over one million dollars, G.C. got on the phone with a bidder from the Mormon Church in Salt Lake City, Utah. G.C. was selling a lot of land to the church's foundation, but he was still way out on a limb by getting a bid over the telephone. While still on the phone with the absentee bidder, G.C. announced a raise on the bid, and the Barnetts got in their car and went home. They got spooked thinking G.C. didn't have a live bid, and as it turned out, he didn't. Doctor Donley was angry with G.C. and so were we. The sale was a done deal at one point, but G.C. overworked a sure thing, and the six-figure commission, outlined in the contract, was never paid. G.C. did eventually collect $10,000 but told me that the money would have to go to cover expenses.

The Colorado ranch auction was the straw that broke the camel's back. We moved on down the road, which turned out to be a blessing in disguise. As for G.C., we parted friends and still are. The experience was educational, intriguing, and in most cases, fun and exciting. Dad, Big Tom, and I got closer than ever, and we also learned that working for someone else had both advantages and drawbacks.

48. The Wrong Track

Understanding that my Dad's life was a procession of friends, events and business ventures, and his complex and busy mind was occasionally difficult to rein in, I found a fitting Father's Day card for him a few years ago. The humorous card said, "Dad, when they made you, they broke the mold." On the inside page, the card read, "Word has it, they beat the hell out of the mold maker, too." I thought Dad would get a kick out of the card, but he took some offense, and said he thought the mold maker had done a pretty good job. After all of Dad's struggles and triumphs, there is little doubt about the mold maker's skill. By the way, I got back on track after that, and tried to put a little more thought into my greeting cards.

Track Section #IV
(2004-2005)

49. A Round-Trip Ticket

This telling of Dad's life history has about come full circle. We left the station in 1971 and told about the Sandy Lake Park years. Then we backtracked and visited Granddad Rush and Mamo in the era when the Old West passed into an age of railroads and horseless carriages. We visited Dad as a child and as a young man, joining his life partner, Mom, and then being thrust into entrepreneurship for a long leg of the journey at old Craterville Park. Later, in those wonderful years at the Rocking R Ranch, new Craterville, and on the rodeo trail, we saw, first hand, what Frank Rush was all about. Boundless energy and a fertile mind allowed Dad to live the prime of his life to the fullest during that time. Good times, tough times, and a move to our new home state of Texas was an adventure which revealed itself over several years, nearly completing the grand tour of the life of Frank Rush.

50. Nearing the End of the Line

Dad's lifestyle changed little over the years; however, he slowed his pace and increased his daily naptime from a few minutes to a few hours as the new millennium settled into place. Dad would go to Home Depot and buy dark wrap-around safety goggles for the boys to wear while they mowed and ran the weed-eaters. He would put on a pair of those goggles and catnap, sitting straight up in his chair, which was located near the pool entrance, the ramp up to the office, and next to the employee time clock. He enjoyed keeping track of everyone who came and went from that vantage point. With the dark wrap-around glasses in place, no one ever knew for sure if he was awake or asleep. We would go by and speak to him, and he wouldn't move. When someone would try to ease by and not disturb him, suddenly he would holler, "Hey, Cowboy, come sit down and let's talk."

He never lost his love for conversation, his interest in making a deal or being a cowboy. In 2002, at age eighty-seven, he went to a horse sale in Gainesville and bought himself a horse to ride. The horse was a nice-looking little paint with a good nature and an easy gait. Danny Arias would saddle his horse, and even though we worried about Dad getting hurt, he enjoyed his lifelong hobby of riding. In his mind, he and his little paint horse journeyed back and gathered cattle and horses on the Rocking R Ranch as he rode along dreaming of another time. Perhaps the little paint horse stirred up the dust in his memory and in an arena as he recalled taking an introduction at his Rocking R Ranch Rodeos or the Wild West Show at Six Flags. He sat tall in the saddle and never fell off.

Pup was another close animal companion of Dad's in his late years. The little Corgy/Blue Heeler dog was a gift for Dad from Tom F and Annesa after Bear, his old Labrador retriever, passed away. Pup was a pest. She would terrorize people visiting the office, and Dad was asked almost every day to remove the animal from someone's pants leg. He would say, "Come on, Pup, let's go ride around, we're in trouble again."

On March 4, 2004, Dad and Pup were eating ice cream late at night. Dad fell in the kitchen and had a very serious head injury. After surgery at Medical City Hospital, Dad was in rehab and skilled nursing care for ten months. He was never able to regain his health to the point that he could return to his beloved home at Sandy Lake Park, even though he had excellent professional care.

People who visited Dad were pleased he was still his old self in most ways. Dad's short-term memory was diminished, but through his final summer and fall, he and I would have long conversations about horses, events, and people he remembered from years long past. Many of the Frank Rush stories in this book were reconfirmed in our conversations, but I continued to be amazed by the scope and details of information that poured from Dad.

Good times return at Sandy Lake

MO SADJADPOUR/Special Contributor

Sandy Lake Amusement Park in Carrollton, owned by Frank and Genelle Rush, opened for the season Saturday. The couple, married 69 years, runs the park for families and corporate picnics. It has 19 amusement rides, miniature golf, paddle boats and Shetland ponies. The pool will open May 25. Sandy Lake is off Interstate 35E at Exit 444. There are also picnic tables, volleyball courts and softball fields. It reverts back to weekends only in September.

Married 69 years and counting, Dad and Mom on the Tilt-a Whirl pose for a news story about the spring opening at Sandy Lake Park in 2002.

Frank and Genelle Rush take a tour on their vis-à-vis
wagon driven by grandson Tom F Self.

Dad and Mom always had plenty of ideas for their annual
Christmas cards. Here they are, looking great with
Tumbleweed, Dad's giant longhorn steer.

Thanks to Suzy for taking this final Christmas card photo of
Dad, Mom and Pup at Vista Ridge Center in Lewisville in 2004.

Whistle Stop for Vista Ridge

One day in 1986, Wayne Ferguson, the mayor of Lewisville and a land developer friend of Dad's, came by the Park and picked Dad and me up in his truck. Wayne said he wanted to show us something of interest. We drove west down Sandy Lake Road and turned north on Denton Tap in Coppell. A couple of miles north, Wayne turned off the road into brushy farmland covering about twelve hundred acres. The property looked like it could be eighty miles from the nearest town, but the work crew was building roads and digging up trees for transplanting. Wayne explained the development was going to be known as Vista Ridge, and a big mall, homes, apartments, and businesses would one day cover the area. Dad told Wayne it looked like a huge task, and he hoped he lived long enough to see it happen.

51. The Last Stop

Even though he made Christmas and New Year's with us, Dad passed away January 5, 2005, with Mom and his family at his side. When Dad passed away, he was at Vista Ridge Nursing and Rehabilitation Center in Lewisville in the heart of the property Wayne Ferguson had shown Dad and me years earlier. Vista Ridge Mall has an annual fireworks show on the Fourth of July, and on occasion, the mall had used Dad's Special Events Sound Truck to play patriotic music to the crowd. The site where the sound truck was parked on a hillside overlooks the Center's location now. The spot where the fireworks were fired is the exact location where Vista Ridge Nursing and Rehabilitation Center now stands. There is action aplenty at the nearby mall and Dad's window overlooked more new construction across the street. He watched the goings on daily and got his wish about living long enough to see the development.

Just behind the center, Mallard ducks swim on the lake. Dad's caregiver Elizabeth, or one of us, would take Dad outside to see the ducks and enjoy the view that included a yet-undeveloped wooded area. There the trees and underbrush remained the same as when Mister Ferguson gave us the tour in 1986.

Doctor Wayne Allen, Dad's close friend and the retired pastor of First Baptist Church of Carrollton, presided over Dad's funeral service in Lewisville, Texas. Doctor Allen told his favorite Frank Rush story: Our family was having a birthday dinner for Dad several years ago at a local catfish restaurant. Doctor and Mrs. Allen happened to be having dinner at the same place. The couple came over to say hello on their way to pay the cashier. Dad, as he did with so many people, reached up and took Doctor Allen's ticket out of his hand so he could pay for their dinner. Doctor and Mrs. Allen thanked him kindly and left. To Dad's surprise, when he went to the cashier to pay for both our meal and Doctor Allen's, there was a $20 bill folded inside Doctor Allen's ticket. Dad was flustered, but he saw an opportunity to get out of Dutch with Doctor Allen and have fun doing it. The next day, Dad walked into Doctor Allen's office at the church, laid an envelope containing fifty-four cents on his desk and said, "There's your change," and walked out.

Mayor Milburn Gravley gave one of Dad's eulogies, and recalled what an impression Dad had made on him and the community of Carrollton. Dad always referred to Mayor Gravley as the only mayor that Carrollton ever had. Factually inaccurate though it is, Dad made his point about his high regard for his good friend Milburn.

Richard Fleming, one of the many young people Dad mentored, gave a eulogy of Dad as well. His words and descriptions of Dad were examples of how Dad changed Richard's life as a young man, as Dad had done for so many young people. Richard spoke with elegance and sincerity that only comes from deep in one's heart.

World famous rodeo performer, J. W. Stoker, trick roped for Dad at the end of the service, while Allison Snyder played "Happy Trails To You" one last time. World Champion Cowboy Roy Cooper was one of the pallbearers, and World Champion Cowboy Larry Mahan attended the service as well. A host of world champion friends, equally famous in the eyes of our family, attended Dad's last Texas production. We then prepared to go to Oklahoma the next day for another service with Dad's Oklahoma friends.

Alan Cartwright and Rory Cowden were on the parade committee with Dad at the Ft. Worth Livestock Show and Rodeo. I was visiting with them after Dad's service in Lewisville, and told them how, for weeks, Dad had asked me to be sure to pick up his Parade Committee Badge at the upcoming parade meeting on January 10. I made the comment, "I wish I had Dad's badge to give him before he is laid to rest." Alan said, "Let me get my phone out of the truck and make a call." Rory said he was coming to Lawton the next day for Dad's other service, and the two of them made arrangements to pick up the badge in Ft. Worth that evening. The next day in Lawton, Rory arrived and handed me the badge before the service started.

In Lawton, Reverend John Webb of the Cache Christian Church gave the sermon and told how Dad had supported his church. Each year, Sandy Lake Park hosts a group from the church for a day of fun and a catered meal, and Dad had donated much-needed items to the church, even though he was not a member.

Rusty Wahkinney, the Comanche Indian whom Dad had hired and mentored at Craterville Park, gave a eulogy and sang a Christian hymn and an Indian memorial song in his native language. Rusty also presented us with a beautiful ceremonial blanket to cover Dad's casket, an Indian tradition steeped in honor and reserved for only those whom they most respect.

Also in attendance was Jay Snider, the son of our dear friends Gene and Lois of Cyril, Oklahoma. When Gene was our rodeo judge at the Rocking R Ranch Rodeos, Jay was a baby. As a grown man, Jay has become a nationally-known cowboy poet. Jay dedicated this poem to Dad after his passing.

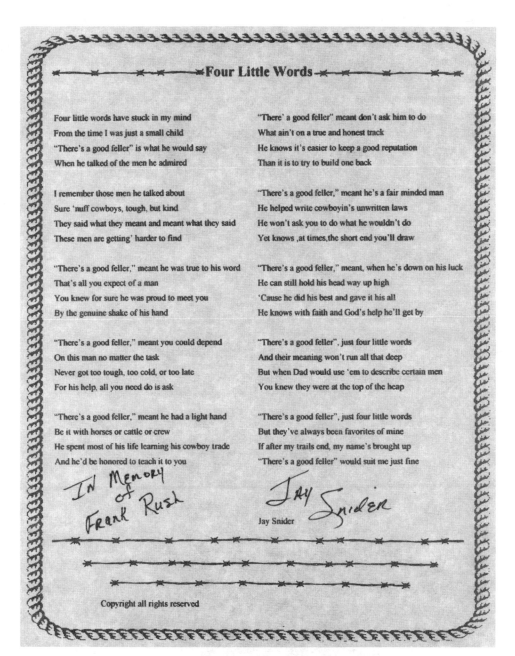

Four Little Words

Four little words have stuck in my mind
From the time I was just a small child
"There's a good feller" is what he would say
When he talked of the men he admired

I remember those men he talked about
Sure 'nuff cowboys, tough, but kind
They said what they meant and meant what they said
These men are getting' harder to find

"There's a good feller," meant he was true to his word
That's all you expect of a man
You knew for sure he was proud to meet you
By the genuine shake of his hand

"There's a good feller," meant you could depend
On this man no matter the task
Never got too tough, too cold, or too late
For his help, all you need do is ask

"There's a good feller," meant he had a light hand
Be it with horses or cattle or crew
He spent most of his life learning his cowboy trade
And he'd be honored to teach it to you

"There' a good feller" meant don't ask him to do
What ain't on a true and honest track
He knows it's easier to keep a good reputation
Than it is to try to build one back

"There's a good feller," meant he's a fair minded man
He helped write cowboyin's unwritten laws
He won't ask you to do what he wouldn't do
Yet knows ,at times,the short end you'll draw

"There's a good feller," meant, when he's down on his luck
He can still hold his head way up high
'Cause he did his best and gave it his all
He knows with faith and God's help he'll get by

"There's a good feller", just four little words
And their meaning won't run all that deep
But when Dad would use 'em to describe certain men
You knew they were at the top of the heap

"There's a good feller", just four little words
But they've always been favorites of mine
If after my trails end, my name's brought up
"There's a good feller" would suit me just fine

In Memory of Frank Rush

Jay Snider

Jay Snider dedicated his poem "Four Little Words"
to Dad after his passing. Jay's work is a special gift
that fits Frank Rush like his favorite cowboy hat.

The Last Whistle Stop for Beans and Badges

Beans Peabshy was the Indian man Dad had mentored and raised at old Craterville. Beans had given me the "Old Timer" pocketknife that Dad had given him as a young boy. Beans had carried the knife every day until he presented it to me a few months prior to his death. I asked a family friend, Ronnie Kitchens, to tell the story about the knife at Dad's final service. We planned to send the keepsake pocketknife with Dad to the "Happy Hunting Grounds."

Also, at Dad's final service, I rose to tell the crowd the story about Dad's Ft. Worth parade committee badge, which Rory had handed me earlier in the day. Dad had collected those badges for years, and I thought it would please him to have that final badge pinned on his lapel for eternity. After Rory had given me the badge, I had held it in my hand, but had not looked at it closely. As I began to tell the story of the badge, and thank Alan and Rory for their help in getting it to me, I read the 2005 stock show motto for the first time. Imprinted on the badge was a fitting epitaph and the title for Dad's life story, "COME HAVE FUN."

Acknowledgements

The recollections of E. Frank Rush, Genelle Rush and May (Mamo) Rush as told to Frank Rush III, the author, are the principal sources for this book. The Rush Family has lived and worked closely together, and the vast majority of information in this book comes from first-hand reminiscences.

This material has been expanded and verified through personal interviews by the author with numerous people and acknowledgement and appreciation is given to the following individuals: Bob Bodenhamer, Herschel Boydstun, Gene Canalizo, Alan Cartwright, Howard Council, Rory Cowden, Shawn Davis, Curt Donley, Dr. Irving Dreibrodt, Lanny Edwards, Wayne Ferguson, Richard Flemming, Merle Frazier, Milburn Gravley, Beck James, Donnie Jordan, Walter Kriss, Larry Mahan, Paul McClung, Jerry McClung, Errol McKoy, Bobby McMillan, Clem McSpadden, Paul Miller, James "Bo" Moore, Bob Parker, Jay Ross, Darrel Royal, E. Frank Rush, Genelle Rush, Vickie Rush, Ralph Segars, Tom Self, Suzy Self, Jim Shoulders, Scott Smith, Georgi Vaughn, Clinton Reeves, Bob Tallman, Rusty Wahkinney, Willie West, Jim "Wild Willy" Windsor, and Hugh Wiersig.

Individuals who related stories but passed away prior to the writing of this book include: Dan Coates, Marvin Bicket, Dr. T. K. Hardy, Bob Kirk, Alma Kirk, Fagon Miller, Milton "Beans" Peabshy, Fred Tennant, May "Mamo" Rush, Dilmas "Dandy" Walker, Maudie Walker, and R. D. Walker. To each of these revered friends and family members, your influence was most valuable.

Permission from the *Lawton Constitution* was granted for the use of various photos. Permission from the *Sunday Oklahoman Orbit* magazine was obtained to reproduce three photos. Permission from the *National Geographic* was obtained to reproduce two photos.

The title sheet of an original music composition "The Sandy Lake March for Symphonic Band" composed by Jerry Nowack, published by

Southern Music Company of San Antonio, Texas, is used as an illustration with permission from Jerry Nowack.

The drawing of Papa Jack Howenstine by Robert A. Gartland which was published in *Papa Jack, Cowman of the Wichitas* by Paul McClung and published by the University of Oklahoma Press, 1973, is used with permission from Paul McClung.

Permission to reproduce various cartoon drawings is granted by artist Roxanna Posey.

Permission to reproduce the photograph of the Meers Store is granted by store owners Marjorie and Joe Maranto and Prairie Production Company.

Publications referenced or used for documentation include *The National Geographic Magazine*, Volume CXI, May, 1957; *The Ranchman* magazine, Vol. 20, No. 2, 1960; Inter-State Arts, Volume 1, Nos. 6-7, 1931; Ethel C. Gray, Editor and Publisher with a reference to a *Southwest Wilds and Waters* item "What Indian Tongues Could Tell," by Frank Rush and Charles J. Brill; *Resourceful Oklahoma*, Oklahoma Planning and Resources Board Publication, 1954, Vol. 5, No. 6.

The image of the parade committee badge from the Fort Worth Stock Show and Rodeo and the 2005 motto wording "Come Have Fun" are used in the text and for the title of this book with permission of W. R. Watt, Jr., President and Manager of the Southwestern Exposition and Livestock Show. Credit for the unusual circumstances that surround the naming of this book are shared, with sincere appreciation, to Alan Cartwright and Rory Cowden.

All other reproductions of brochures, advertisements, poetry, original music scores and photographs are property of the Rush family.

Special appreciation is given to Jay Snider for allowing his poem "Four Little Words," written in honor of E. Frank Rush upon his death, to be included in this book. I also recommend Jay's cowboy poetry CD *Of Horses and Men*. Order one by e-mail at jay@jaysnider.net.